G000164767

JUSTIFICATION BY FAITH

JUSTIFICATION BY FAITH

Thy righteousness is
like the great mountains
PSALM 36:6

THE APOSTOLIC FOUNDATION
OF THE
CHRISTIAN CHURCH

Volume Six

JOHN METCALFE

THE PUBLISHING TRUST
Church Road, Tylers Green, Penn, Buckinghamshire.

Printed and Published by
John Metcalfe Publishing Trust
Church Road, Tylers Green
Penn, Buckinghamshire

—

©John Metcalfe Publishing Trust 1987
All Rights Reserved

—

First Published 1987

—

ISBN 1 870039 11 4

—

CONTENTS

THE
INTRODUCTION

JUSTIFICATION BY FAITH

THE INTRODUCTION

I

Justification and the Epistle to the Romans

JUSTIFICATION is a doctrine that was revealed to the apostles by the Lord Jesus Christ from heaven. It is a heavenly doctrine, it is divine in origin. The revelation of justification was committed first to the Apostle Paul, the apostle to the Gentiles. By the heavenly and spiritual openings of the Father it was given to him to see the Son of God seated in glory. In the light that shone from heaven Paul's spiritual vision perceived the full implication of that Person in that posture in that place. The implication of this to the individual shines forth in the doctrine of justification by faith. The implication to the company stands in the truth of the body of Christ, the church.

1

What Paul the Apostle saw in Christ, pertaining to the individual, he wrote in a book. That book is called The Epistle to the Romans. It is true that the apostle refers to justification in other epistles. It is true that he defended the doctrine with particular vehemence in Galatians. It is also true that justification occurs in the writings of other apostles. Nevertheless it is certain that in the Epistle to the Romans the divine revelation of justification was translated uniquely into written form. Romans is the apostolic letter corresponding to the heavenly vision that Paul saw.

There are two words in the Greek New Testament which have been translated 'justification' in the English. The first is *dikaiōma*. This word occurs ten times, and to translate it four different English words have been used, of which one is 'justification'. Half the number of references to *dikaiōma* are in Romans. It is in that epistle that the word has been translated 'justification', Rom. 5:16.

The second word is *dikaiōsis*. This word is found twice in the original language, and both times it has been rendered 'justification' in the English. *Dikaiōsis* is exclusive to Romans, and appears firstly in Rom. 4:25, and lastly in Rom. 5:18.

The word translated 'justify' in the Greek New Testament is *dikaioō*. This occurs forty times spread over ten different books. But not spread evenly. Fifteen times the word is found in Romans. Eight times in Galatians. That leaves seventeen occurrences for the remaining eight books. From this it is clear that the word *dikaioō*, 'justify', appears predominantly in Romans.

Because righteousness is the foundation upon which justification rests, this word is of particular significance to the doctrine. *Dikaiosunē*, uniformly translated 'righteousness' in the New Testament, occurs over ninety times. No less than thirty-five of these occurrences are in Romans.

2

Such instances of the various words connected with justification serve to illustrate the truth that this doctrine is taught primarily in the Epistle to the Romans. Romans is the book in which the Apostle Paul committed to writing the heavenly revelation of Jesus Christ the Son of God, in its bearing upon the individual in Christ. This is the revelation that Paul called 'justification', asserting always and in every place that it is by faith without the works of the law.

It follows that rightly to understand justification one must grasp the argument of Romans. The epistle is neither an academic treatise, nor a text book on justification. Romans was written to the saints, it was written for a purpose, and to further that purpose Paul brings in the doctrine. Thus justification is displayed in a certain perspective, and that perspective is the Epistle to the Romans. The observation of this point is essential if one is to grasp the doctrine. Justification is applied in a context, not stated as a subject. Then the book must be understood as a whole, the doctrine must be distinguished in and of itself, and there must be spiritual discernment in drawing out the substance of the teaching.

In the Epistle to the Romans mankind is called to account before God. Man is to give an account of himself, he is brought to the light to answer for his state before God. All superficialities, the whole veneer of outward religion, everything is swept aside: the heart is made bare: mankind is seen as responsible to God, as having to answer to God. He is made to stand at the bar of divine justice. Romans appears as the moral counterpart of the great white throne in the day of judgment.

There will be no other things required of men, no different a standard of justice, in the 'day of wrath and revelation of the righteous judgment of God', than that which appears in this epistle. In Romans, Paul the Apostle faithfully brings before mankind, in anticipation of the event, the fact of judgment, the standard of judgment, and the sentence of judgment.

The apostle formally commences the argument of the epistle with the words, Rom. 1:18, 'The wrath of God is revealed from heaven against all ungodliness and unrighteousness of men.' That is the background of the gospel. It is the revelation of the righteous wrath of God. This is expounded from Ch. 1:18 to Ch. 3:20. Only then does the apostle commence to preach justification. There is a context to the proper declaration of justification, that which precedes and that which succeeds the doctrine. Here, that which precedes occupies the best part of three chapters. And that is not the gospel which ignores it. The wrath of God against all ungodliness and unrighteousness of men preceded the gospel, and, indeed, was the cause of the gospel. Because of this wrath, God sent his Son to save sinners. That is, save them from wrath. Then the wrath upon man preceded the coming of the Son. Wrath was upon mankind, revealed from heaven, without the gospel, and before the gospel appeared.

If so, what was the cause of this wrath? 'All ungodliness and unrighteousness of men.' That is, the behaviour of mankind, both among men and before God. It is not the fall of Adam, but the will of man that is brought to account. Paul opens his argument with what is moral, not constitutional. The introduction of the fall, and of inbred sin, commences in the fifth chapter, not the first. Here it is personal accountability. What is voluntary, not involuntary. Here it is what man chose: he willed this. It is the will of men, their own choice, that is brought into judgment.

The whole issue of the judgment is one of man's wilfulness under accountability to God. If man should claim ignorance, God charges deliberate blindness upon mankind. Man is wilfully ignorant of his responsibility towards God. The apostle brings in man as guilty, and leaves him speechless. God must be justified in his saying that 'The wrath of God is revealed from heaven', and clear in his judgment 'against all ungodliness and unrighteousness of men'.

How shall God be justified? Paul opens the eyes of the blind, reasoning of sin, righteousness and judgment to come. He shuns not to declare all the counsel of God. He will justify God on the one hand, and leave man speechless on the other. Then he must demonstrate man's responsibility, his accountability, and do so by indicating the light to which man is under obligation.

In Ch. 1:19 Paul shows the reason for the wrath of God, commencing with the word 'Because'. Because that which may be known of God is, firstly, manifest in them; and, secondly, shown unto them. Manifest in whom, and shown unto whom? The Gentiles in particular, though not excluding the Jews: mankind generally.

What is it that is manifest in man? The light from God which shines within, the denial and abuse of which brings down the wrath of God. It is the inward light of consciousness, the work of the law written in the heart, the first truths that dawn with the awareness of reason and accountability. Here is an interior light, manifest in mankind, showing 'that which may be known of God'.

This light glows deep in the conscious awareness, it is reflected dimly in the conscience, it manifests that God is, that he has rights, that eternity exists, that there is a day of reckoning, that one is accountable. From this light come the questionings, What am I? Who am I? Where am I from? Where am I going? What is death? What is beyond death? Who is God? What is God? Where is God? How may God be known? That is 'manifest in them'.

Likewise there is that which is 'shown unto' mankind, illuminating 'that which may be known of God'. This is the light that shines from heaven, reflected in the things formed on earth, and diffused throughout the creation. It is the light of the glory of God, refulgent in the things created and made, and testifying infallibly of the Creator of heaven and earth, things 'shown unto' men. And because of man's ignoring these things, abusing them, contradicting them, and denying 'that which may be known of God', the wrath of God finds sufficient cause, without or before the coming of Christ, without or before the hearing of the gospel, enough cause, in that man spurns such glory, and rejects it, enough cause to smoulder and burn from heaven against the day of retribution and vengeance of Almighty God. Enough is shown, shown in the creation of the world, shown in the things that are made, shown in his invisible presence, shown in his everlasting glory, shown in his eternal power and Godhead, to leave mankind without excuse.

Nevertheless the will of man denied the glory of God. Negatively, mankind glorified him not as God, and neither were men thankful. Positively, men became vain in their reasonings, their foolish heart was darkened, and, professing themselves to be wise, they became fools. Man's heart foolish? Darkened? Man became a fool? Ignoring the glory of God in the things created and made, which had been shown unto them, suppressing, contradicting, despising, the light that shone within, that had been manifest in them, men turned to what was vain, light, airy and outward, forsaking their own mercy and cleaving to lying vanities.

Wherefore God gave men up, who had given him up, God gave them up to the lusts of their own hearts, to their own vile affections, and to a reprobate mind. That was their will, and this was his will. Hence to the wilful impenitence and hardness of heart in man, the wrath of God was revealed from heaven judging every man according to his works. The stiff-necked, hard-hearted, impenitent world, religious or irreligious, with the law or without the law, Jew or Gentile, all alike were warned of the folly of ignoring the light of God's righteous judgment.

For his judgments are made known, his judgments are in all the earth, he will render to every man according to his deeds. Shall not the Judge of all the earth do right? His judgment upon the life and work of the righteous, who by patient continuance in well doing seek for glory, and honour, and immortality, is declared to be 'eternal life'. But his judgment upon the life and work of the unrighteous, who are contentious, who do not obey the truth, the apostle pronounces as 'indignation and wrath'. Thus is declared the recompense due to all the earth from the Judge of whom it is said, 'Righteousness and judgment are the habitation of his throne.'

Following the judgment, comes the everlasting sentence: 'Tribulation and anguish upon every soul of man that doeth evil, of the Jew first, and also of the Gentile; but glory, honour, and peace, to every man that worketh good, to the Jew first, and also to the Gentile: For there is no respect of persons with God', Rom. 2:9-11.

Then where does mankind stand before such a Judge, before the judgment of that great day? Saith Paul, 'Without excuse.' What of the law? 'What things soever the law saith, it saith to them who are under the law: that every mouth may be stopped, and all the world may become guilty before God.' The law? 'By the deeds of the law there shall no flesh be justified in his sight: for by the law is the knowledge of sin.' What of those without the law? 'There is none righteous, no, not one.' 'There is none that understandeth, there is none that seeketh after God.' 'There is none that doeth good, no, not one.' 'There is no fear of God before their eyes', Rom. 3:18.

With such a view of man, such a sight of the judgment of God, such a prospect of the day of judgment, and such a revelation of a fixed, immortal state, enduring to everlasting eternity, one might suppose Romans to be the most fearful, the most negative, the gloomiest of epistles; but it is not.

Romans is an epistle that is full of grace, full of triumph, it is positive, it is an epistle that rings with the sound of victory. Is man by nature found guilty, cursed under the law, shut up to judgment? Grace abounds to lift man into a new standing, having righteousness and life in Christ. Does man stand under condemnation and judgment? The word resounds through the epistle, 'It is God that justifieth. Who is he that condemneth?'

'Who shall lay anything to the charge of God's elect?' In no other epistle is election more strongly emphasised, more intimately connected with the salvation of God. In the third chapter as much as the ninth, election gives basis, substance and validity to the argument of the apostle. The choice, the will, the redemption of God in Christ Jesus redound to the praise of the glory of his grace, whilst a justification for all the elect appears as the only justification that can stand for time and eternity, overturning all the oppositions of devils and men. What an epistle! So mighty, so strong, so powerful, yet so full of pity and tender mercy to the weakest of conditions. 'Who shall lay anything to the charge of God's elect', cries Paul, 'It is God that justifieth. Who is he that condemneth?' That accuser shall never be found who can uphold one single charge against those that are established by faith in this holy doctrine.

Romans views man in the light of his personal accountability. It takes up the individual. The majority of the epistles deal with the church, having to do with the company. They take up a corporate position, they speak to the assembly, the congregation. The Epistle to the Romans, however, addresses the individual. It is a question of what answers to baptism. That is personal. Baptism may introduce one into a company, but it, itself, is personal. Baptism is the figure in which one is depicted as buried with Christ, and, having been buried, raised up with him in newness of life.

'Buried with him by baptism into death.' That is the answer to everything that was raised against one in judgment.

The wrath of God, the judgment, had been revealed. Now, with equal justice, God has provided the perfect answer. It is one's identity with Christ in his death. There is no accusation against the individual in Christ that death has not answered, no charge which it has not silenced with justice, and no sentence from which it had not obtained absolute acquittal before the throne of God.

Before, the individual, taken up, was found to be lost, guilt-worthy, unable to open his mouth, condemned and without any justification before God for having existed at all. Now, through death in Christ and with Christ, he is saved, justified, a new song is put in his mouth, he magnifies God, his goings are established, and he views with joy the bright hope of the glory and of the world to come.

Everything in Romans is through the death of Christ. It is true that one sees onself risen with Christ in newness of life, and that the nature of that life stands in freedom from the law of sin and death. It is also true that—by the mercies of God—the saints find themselves in a company, in one body, with many members. But these are things glimpsed, these are the consequence; such things show the light of the glory beginning to break, the glorious prospect before those who have been crucified with Christ. His death is what is central, and their death in him: they have been buried with him. That is the answer to every moral question, to the very judgment itself, in the light of the great white throne: crucified with Christ. Buried with him by baptism into death.

It is this that brings in the body of Christ. Nothing less and nothing else. Upon the hearing of this by faith, there follows the baptism of the Holy Ghost. Hence Romans, dealing with the individual in the light of the judgment of God, is the true evangelist's message. Anything else is false. But the true evangel brings, and must bring, the faithful to one body in Christ as a reality. So that forgiveness, remission, justification,

propitiation, reconciliation, redemption, adoption, substitution, sanctification, can neither be preached nor received in
isolation from the truth of the company to which these things
inevitably lead, and which they bring in. It is impossible that
the true evangel should result in continued individualism
and independency. The gospel unites us and must unite us in
one body with many members. Salvation is preached with an
end in view. The church is in view. It is the church that is the
pillar and ground of the truth, nothing else. The church
which is his body, the fulness of him that filleth all in all.

This appears at the close of the epistle, Rom. 16:25. It is not
expounded but it is indicated. We are brought to a mystery.
This mystery is made known by revelation. It is the mystery
of the fellowship. It is that assembly, the house of God not
made with hands, indwelt by the Father and the Son, and
united in the life and power of one Spirit. This is what the
preaching and teaching of the evangel, the gospel, achieves.
This is what evangelism properly so-called achieves. This is
what the evangelist who is sent of God achieves. And it is
what the evangel maintains. Death with Christ and in Christ
is the basis of the fellowship of the mystery. It is what is
depicted by baptism, and set forth in Romans.

The Lord's supper is not mentioned in the Epistle to the
Romans. The Lord's supper is for the company, it is the communion of the body of Christ. The epistle in which the supper
is mentioned is the first Epistle to the Corinthians, which
takes another position in Christ altogether. In Romans, the
death of Christ is studied, together with our death in him. By
grace in Christ we are judicially slain, and buried, by a death
and burial that meets and answers all responsibility through
him who loved us, and gave himself for us.

Romans is a book about death, it studies death in Christ. It
is a book that studies the death of Christ for the individual,
and the individual's death in Christ. Christ died for him, and

he died in Christ. What a wonderful peace this gives, what a tremendous salvation, what assurance this brings to the conscience. How marvellous is the Epistle to the Romans!

The book takes up the faith of the individual, it plunges him into the waters of death, it carries him down into the tomb of Christ, it buries him in the depths of the death of Christ. He has died with Christ, he is buried with Christ. That is the position Romans takes. Buried with him by baptism into death. That is not Christ dying for him, it is his dying with Christ. It is not Christ being buried for him, it is his being buried with Christ. But if he is buried, then he is taken out of sight: the man has disappeared from view. From view of what? Why, from view of the law, from view of the curse, from view of sins, guilt, rebellion, from view of the old man, of Adam, from view of sin, the world, corruption and death, and from view of the great white throne in the day of judgment.

The saints are dead and buried to it all, they are out of sight in that chamber of death called the tomb, and they cannot be brought back from the sepulchre to face the charges of the accuser, or the sight of that to which they have died, any more, world without end, Amen.

When a man is dead, the law brings no more charges against him, and neither does it require any more from him for ever. It cannot. The ultimate sanction of the law is death, and when that sanction has been brought into execution, that is the end of any relationship between the law and the man upon whom the death penalty has been executed. Will they bring him back into court? By this time he stinketh. It cannot be. He has answered to the grim reaper, and the law has nothing to say, nothing to require, nothing to demand of a corpse. That is the place of all who are 'buried with him by baptism into death'. It is the position of Romans.

In the first Epistle to the Corinthians a company is seen. 'Even as the testimony of Christ was confirmed in you.' That is, 'you', plural. Not 'thee', singular. It is the assembled company, plural. A fellowship is seen, in the wilderness of this present world. In a figure it is the pilgrim company, passed over the Red Sea by faith, now entered into the wilderness, bound for the distant promised land beyond the river Jordan. However, once separated from Egypt, once entered as a body upon the pilgrim way, the testimony, 'the pattern shown on the mount', comes down, 'even as the testimony of Christ was confirmed in you'. The Holy Ghost fills the body, Christ above in glory administers the Spirit to the separated company below, gifts are given, guidance obtained, truth ministered, a pillar of cloud and fire, by day and night, goes before.

The Lord's supper shows the people's severance from Egypt in the past, their unity in the wilderness at present, and their entry into the land of promise in future. The testimony came down in Chapter one, love fills the saints in Chapter thirteen, the descended Spirit from the headship of Christ forms the body and guides the assembly in Chapters twelve and fourteen, and the entire company is raised up to ascend in Chapter fifteen.

Here are special provisions for the time of pilgrimage. Gifts, prophecies, signs, the principles governing differing ministries, the manifestation of the Spirit, the Spirit himself, the distinction between male and female, the Lord's supper, provision for the ministry and service of women: here is the pillar of cloud, there the pillar of fire. As many as are led by the Spirit of God, these are the sons of God. The Spirit leads into all truth. This lowly, pilgrim, sojourning company, meek, submissive to the truth in the love of it, this is the company that the Holy Ghost owns, in which he dwells, and none other. It is the church of God on earth.

In Colossians the emphasis is otherwise, and so a different position in respect of the union of the saints with Christ is seen. In Colossians the saints are risen with Christ, that is the opening position, it answers in them to Christ risen from the dead, but seen on earth. Through his inward life they are sustained on earth by him from glory. There is an interior living union, they live by him, who is invisible, above in the heavens. Their life is hidden. But hid with Christ in God.

In Ephesians the position of the saints is not on earth at all, in the counsels of God they are outside of this world. Everything is dead on earth, the world already judged, all who live before God are ascended with Christ in the heavenly places, the saints are seated with Christ in glory. Here, their position corresponds with his. God's eternal purpose has already come in, the saints answer to it even now, eternal things are come to pass, and the light, power and spirit of them govern the church, as seen in the faith and love of the saints at Ephesus.

But all is based on his death. Did Christ die, and was he buried? And was his death and burial for the saints? Then they also died, and they too were buried, with him. Constantly one must return to the position in Romans. Here all that is to be revealed of death and burial in Christ, is brought to light for faith, the faith of God's elect.

But having died, did Christ rise, and was he forty days on earth in the power of an endless life from the other, far, side of death? Then the saints are risen with him, that life is theirs, not distinct from the Head, but ministered and flowing down from the Head in living union to all the members. But he is hidden above, they are visible below, and the world believes them not. Well, it believed him not.

But it is all true, and they are in the power and good of that which is true, risen with Christ, seeking the things which are above, where Christ sitteth on the right hand of God. Yet not remote. Christ is our life. As to our body, when he shall appear, we shall be like him. Now, within, his life, risen, fills the body. Here is found the position in Colossians. But all is based on his death. All rests on what is revealed in Romans.

What of Ephesians? It is the same. Did Christ ascend? Then the saints ascended, seated with Christ, above in heavenly places. All is judged and passed away below in the counsels of God, whilst faith lays hold upon God as the God of our Lord Jesus Christ, and upon the Father as the Father of our Lord Jesus Christ, so that everything that was brought to pass in the Head might find full response, and receive abundant answer, in the whole body. But ascension commenced in the lower parts of the earth. All is based on death, rooted in burial, and grounded in the revelation conveyed by Romans.

How important it is to ponder and meditate upon all God's ways in Christ. To be rooted and grounded in him. Paul stood at the sepulchre, so to speak, and in spirit looked into the grave at the dead body of Jesus. In retrospect he looked, he gazed, he pondered, he perceived. He cried 'Our old man is crucified with him!' Jesus' body lay still, shrouded, alone. But in the Spirit Paul perceived a further crucifixion; he saw together with the body of Jesus 'our old man'. Who else had seen that? But Paul saw, with heavenly vision he perceived the flesh, the fall, the world, the judgment, the great white throne, the lake of fire. Yet all taken away, absorbed, removed, gone in the still, shrouded figure in the sepulchre. What a death! But it does not yield its secrets, nor the Spirit his mysteries, to the casual gaze.

What a death! Someone may object, Yes, but his body is not in the tomb now. Neither was his body in the tomb when the two angels sat, one at the head, and one at the feet, where the body of Jesus had lain. Like Paul, the angels sat still, and lingered long, contemplating the place where the body of

14

Jesus had lain. They took in his death. From his head to his feet, with angelic vision they took in the length, the breadth, and the depth of that death and burial, despite the emptiness of the tomb. And so did Paul. And so should we. It may be said, But it is not given to us to have such vision. No, but it is given to us to have the Epistle to the Romans.

Sin and death came in by Adam, appearing in all his seed. The will of man under responsibility brought forth sin, and, in the sight of God, nothing but sin. Upon this the wrath of God is revealed from heaven. But now, righteousness and life have come to light by Jesus Christ. Not only are sins remitted, not only is pardon proclaimed, not only is God declared to be propitious, but the very thing that was lost has been brought in far more abundantly by Jesus Christ.

Did Adam bring in the sin of man? Christ has brought in the righteousness of God. Did death come in by the one man, Adam? Everlasting life has been brought in far more abun-dantly by the other man, Christ Jesus. This is the doctrine, and the manner of teaching, that is declared in the Epistle to the Romans. This is the context of Romans. But at the heart of the epistle, in the centre of that context, one great truth rad-iates and pulsates with the light of the glory of God. And that truth is summed up by the phrase, The doctrine of Justification.

PART ONE
THE PROLOGUE

THE PROLOGUE

II

Righteousness and the Gospel of Christ

IN the Epistle to the Romans the Apostle Paul makes a statement about the gospel that is fundamental to the
understanding of justification. It is this: 'For I am not
ashamed of the gospel of Christ: for it is the power of God
unto salvation to every one that believeth; to the Jew first,
and also to the Greek. For therein is the righteousness of
God revealed from faith to faith: as it is written, The just
shall live by faith', Romans 1:16,17.

Paul affirms that he is not ashamed of the gospel of Christ.
What gospel is this? It is the 'gospel of God concerning his Son
Jesus Christ our Lord, which was made of the seed of David
according to the flesh; and declared to be the Son of God
with power, according to the spirit of holiness, by the
resurrection from the dead', Romans 1:3,4.* The Son of God
and seed of David, Jesus Christ, is the subject of the gospel.

*See 'The Son of God and Seed of David', John Metcalfe Publishing Trust.

19

That the Son of God was made of the seed of David, shows the pre-existence of the Son—as Son—in the deity. It shows his incarnation, as well as the nature of his manhood. The verses go on to imply the death of the incarnate Son of God, in that they speak of his resurrection. Likewise they declare his power, and show forth his risen glory. Of this gospel Paul was not ashamed.

'I am not ashamed of the gospel of Christ.' The gospel is that which declares the divine Person and nature of the Son, his human nature, and the union of both natures in one Person. The gospel speaks of his virgin birth, his perfect life, his spotless sacrifice, his substitutionary death, his bodily resurrection and his ascension into heaven. From the glory this gospel affirms that Christ is the wisdom of God, which wisdom stands in justification, sanctification and redemption. This is the heavenly wisdom that shall be both vindicated and consummated at the glorious appearing and coming again of the Son of God from heaven. Of this gospel Paul was not ashamed.

The apostle could not say, however, that he was unashamed when he was under the works of the law. Though at first, in his ignorance and boasting, he thought he had nothing to be ashamed of under the law, later he found that this false confidence was due to the veil upon his heart and the blindness of his eyes. Dead and insensitive, going about to establish his own righteousness, justifying himself, he had been proud of his religion. But when the commandment came, that is, into his inward parts, breaking up the great deep, sin revived, and he died. Then he was ashamed. The law required him to bring forth righteousness from the flesh, it taught him to look to the interior, and find strength within himself: 'This do, and thou shalt live.'

Yet what he found within was not strength, but weakness; not life, but death; not light, but darkness. The motions of sin wrought in him, and what had promised to give life, proved to be death. The law was subjective, setting him on to states within and works without which he had strength neither to order nor to perform. He performed the very things that he would not, and discovered the very states that were the opposite to those for which he longed. He found himself carnal, sold under sin. Ashamed. He was so ashamed.

But he was not ashamed of the gospel of Christ. What a difference from the law! Whereas the law had taught and required him to look within himself for ability, the gospel taught him to look outside of himself for a Saviour. Light shone from heaven: a voice came from above: justification was in Christ: life flowed from on high: all was outside of himself. Everything was from the glory. What relief this brought to Paul. He had been prostrate on the earth, sunk in deep pits, shut up in prison, trapped in the body of sin and death. He had beaten at the gates of brass, he had torn at the bars of iron, he had groped for the wall like the blind, he had wasted his years in the prison-house, he had groaned, cried, sighed: but there was none that would hearken; none came to his aid.

Till Christ reached down from above. He sent from above, he took him, he drew him out of many waters: he lifted Paul out of guilt, fearfulness, and trembling: he cleared him from condemnation and wrath, he lifted him up and set him down in safety. This was the power that was in the gospel. It bestowed redemption from above, it commanded justification from the glory, it brought reconciliation from heaven, it sent salvation from on high, and Paul was accepted in the beloved, unashamed.

Paul was not ashamed of the gospel of Christ, because that gospel could do what the law could not do. The gospel removed the distance between God and man, took away the old veil, broke off the old yoke, removed the intolerable burden, brought deliverance from sin, peace with God, entrance into the holiest, and communion with the Most High.

21

Paul was unashamed of the gospel because by it he was just-ified from all things from which he could not be justified by the law of Moses. He found liberty at the cross, he had been set free from the man of sin and death. He found pardon through the blood of Christ, for by it mountains of guilt and iniquity had been removed and covered over. He found heavenly power in the spiritual touch of the ascended Son, as the leper found on earth when Jesus touched him; and as the woman found who but touched his garment, and was healed: for 'as many as touched him were made whole'. Paul found a fulness in his deity, a nearness in his humanity, and an intimacy in his Person, which defied all expression, beyond tongue to tell. He found the hope of the resurrection in Christ's return, with death, the grave, and hell itself con-quered, swallowed up, abolished, when the Lord of glory should raise the saints to glory, bringing in the elect to the everlasting inheritance of the world to come. How should Paul be ashamed of such a gospel? 'I am not ashamed of the gospel of Christ.'

Paul affirmed the gospel to be definitive of Christ and his work, the 'form of sound words'. It was 'the gospel' of Christ, Romans 1:16, that is, it had content, there was order to it which defined what it had to say about Christ. The law con-cerned oneself, and what was required of oneself: but the gospel concerned Christ, and what was accomplished by him outside of oneself. The gospel therefore did not tell Paul what to do: it declared what Christ had done for him.

The apostolic gospel reveals what Christ has done, and it does so in doctrinal terms. It is the doctrine of Christ. It is definitive. It does not leave one on shifting, changeable sands, but upon immoveable, unchangeable rock, the Rock Christ Jesus. The gospel declares Christ's deity, his Sonship, his manhood, his birth, baptism, transfiguration, visitation, his death, burial, resurrection and ascension. It declares Messiah and the Kingdom of Heaven, the Servant and the

Service of God, the Saviour and the Grace of God, and the Son of God and Everlasting Life. The gospel reveals the ministry, priesthood, sacrifice, advocacy, headship, kingdom, inheritance, and glory of Christ, in a word, it definitively declares his Person and work, on earth and from heaven, for time and eternity, in this world and the next.

Romans 1:16 tells us that the gospel is 'the power of God unto salvation'. Paul says, I am not ashamed of the gospel of Christ, for 'it' is the power of God unto salvation. Then, the power of God is not something apart from the gospel, because the gospel in itself—'it'—is God's power unto salvation. Practically, men deny this. They think that the power is in the Prayer Meeting, the Revival Meeting, the Breaking of Bread, the Crusade Meeting, the Fellowship Meeting, or, at least, in the Church. They suppose it to be in traditions, 'sacraments', in the 'Ministry'. Or in theology, commentaries, sermons: for it is to libraries, to learning, to others, in practice, that man looks for help, as if there were no power directly from God. But there is power directly from God: and it is in the gospel.

Others suppose that power is in what they presume to be manifestations of the Spirit, visions, tongues, as they think of them, the Second Blessing, as it is called, the 'Baptism of the Holy Spirit', as some say, or dreams, feelings, excitements, or other forms of subjective experience. So they confound the right way, these people whom God never taught, who know nothing at all, and who lead others into confusion away from a gospel they neither understand nor were called to preach. But it is that gospel, and that gospel alone, which the apostle calls 'the power of God unto salvation'.

The gospel itself, the gospel of Christ, is where the power of God lies, because it is that which God owns, that by which Christ is revealed, and it is that to which the Spirit bears witness. This was abundantly illustrated in the days of Christ's flesh. The word which Jesus spoke was effective, dynamic: authority was in the gospel. It drew the publicans, sinners, and the harlots. It lifted the fallen, the penurious, the beggar from the dunghill. And it set them among princes. The gospel in the mouth of Jesus Christ really saved the lost. If this was not the power of God unto salvation, what was?

In the ministry by which Jesus set forth the power of God in the gospel, water was turned into wine: one at death's door was raised up again by a word spoken at that same moment many miles away: another was healed who had been stricken on a bed of paralysis thirty-eight years. By the power of God in the gospel the storm was stilled, the waters calmed, and five barley loaves and two small fishes fed five thousand with baskets over and to spare. This same word brought bread from heaven, water from the rock, gave the flesh and blood of the Son of man to perishing sinners, delivered from Moses' law, brought in Abraham's promise, and bestowed on the heirs of faith an everlasting inheritance. The power of God unto salvation made men free indeed, raised up from corruption and death to eternal life, proclaimed the resurrection and the life, brought in sonship, led into the Father's house, established union with the Father and the Son, and united all the children of God in one, world without end, Amen. If the gospel that achieved such things as this be not the power of God unto salvation, then what is the power of God unto salvation?

Paul the Apostle stresses that the gospel is the power 'of God'. There is nothing of the power of man, or will of the flesh, here. Salvation belongeth unto the Lord. Hence it is said, 'God hath chosen you to salvation through sanctification of the Spirit and belief of the truth', II Thess. 2:13. It was the Lord that added daily to the church such as should be saved; men did not add themselves, and neither could others do the adding. This was the kind of addition that was divine. As many as were ordained unto eternal life believed, and none other.

In the gospel, all is of God. The gospel is the power of God, not of man. The Lord could say, 'I have much people in this city'. This was long before that people knew him, or knew of the gospel. He had first loved them, then bought them, and so saved them. Long after all this, he sent Paul to call them. They knew nothing of these things. Not until they heard Paul preaching. 'How shall they hear without a preacher? And how shall one preach except he be sent?' But when Paul preached the gospel, that was the power of God unto salvation to them with a witness.

The gospel was of God, and of God's power, first and last. All flesh had corrupted his way utterly upon the earth, there was none that did any good, no not one. Yet God had chosen out the vessels of mercy, distinguishing them from the vessels of wrath, and by his power was to prepare them for glory. And since he was the Potter, who can complain about that? As to the power by which he prepared the clay, the earthen vessels, it was that power of God unto salvation called the gospel.

Will the clay vessels complain? They will not. They know that without the power of God in the gospel they would have been lost, but now they are saved. Then, seeing the way in which they would have destroyed themselves, they cannot be too heartbroken, too convicted, too dependent, too helpless, they cannot feel their depravity and inability too strongly, they cannot too heartily give glory, thanksgiving, and praise to God, cannot cry too loudly, 'Grace, grace unto it!'

As to the world, far from desiring the power of God unto salvation, the world, and the worldly in religion, want self-will, they want the arm of the flesh, they want the power to be of man, they glory in self-reliance, and triumph in self-dependence: what have they to do with the power of God unto salvation? If they want salvation, they will fetch it for themselves. The world chooses self-justification, its religion is self-righteousness, these are the very things at which the world aims, self-glory is all its boast, and conceit. Opinions, notions, theories, these the world will put for religion, as it presumes to think its haughty way to heaven. The world has no time for election, predestination, the sovereign power and majesty of God, no, it will stand in its own power and strength. And as they desire, so shall it be done unto them.

To the world the gospel is foolishness, and, in view of all the latent goodness and strength in man, the power of God superfluous. The will of man is adequate. The provision of a gospel is all very well in its place, but no power is needed in connection with it, power is in man. But to us who are saved power is not in man, power is in God; as to us, so lost and helpless are we, that had not God exerted his power in the gospel, we had never been saved. To us who are saved the gospel is the power of God and the wisdom of God.

For the foolishness of God is wiser than men, and the weakness of God is stronger than men. Hath not God chosen the base, the weak, the despised, and the things that are not, to bring to nought the things that are? This is our calling, it is by the power of God, it is in the gospel, it is all of God, and, saith Paul, 'Ye see your calling, brethren'.

The gospel, declares the apostle, is the power of God unto salvation. Salvation is that which the power of God effects by the gospel. When the gospel is believed in the power of God, salvation is the inevitable consequence. How great is this salvation! What great and numerous enemies combine to array themselves against man, without and within, in this world and the next! It is the revelation and destruction of these enemies, together with our deliverance from them, that is at the heart of salvation.

Satan, the chief and head of all other enemies, rages against the gospel, and against those called by the gospel. Satan attacks both the saints and the church, urgent to bring down wrath against the people of God. He storms, as in a court of law, to bring in the sentence of death, and to that end accuses the elect day and night before God. He appears as the prosecuting counsel—*Diabolos*—at the great Assize, arguing his case with forensic brilliance. He develops his charges with devastating skill, raising point after point with deadly effect, bringing out the spirituality, the holiness, the justice, the goodness of the law; observing the impartiality, the rectitude and the obligation of the Judge; exposing the carnality, the worldliness, the corruption of the elect.

How this *Diabolos* appeals to every precept of the penal code, crying up every sanction, calling down every penalty, lauding the universality, insisting upon the impartiality and expounding the immutability of the whole law, the ten commandments, the two commandments, and the great commandment. This Prosecutor would bring in every judgment, the entire testimony, all the statutes, each precept, as he labours to overturn the election of God. He would appeal to the duty of the Judge, the unchangeableness of the law, the absoluteness of justice, the rectitude of the throne, the resolution of the Lawgiver: Oh, what a pleading for condemnation, till at last he folds his arms, rests his case, expectant of triumph in the issue.

But to no avail. An Advocate appears: Jesus Christ is his name; the brief for the defence is the gospel itself. Now, if never before, men shall see that this same gospel is the power of God unto salvation to every one that believeth! By the gospel of God the Advocate shall answer every question, of God or man, in heaven or on earth, in time or eternity. By this gospel he shall silence every plea, each accusation on the ground of sin, death, the law, the curse, the nature and duty of man, or the obligation and impartiality of the Judge. The state of human nature in the fall, the entanglement of humanity in the man of sin and death, all shall be answered, and answered to perfection, by the gospel Advocate. Because it, the gospel, in the mouth of Jesus Christ the Righteous, provides the perfect answer to every charge. The words 'Case dismissed' must and shall ring across the vault of heaven, sounding to the depths of eternity, with every charge, all argument wholly overturned, and the Prosecutor brought to shame and confusion by the word of the truth of the gospel. In that day it shall appear, and of the gospel it shall be said, 'It is the power of God unto salvation.'

Wherefore? Hear the Sentence of the Judge, sounding back from that world to this, echoing from the brink of eternity into time through the prophetic ministry of the Apostle Paul: 'Who shall lay anything to the charge of God's elect? It is God that justifieth. Who is he that condemneth? It is Christ that died, yea rather, that is risen again, who is even at the right hand of God, who also maketh intercession for us.'

'Who shall separate us from the love of Christ? shall tribulation, or distress, or persecution, or famine, or nakedness, or peril, or sword? As it is written, For thy sake we are killed all the day long; we are accounted as sheep for the slaughter. Nay, in all these things we are more than conquerors through him that loved us.'

'For I am persuaded, that neither death, nor life, nor angels, nor principalities, nor powers, nor things present, nor things to come, nor height, nor depth, nor any other creature, shall be able to separate us from the love of God, which is in Christ Jesus our Lord.'

For this cause Paul affirms that the gospel is the power of God unto salvation. So it shall appear in that day, and so faith appropriates it at this present. Should someone enquire, Wherein is the strength of this gospel, that it should be called God's power unto salvation: in what particular does the power lie: what precisely are the seven uncut locks which hold the secret, the very heart of gospel strength, the cause of its being able to effect so great a salvation? The answer is, Justification by faith.

This the apostle plainly teaches, in the following verse declaring the reason for his statement that the gospel is 'the power of God unto salvation', Rom. 1:16. What is this reason? What basis does Paul give for such a statement? 'The gospel', saith he, 'is the power of God unto salvation to every one that believeth; to the Jew first, and also to the Greek.' 'For'—mark that, 'For': for this reason—'therein is the righteousness of God revealed from faith to faith', Rom. 1:17.

Clearly the revelation of the righteousness of God in the gospel is given as the cause of its being the power of God unto salvation. It is because of the righteousness of God. It is because of justifying righteousness. Remove the revealed righteousness of God in the preaching of the gospel, and at a stroke justification is overturned, the gospel is made void, the power of God is annulled, and salvation become of none effect. Why? Because the gospel being the power of God unto salvation depends upon the righteousness of God having been revealed therein. Take that righteousness from the gospel and all is lost. Yet in modern evangelism, in contemporary evangelicalism, in the current 'evangel', the righteousness of God has been taken away. Justification by faith has been made irrelevant, it has been removed, and, what is worse, it has been perverted out of all recognition by the 'sleight of men, the cunning craftiness, whereby they lie in wait to deceive', who are the leaders of the latter-day antichristian apostasy.*

It cannot be emphasised too often or too strongly that, according to the apostolic doctrine, the revelation of the righteousness of God in the gospel is the cause of its being powerful. Righteousness of God is revealed in the gospel: that is why it is the power of God, that is why salvation is effectual, and that is why Paul is not ashamed of the gospel of Christ.

*See 'The Elect undeceived', John Metcalfe Publishing Trust.

Omit that revealed righteousness, or the preaching of it, and the gospel becomes nothing but an empty husk, a lifeless shell. Here is the very heart of the doctrine of the gospel. It is the gospel.

The first seventeen verses of the Epistle to the Romans constitute the preamble to the full and proper exposition of Paul's doctrine. Here, so early in the epistle, two separate passages give the apostle's summary of the gospel. Firstly, Rom. 1:3,4. Paul shows that the gospel concerns the Person of God's Son, possessed of both divine and human nature, raised from the dead, and declared to be the Son of God with power. Secondly, Rom. 1:16,17. The gospel Paul received is the gospel of Christ, it is the power of God unto salvation, and therein the righteousness of God is revealed from faith to faith. So that in the Person of the Son, the righteousness of God is revealed from faith to faith, and this summarises the gospel. Leave out any part of this summary and it is less than another, it is altogether an accursed gospel.

The gospel therefore is not that travesty which for the past century and a half has imperceptibly taken its place in the interests of the 'results' of mass evangelists, particularly from America. This Arminian appeal system does not contain the doctrine of the gospel. It is the crusade or campaign method, using charismatic personalities, crooners, togetherness, jokes, craftiness, compromise, soft singing, sweet music, gentle pressure and unoffending coercion to get people to 'the front'. But where is the doctrine of justification by faith? Where is the revelation of the righteousness of God? Where is the truth of the Person and work of Christ, the doctrine which formed the saints and the early church? People know perfectly well this system evades the righteousness of God, just as it ignores the evangel, the evangelist, and the evangelism of the New Testament. Not only does it ignore these things, it supplants them by what is clean contrary to the apostolic authority given by the Holy Ghost in the scripture.

In the summary of the gospel revealed to Paul, great value lies in the setting forth of things that are essential: the essence of the gospel. It is not that other truths are not vital, they are, but what encompasses all other truths, and therefore stands out as the *sine qua non*, is the revelation of the righteousness of God. That revelation takes in everything else, but nothing else takes in that revelation. Hence Paul makes it central. The forgiveness of sins is vital to the gospel, but the righteousness of God encompasses it and transcends it. Righteousness tells me how sins are forgiven, by whom, through whom, why, and with what effect. It shows the condition of those whose sins are forgiven. The heart of the declaration of the gospel is not pardon, peace, remission, though none of these things can be omitted without great harm, but at the heart, encompassing all these things and transcending them, at the heart of the gospel lies the revelation of the righteousness of God.

The gospel itself is not the declaration of the forgiveness of sins, although in and by the gospel remission of sins is preached in the name of Jesus Christ. But the gospel itself is the declaration of the righteousness of God. That declaration reveals how God can forgive sins in righteousness. It is not a part of but the whole of the gospel. The preaching of the gospel is not the declaration of a part, but the exposition of the whole. How can God forgive sins? How can he pass over his own revealed wrath from heaven? How can he pardon sinners consistent with his own nature and attributes?

The gospel, properly so-called, faces the real issue: the nature of God. And, facing it, the gospel answers every question triumphantly with the divine revelation of God's own righteousness. Whereas false gospels, partial gospels, other gospels, always begin and end with man. And they always degenerate over time. Because with man-centred false or partial gospels the appeal is always to self-interest at the expense of divine truth. But the gospel of Christ declares the righteousness of God.

31

The gospel, properly so-called, is based and established upon this sure foundation: the righteousness of God—without the law—manifested by faith of Jesus Christ. In the gospel it is God's righteousness that has been revealed, it is God's righteousness that is to be declared doctrinally, and it is God's righteousness that is to be grasped intelligibly by faith in the gospel. This declaration of the righteousness of God in the preaching of the gospel is at the heart of the gospel. Where this is missing, justification is missing, power is missing, salvation is missing, the gospel is missing, and God is missing.

Such vital things missing? If so, then the unrighteousness and ungodliness that must follow in the professing church will resemble the spiritual conditions before the Reformation. Only, because now it is a going back on light, not a coming out from darkness, conditions will be much more deceptive, the moving spirit will be much more subtle, the guile of men will be much more persuasive, and the darkness will be final: irrevocable.

Christendom will rise up in libertarianism: and the word of God shall sink down in bondage. Roman Catholicism will reign as queen: and Christ shall be deposed as King. The Pope will embody authority: and the Holy Ghost shall be blasphemed as sectarian. False teachers will swarm in: and the ministers of the gospel shall be cast out. And these things shall come to pass chiefly, knowingly, because the eucharistic mass—over the blood of ten thousand martyrs—will be exalted: and justification by faith shall be debased.

Now, justification by faith was the burning issue of the New Testament. It was the burning issue of the Reformation. Then, since the righteousness of God by faith of Jesus Christ unto all and upon all them that believe has been degraded and debased in our time, ought it not to be the burning issue of all with eyes to see, and ears to hear, in our own time, and in the present generation?

III

Righteousness of God Revealed

WHEN the Apostle Paul speaks of the revelation of the righteousness of God, Romans 1:17, he is not speaking directly of justification by faith. Neither is he speaking of faith being counted for righteousness. Nor of righteousness being imputed to the believer. He will speak of these things as he continues to expound the doctrine, but in this place he addresses himself to the fact that, before justification could become a reality, righteousness of God must be brought in and established by the death and resurrection of Jesus Christ in the gospel.

The imputation of righteousness, or a person being accounted righteous before God, though a sinner; the justifying of a person that believes, though he be ungodly; the accounting of a person's faith for righteousness, though he were unrighteous: all these things become effectual after Christ ascended on high, with the doctrine of the gospel complete in itself. By the gospel, the justification of the ungodly, faith being counted for righteousness, and righteousness being imputed to the sinner, are things that continue to this very day. But the gospel itself was concluded as an entity two thousand years ago.

The fact that people are still being justified two thousand years after Christ rose from the dead, neither adds to nor subtracts from the completeness of the gospel preached. The gospel was complete in itself from the beginning. Thereafter people may believe, but their believing neither increases nor diminishes what they believe, namely, the gospel itself. The doctrine of the gospel was already concluded, and was an entity, the sum of all its parts, when Christ died and rose on high. The fact that by believing the gospel countless multitudes have since been justified does not add one jot or one tittle to that gospel.

Now Paul is saying in this summary, Romans 1:16,17, that 'therein'—that is, in the gospel—'righteousness of God is revealed'. Then it must already have been revealed as an integral part of that gospel. Therefore what Paul refers to is nct justification by faith as such—because that has continued to take place from that day to this—but the righteousness of God brought to light in the gospel when Christ died and rose again from the dead. It is this that is the ground and basis of the justification of all that ever did or ever should believe from the creation of the world to its dissolution.

Hence when Paul states that 'therein'—in the gospel of Christ—'the righteousness of God is revealed', he is speaking of the foundation upon which afterwards God would justify sinners. He is speaking of Christ's bringing in the righteousness of God and establishing it in the gospel so that from the beginning of time to that day, and from that day to the end of time, righteously God could pass a sentence of justification upon every one that ever did or ever should believe. It follows that he is not speaking of men being justified, but of righteousness being established so that men could be justified.

That is why, in summarising the gospel, Paul discards all else and focuses upon this one thing: Christ had brought in an everlasting righteousness which was to become the very foundation of the gospel which henceforward was to be preached in all the world. By the time Jesus said to the eleven, Go ye into all the world and preach the gospel to every creature, that gospel was complete. Its doctrine was concluded. In the evangelical doctrine of the gospel the righteousness of God, brought in by the death of Jesus Christ, was already revealed. When the eleven went forth and preached the gospel, by believing, men were justified by faith. But the revelation of the righteousness of God, declared in the preaching of the gospel, preceded their being justified by faith. That righteousness of God revealed in the gospel, foundational to men being justified thereafter, is that of which the Apostle Paul is speaking in Romans 1:17.

In order to understand the apostle's doctrine that 'therein'—in the gospel—'the righteousness of God is revealed', it is necessary to answer certain fundamental questions. The first of these questions is the basic enquiry, What is righteousness?

In the Hebrew of the Old Testament there are some four or five words belonging to the same family conveying the idea of 'right' or 'righteousness', particularly *Tsedaqah* and *Tsedeq*. The words that make up this group, translated Righteous, just, right, righteousness, and so on, occur over five hundred times. Such words come from an original meaning of Hard, even, straight, perfect, fair, true. A physical idea associated with the root of the word is that of a straight path, and, even more vivid, of the stiff straightness, the rigidity, of a lance. Hence the concept of the word is To be right, straight, to speak the truth, be upright, to have the quality of righteousness or uprightness.

Likewise the Greek of the New Testament provides a family of words which, though more complex, denotes the same idea of Right, righteous, just, righteousness. To this group belong the words *dikaios, dikaiōma, dikaiōsis, dikaioō,* and *dikaiosunē*. The number of occurences of the entire group exceeds two hundred, spread throughout the New Testament, with the meaning running through and embracing Right, just, righteous, justify, justification, and righteousness.

The Shorter Oxford English Dictionary gives the following definition of the word Righteousness: 'The quality or condition of being righteous; conformity of life or conduct to the requirements of the divine or moral law; *spec.* in *Theol.* applied, e.g., to the Perfection of the Divine Being, and to the justification of men through the atonement'.

From all of which it appears that righteousness may be spoken of God or men, and that it may be considered objectively or subjectively. In itself, righteousness is the description of that quality in a person habitually conformed to right. The idea of right therefore precedes the development of righteousness and is inherent in the use of the word.

Objectively, right refers to a rigid, inflexible rule or standard: it is the objective rule of righteousness declared either in accepted custom or precedent, or in oral or written law. Such a rule has nothing to do with mercy or repentance. It is the standard, the rule, it is to be kept, it is a law, and conformity to it is called righteousness. Nonconformity requires punitive sanctions in order to uphold the idea, necessity and worth of law.

Subjectively, right refers to the 'first truths' in the consciousness, that which may be known of God made manifest in men, the work of the law written in men's hearts. This inward light or awareness answers to the relative being and rights of both God and men, and one's obligation in consequence of this awareness. Of these things conscience is the natural monitor. This interior rule addresses not only bodily and outward action, but interior states, conditions and intentions. What determines a person's righteousness is conformity to this inward rule not only outwardly in conduct but also inwardly in heart, not only in some things but in all things, not only to oneself and to man but also to God and the divine glory. That is true righteousness.

The next question that arises from the statement that 'therein'—in the gospel—'is the righteousness of God revealed', Rom. 1:17, follows naturally: What is the righteousness of God?

The righteousness of God made known in the Old Testament, is seen in the judgment called forth from God by the works of men or of nations, for good or for ill. This appears particularly under the law. It is not the exposure or full manifestation of the righteousness which is hidden in God himself, making known what is intrinsic to his Being, but it is the appearing of his righteousness in answer to given behaviour or activities of men, extrinsic to himself. Of course this shows that he is righteous, and it is righteousness as such, but it does not reveal the depth of the quality of righteousness proper and unique to the divine nature; that, like everything else, remained shrouded, unrevealed, behind the veil.

What is seen is that God is righteous in dealing this way, or that way; in judging so, or thus: that he is consistent in his judgments: that he loves righteousness in men, and hates iniquity. But all this is reactive to men. By the things in Israel, or on earth, it is true that what he is in himself is drawn out, but it is his relationship to men that draws it out, it is his office as Judge that brings forth what he is in respect of what men have done. It is not the revelation or exposure of what he is in himself. That belongs to the gospel.

Under the law righteousness of God appeared as that judgment in God whereby he determined the discrepancy between the external rule of the law, and the degree to which man had conformed with or erred from that law. God is Judge. He judges according to the law, and judges men by that law. His judgment is according to righteousness. But the measure of the righteousness by which he judges is the rule of righteousness for men. In so judging, he appears as righteous, and protests his righteousness: 'Shall not the Judge of all the earth do right?'

But this is certainly not the revelation of his intrinsic divine righteousness. That is, the law did not, and could not, make known righteousness within the deity, proper to the divine Person himself. Only the Son of God in the gospel could make that known. 'Therein is the righteousness of God revealed.' What is seen under the first covenant is his judgment of righteousness in man and upon the earth. That is what comes to light in the Old Testament. It is God's righteous judgment of the measure of conformity or nonconformity in man to the rule of righteousness which God had given to him. It is this that is manifest under the law. The conduct of man, good or bad, brings God's righteous judgment to light.

The righteousness proper to divine Persons, true within the divine Being, was neither seen nor known as such: what he is in himself, the divine nature intrinsically, remained veiled. Righteousness of God was not revealed for what it is in itself in the Old Testament, nor could it be, until the revelation of the gospel of Christ. Before this, righteousness of God was limited in its manifestation to the fact of law, the actions of man, and the consistency of the judgments of the Judge upon men and nations, particularly in Israel.

Except, of course, for passages prophetic of the gospel, and of the revelation to be made known under the gospel. What was foreseen in Moses, the psalms and the prophets was that God, in righteousness, should be revealed in an entirely new way, but that that way was a mystery. Not that the righteousness of God would change: it would be unveiled. How, none could conceive. It was known that Messiah, when he came, should bring in this revelation of the righteousness of God, and that he should bring it in by finishing the transgression, making an end of sins, and making reconciliation for iniquity. The righteousness brought in by Messiah would be everlasting, Dan. 9:24.

Furthermore it was declared by them of old time that this future, evangelical righteousness would pertain to the seed of

Abraham, the father of the faithful, who 'believed God, and it was counted to him for righteousness'. Then, it was to be an accounted righteousness, and, as opposed to any conceivable righteousness known by the law, or without it, this was the righteousness of faith. Moreover, the Lord, JEHOVAH, should be the righteousness of his people, and he should put that righteousness upon them as a man puts on a robe. But seeing that all their righteousnesses were as filthy rags, how these things could be, they could not imagine. It was all a mystery. Nevertheless this mystery was spoken of by the prophets, and, understanding nothing, those that were of faith believed every word of it, as may be observed in the eleventh of Hebrews.

Though in the Old Testament God was seen to be righteous as Judge in judging men and upholding law, it was men and law with which that righteousness was concerned. But that Judah, Israel, and Jerusalem in the days of Messiah should be called by the name of 'The LORD our righteousness', Jer. 23:6, 33:16, or that the seed of promise should be covered with 'the robe of righteousness', were things yet to be revealed. Well, now, in the gospel, these things are revealed. What has been revealed, therefore, cannot, by definition, be that which was known of God's righteousness under the Old Testament. Neither can it be on a legal principle. Otherwise, where were the revelation? But the unsearchable, the infinite, the invisible, the intrinsic divine righteousness proper to the divine nature, that is what has been revealed in the gospel. And, if so, not to judge, but to justify.

Although God judges righteously, and, as Judge, justly requires all the rigour of the righteous sentence against transgressors under the Old Covenant, although he magnifies the law and makes it honourable, although, far from making it void—God forbid!—he establishes the law, nevertheless the revelation of the righteousness of God in the gospel utterly eclipses everything made known from Genesis to Malachi. By

Jesus Christ in the gospel the righteousness of God without the law is manifested in a way that is entirely transcendent. This evangelical revelation includes all that ever was seen under the law and the prophets, honouring every line, text and book of those scriptures, but it soars above and beyond the entire Old Testament as far as the heavens are above the earth. And this is no more than what was promised of old time, when the ancient prophet spake forth, saying, 'Eye hath not seen, nor ear heard, neither have entered into the heart of man, the things which God hath prepared for them that love him.'

IV

Righteousness Revealed from Faith to Faith

PAUL, unashamed of the gospel of Christ, informs us that it is the power of God unto salvation, and for this reason: 'therein is the righteousness of God revealed from faith to faith', Rom. 1:17.

From faith to faith? What does the apostle mean by saying the revelation of the righteousness of God in the gospel is 'from faith to faith'? From whose faith to whose faith? Or does he mean a certain increase of faith in the same person? How can that be? Then what does this passage mean?

Whatever it means, one thing is clear at the outset, and that is the decisive way in which the apostle puts the entire emphasis upon faith. This indicates that it is nothing to do with works. Faith is always contrasted with works. It is by believing, not doing, that the righteousness of faith is revealed. It is not by the works of the law, but by the hearing of faith. Now faith and works are subjective. The one comes from within the believer, and the other from within the doer. The one entails an inward rest, the other an inward exertion. Of necessity they are opposites.

Again, faith and works each pertain to an object. They do not subsist of themselves. They are called forth by what is plainly objective. Objective to faith is the gospel of Christ. Objective to works is the law of Moses. These two things, the gospel and the law, are always set in opposition. They are

41

contrary in principle the one to the other. The law was given by Moses, but grace and truth came by Jesus Christ. The law was given on mount Sinai, but grace is promulgated from mount Zion.

Law and gospel are always set the one over against the other. So that just as faith and works are things subjective, and, as such, opposed the one to the other, so also gospel and law, objectively, are things that stand in complete contrast. Faith comes by hearing, that is, of Christ in the gospel; but works come by doing, that is, the rule prescribed by the law. And these contrasting things, whether subjectively or objectively, never subsist together.

'For the promise, that he should be heir of the world, was not to Abraham, or to his seed, through the law, but through the righteousness of faith', Rom. 4:13. The law and the righteousness of faith are opposed. The promise to the heirs was not through the law, it was nothing to do with law, it was through the righteousness of faith, it was altogether to do with the gospel. If these two things are not in contrast, then what is in contrast?

'For if they which are of the law be heirs, faith is made void.' Why? Because the law, objectively, calls for works, subjectively, from those under the law. It does not and it cannot call for faith. It makes faith void, because it does not require rest, it demands activity. But faith requires rest. Then the law has nothing to do with faith, everything to do with works. By the objective legal rule, of necessity faith is made void and works must be activated. But then, righteousness is not by works. Saith Paul, 'It is of faith, that it might be by grace; to the end the promise might be sure to all the seed.' Nothing to do with works.

Once more, 'Christ is the end of the law for righteousness to every one that believeth', Rom. 10:4. If Christ is the end of the law for righteousness, it follows that this is the end of works. For the law demands works, but the gospel calls for faith. And as to faith, to every one that is of faith, that believeth, the law is ended, Christ is the end of it. Righteousness, by faith, revealed in the gospel, has been effected. Then why go back to the law to strive for a righteousness which can never be achieved, when the gospel proclaims a gratuitous righteousness far higher in character than the law ever envisaged? The law demanded righteousness but brought condemnation: the gospel bestows righteousness and secures salvation. How can a man be delivered from the one and brought to the other? Christ is the end of the one for righteousness, and the fulness of the other to everlasting glory. What a contrast!

Grace and law, faith and works, likewise grace and works, law and faith, are diametrically opposed: these things can never subsist together. 'If it be by grace, then it is no more of works', Rom. 11:6. Why not? 'Otherwise grace is no more grace.' Grace begets faith, and faith hath ceased from works. Then if righteousness be by grace, manifestly it cannot be by works, because grace cannot require works. Contrariwise Paul says, 'If it be of works, then it is no more grace.' Why not? For the same, and obvious, reason: 'otherwise work is no more work.' Not only are grace and works seen to be opposed and incompatible, but that opposition and incompatibility form the basis of the apostle's argument.

'Knowing that a man is not justified by the works of the law, but by the faith of Jesus Christ', Gal. 2:16. Here the works of the law, and the hearing of faith, are contrasted. They cannot abide together. It is one or the other. Faith is opposed to works. Law is contrary to grace. They are opposites. And the revealed righteousness of God is of faith, and all of faith, 'from faith to faith'. Then, works are excluded, utterly excluded, and perpetually excluded. Otherwise, 'grace is no more grace.'

That is the first thing to be seen in the apostle's teaching that the revelation of righteousness of God in the gospel is 'from faith to faith'. That this excludes works. That it is nothing to do with the law. That everything is of faith, from first to last. And that all is of grace. And that law and works, grace and faith are utterly and absolutely incompatible, they can never exist together. Here then is the ground that is exclusive to faith, Rom. 1:17, 'from faith to faith'.

But—to return to the question—What does this mean? The phrase 'from faith to faith' has greatly perplexed theologians and commentators. The traditional interpretations show this, and it may be seen from the views expressed by Luther and Calvin respectively.

Martin Luther, delivering his lectures on the Epistle to the Romans, states, 'The words from faith to faith have been interpreted in various ways. Lyra gives the meaning, 'from unformed faith to formed faith'; but I do not believe it possible for anyone to believe by unformed faith. Others explain the words thus, 'from the faith of the Fathers of the Old Testament, to the faith of the New Testament'; this exposition may be accepted, though it may be contested: it cannot possibly mean that the righteous man lives by the faith of his ancestors. The fathers had the same faith as we: there is only one faith, though it may have been less clear to them.

'The words evidently mean: the righteousness of God is entirely from faith, but in such a way that there is constant growth and greater clarity—as in II Cor. 3:18, 'We are changed into the same image from glory to glory'; and Psalm 84:7, 'They go from strength to strength.' Just so the words 'from faith to faith' signify that the believer grows in faith more and more. Likewise 'He that is righteous can be justified still', Rev. 22:11, so that none should think that he has already apprehended, and hence ceases to grow.

'Saint Augustine explains these words in the eleventh chapter of 'On the Spirit and the Letter', thus, 'from the faith of those who confess it with the mouth to the faith of those who prove it by their obedience.' And Burgos interprets the passage by saying, 'from the faith of the synagogue (as the starting point) to the faith of the church (as the finishing point).' But the apostle says righteousness comes by faith; yet the heathen did not have a faith from which, so as to be justified, they could have grown into a further faith.' So much for Luther.

John Calvin comments as follows: 'But instead of the expression used before by the apostle he now says 'from faith'; for righteousness is offered by the gospel, and is received by faith. And he adds 'to faith': for as our faith makes progress, and as it advances in knowledge, so the righteousness of God increases in us at the same time, and the possession of it is in a manner confirmed. When at first we taste the gospel, we indeed see God's smiling countenance turned towards us, but at a distance: the more the knowledge of true religion grows in us, by coming as it were nearer, we behold God's favour more clearly and more familiarly.

'What some think, that there is an implied comparison between the Old Testament and New Testament, is more refined than well founded; for Paul does not here compare the Fathers who lived under the law with us, but points out the daily progress that is made by every one of the faithful.' Calvin: Commentary on the Epistle to the Romans.

Broadly speaking, Luther and Calvin agree that the words 'from faith to faith' apply to the same individual. The phrase refers to the same person, indicative of his growth in faith. Only Calvin adds, 'As faith makes progress, and as it advances in knowledge, so the righteousness of God increases in us at the same time.' This is a glaring and dangerous error. Far from increasing in us, righteousness of God is never said to be in us at all. The doctrine is that the righteousness of God by faith of Jesus Christ is 'unto' all and 'upon' all them that believe, Rom. 3:22. But that is a very different thing from being 'in' them that believe. Justifying righteousness is imputed not imparted to those that believe. Whereas faith is imparted not imputed to those that believe. To confuse these two things together is to darken counsel without knowledge, disseminating error which brings down darkness on this the most vital of all issues.

Luther and Calvin are in agreement, however, that the words 'from faith to faith' apply to the same person. Both give the meaning, from a believer's (first) faith, to his (increased) faith. Two texts are proposed to support this view. The first is II Cor. 3:18, 'Changed from glory to glory', and the second Psalm 84:7, 'They go from strength to strength'. These texts are supposed to confirm that the words 'from faith to faith' apply to one and the same person. However, this supposition ignores the different grammatical structure in the case of both texts, and the different Greek in the case of the Corinthian text.

Take first the case of the Greek in the Corinthian text. The words 'from' glory 'to' glory, II Cor. 3:18, whilst being the same in the English 'from' faith 'to' faith, Rom. 1:17, are not the same in the Greek. This has been overlooked due to eagerness to find support for the supposition that 'from faith to faith', Rom. 1:17, refers to the increase in faith of the same person or persons. Of course the words 'from glory to glory', II Cor. 3:18, do refer to the increase in glory of the same person or persons. The same persons pass from the glory of the Old Covenant, which has faded away, to the glory of the New, which is everlasting.

However, the prepositions read *apo* 'away from', and *eis* 'unto'. Hence, 'Away from glory, 'namely, away from the veiled and passing glory of Moses' countenance, 'unto—or into—glory', that is, unto the everlasting glory shining for ever without a veil in the face of Jesus Christ. So that a parallel between the passages in Rom. 1:17 and II Cor. 3:18 can hardly be drawn, since the prepositions differ in the original.

However, that is the least of the arguments against the traditional interpretation—of Rom. 1:17—that the twice-mentioned faith indicates 'from a believer's (first) faith to his (increased) faith'. How could Calvin and Luther, of all people, have credited such an impossibility? Because of Augustine, whom they favoured? But a moment's consideration should have shown them the far from untypical inconsistency of that revered papist prelate. How can a believer's 'first' faith be 'out of'—*ek*—faith? Out of what faith? Out of the faith he had before he came to faith? Out of whose faith? The faith of others 'before faith came', Gal. 3:23?

The reformers support their notion 'from beginning faith to mature faith' by drawing a comparison with texts that show but the most superficial association of ideas. They compare II Cor. 3:18, 'from glory to glory', and Psalm 84:7, 'from strength to strength'—indisputably referring to the glory and strength of the same party, not of two different parties—with Rom. 1:17, 'from faith to faith', supposing to have proved thereby that the faith in question must also be that of the same party. Luther and Calvin, at a loss otherwise to explain the phrase in Rom. 1:17, have run together 'from faith to faith', 'from glory to glory', and 'from strength to strength'. Yes, but they have fallen into the trap of assuming that, because of an apparent similarity in phraseology, what applies to two of the texts necessarily applies to all three texts.

But the subject in II Cor. 3:18 and Psalm 84:7 is the increase of the people of God. They go from strength to strength, and they go from glory to glory. But that is not the case in Rom. 1:17, where the subject is not the people of God at all, but the righteousness of God. How is the righteousness of God revealed? Answer, 'from faith to faith'. The interpretation of II Cor. 3:18 and Psalm 84:7 is irrelevant to this. That is about persons. Whereas Rom. 1:17 is not about persons.

It is not that believers go from faith to faith, but that the righteousness of God is revealed from faith to faith. 'It' is revealed—*ek*—'out of' faith, and 'it' is revealed—*eis*—'unto' faith. This passage cannot be so lightly dismissed as Calvin, Luther, and the commentators suppose to dismiss it, relegating its meaning to 'the faith of the people of God'. This passage is not about the faith of the people of God. It is about the revelation of the righteousness of God.

The interpretation of the phrase 'from faith to faith', Rom. 1:17, depends upon the proper observation of the preceding verb. That verb is 'to reveal'. The subject is the righteousness of God. It is this that is to be revealed. The phrase 'from faith to faith' is an amplification of the verb 'to reveal': the subject, the righteousness of God, is revealed in this way. 'From faith to faith' is not some detached, non-contextual afterthought. It is a vital exposition of the act of revelation, amplifying the manner of that revelation. The verb concerns the subject of God's righteousness, not the faith of the believer: it is speaking of the way in which the righteousness of God is revealed.

Thus the phrase 'from faith to faith' does not amplify the way in which the believer believes, but the way in which God's righteousness is revealed. The verse deals with the coming to light of God's righteousness in the gospel, not the coming to light of the faith of those that believe. 'Revealed' is not about a believer, or a believer's doing something, it is about God, and God's doing something. It is not how we believe, but how God has revealed his righteousness. That is the point. The righteousness of God is revealed. How is it revealed? From faith to faith. The phrase applies to the revelation, the unveiling, of God's righteousness.

'From faith to faith' does not speak about people believing, although 'from strength to strength' does speak about people going onwards, just as 'from glory to glory' speaks about people changing from one state to another. But this is not the case in Rom. 1:17. Here it is a case of something being unveiled, of revelation, that is, of the quality of righteousness in the character of God. The verb tells you this has been revealed. And the phrase 'from faith to faith' tells you how it has been revealed.

Generally speaking, the phrase 'from—out of—faith unto faith' has been read as if it meant the same person's faith. But this cannot be. Such a view makes nonsense of the words, and, worse still, it prevents the understanding of the apostle's doctrine.

It is impossible that a person should believe 'out of' faith. Out of whose faith? Somebody else's? Out of what faith? The faith he had before he believed? How absurd. The preposition translated 'from' or 'out of' does not direct us to a person's faith at all. It directs us to the revelation of the righteousness of God. It is this that is 'from' or 'out of' faith.

Is it possible that so great a matter as the righteousness of God could be revealed 'out of' or 'from' faith? Yes, for that is what the verse is saying: The righteousness of God is revealed 'out of faith'. Then out of whose faith? The faith of the people of God? Your faith? Mine? Absolutely not. The righteousness of God had been revealed in the gospel long before I believed, or you believed. Then the faith spoken of cannot be our faith. Out of the apostles' faith? But Paul the Apostle says 'the righteousness of God is revealed'. Then it was revealed in the gospel before he, or any other apostle, believed. The gospel was what they believed, just as the gospel is what we believe.

And, indeed, however holy or apostolic, where is the man whose faith could bring to light God's own righteousness? This pertains to none other than he whose faith brought to light the gospel itself, he who commanded the gospel to be preached in all the world.

And whose faith is that? Whose faith, found equal to the revelation of the righteousness of God? Whose faith, equal to laying the foundation and bringing in the topstone of the gospel? It is as clear as the sun at noonday that the apostle refers to the faith of Jesus Christ. The righteousness of God is revealed, and revealed once and for all, by the faith of Jesus Christ in the gospel. How is it revealed by Jesus Christ in the gospel? It is revealed, *ek*, 'out of' faith. It is, 'out of' the faith of Jesus Christ. But, to whose faith is it revealed? It is revealed, *eis*, 'unto' the faith of all that should believe the gospel.

Ek shows that the righteousness of God is revealed 'out of' faith. It is 'from' faith, this revelation. But such faith cannot possibly be ours. Why not? Because, firstly, our faith does not and cannot bring to light the righteousness of God, it is not equal to such a thing. Secondly, our faith is in a righteousness that has been revealed; it existed for us to believe, righteousness is already revealed in the gospel. And, lastly, it is obvious that the faith that brings to light what is to be believed, cannot be the same faith as that which believes what has been brought to light.

The literal translation of the phrase in question might well read 'Out of faith unto faith', but because such wording was unintelligible to the translators—just as it was to the commentators—they have given the weaker 'from faith to faith'. It is certainly true that the Greek will bear that rendering. But if accuracy were to be studied, in this context, the phrase ought to read 'out of faith unto faith'. If so, then the faith concerned cannot refer to the same person: faith cannot come out of a believer's faith unto that believer's faith!

In the New Testament the word faith is used of two distinct parties. The one is that people brought to belief, the other is Jesus Christ himself. In Rom. 1:17 it has been clearly shown that faith cannot refer to one party only: of necessity two different parties are in view. The revelation of the righteousness of God is 'out of' the faith of the one, and 'unto' the faith of the other. The object of faith differs in each case. But it is obvious that the party whose faith rested in his God, 'out of' whose faith would be revealed the righteousness of God, must be the Son of God's love.

This cannot refer to the faith of the other party, the believer, because the righteousness of God simply is not 'out of' the faith of believers. It is 'unto' the faith of believers. The faith of believers cannot possibly be said to precede the revelation of the righteousness of God. The faith of believers rests in the revelation of the righteousness of God. The righteousness is there, it is preached in the gospel, and this is what is believed when one is justified by faith.

It is impossible that our faith should be that 'out of' which the righteousness of God comes to light. Our faith is in a righteousness that has already been brought to light, set forth in Jesus Christ for us to believe.

The use of the preposition *ek* indicates a faith by the exercise of which an unknown, veiled righteousness was to be revealed. Righteousness of God is revealed 'out of' faith. The expression, quite excluding the faith of believers, shuts us up to the faith of Jesus Christ.

What do we understand by the faith of Jesus Christ? Not that his faith is imputed to us, but that when in our place and on our behalf he submitted passively by faith to the just judgment of the righteousness of God, that faith was honoured, the just judgment of God's righteousness against us was outpoured upon him. His faith brought down the righteousness of God which thereafter should be accounted to those for whom he died.

His faith therefore revealed the righteousness of God in an entirely new way, in an evangelical way: a way which brought divine righteousness to light 'out of' his faith. Not that the faith of Jesus Christ is accounted to us; it is the righteousness of God by faith of Jesus Christ that is accounted to us: just as it is this that is revealed 'unto' the faith of the believer.

There are many passages, implicit and explicit, in the gospels and in the epistles, speaking of this very thing. Indeed, there are many passages, implicit and explicit, which shut us up to this very thing. The truth is, the gospel must be brought in on the principle of faith, just as it must be preached on the principle of faith. It is 'the faith'. 'The faith once delivered to the saints.' Works, the law, are utterly excluded from the gospel, save that by faith of Jesus Christ at the cross the law is magnified, made honourable, and established, by the same work through which believers are freely justified by faith, and divine righteousness put to their account, world without end.

That righteousness, that justification, however, was wrought wholly by faith, just as it is conveyed wholly to faith. It was out of faith and unto faith. It was from faith to faith. Jesus Christ brought in the gospel, the whole gospel, and nothing but the gospel, through his faith, and he presents the gospel, the whole gospel, and nothing but the gospel to the faith of believers. There is no alternative meaning that can bear weight in the apostolic doctrine of Christ in the New Testament. That is what we believe.

From the beginning of his ministry until the cross the faith of Jesus Christ was never so tried—not even in the temptation in the wilderness—as it was at Gethsemane. That was the hour of darkness. Yet against that darkness the radiance of his faith was more luminous than ever. As the darkness closed about him, he went forward a space, and fell prostrate, being in his manhood tried to the uttermost. Here it appears that, though he were a Son, he should learn obedience by the things which he suffered. Yet in that hour of weakness his faith appeared the more strong. His sweat was as it were great drops of blood falling to the ground. 'Father, if it be possible, take this cup from me.' What language is this? Of works? 'Nevertheless, not my will, but thine be done.' This is the language of faith. It is the language of submission to the will of God, the language not of him that willeth, nor of him that worketh, but of him that believeth.

The law saith, This do, and thou shalt live. Jesus said, Not my will but thine be done. The law was for the work of a servant. The Father's will was for the faith of the Son. The death of the cross was before him. This was the Jews', the rulers', hour, and the power of darkness. The faith of Jesus Christ looked into that darkness, and saw the cup that he must drink. 'Father, if it be possible, let this cup pass from me.' But for this cause came he unto this hour.

'Not my will, but thine be done', prayed Jesus. This was the language of faith, and this was the path of faith. He knew of the cross, of the piercing of his hands and of his feet. He knew of the spiritual, the mysterious cup that should be lowered from heaven during the hours of darkness. He knew that he must drink of that cup, drain it, sip by sip, hour after hour, till the last drop of its terrible contents should have passed through his inmost soul. What law required this? This was the work of God, and by faith he knew what was before him. His pathway was the pathway of faith, not of works. In weakness he bowed by faith to the will of the Father, not, in strength he rose to labour by the works of Moses. His faith was not that he should do anything, but that the Father should do to him all that for which he had come into the world.

He went by faith to Golgotha, believing that when he was hung up on the tree, bowed in passive faith, hanging suspended between heaven and earth, God would make him to be the great sacrifice for sin. He knew then, his faith knew then, what should begin to happen once they had driven the nails through his hands and through his feet.

For three hours of daylight he was exposed to the mockery of professing religion, to their insulting persecution, to their abuse of his faith, to their pouring their envy and hatred upon him. But when the sun ceased to give her light, when darkness covered the earth, then he knew that the hour had come indeed. Then began the mysterious, the supernatural, the divine transaction between the Father and the Son whereby in his manhood all the sins of believers, from the beginning of the world to the end of it, should be gathered up, heaps upon heaps, as great mountains, and laid upon the believing soul of the Son of man. He believed that the LORD would lay upon him the iniquity of us all, and it was so. He believed that God, through his suffering, should take away the sin of the world, that he should be made sin, and so it came to pass.

He believed that God would call down upon him the curse of the law, that the lash of the broken law should be laid upon him, that he should be wounded for our transgressions, that stripes should be laid upon him by which we should be healed. He believed, and, according to his faith, it was done unto him. He bore the wrath of God, so that from the firmament of heaven, from the heights of the deity, to the lower parts of the earth, to the depths of humanity, there pressed down and rose up upon the great Believer hanging between heaven and earth all that his faith had anticipated when he had said 'Father, if it be possible, let this cup pass from me: nevertheless, not my will, but thine be done.'

By faith he endured, as seeing him who is invisible. By faith he crossed the Red Sea of God's righteous judgment and vengeance upon mankind. By faith he prevented the waters of Jordan, the rolling tide of death, alone in the river bed, whilst his people, whose sin-bearer he had become, passed mysteriously before his face, till the last one was over, safe, in the promised land. By faith he gave the great shout of victory, 'It is finished'. By faith it was finished. By faith he made an end of sins, by faith he made reconciliation for iniquity, by faith he finished the transgression, and by faith he brought in ever-lasting righteousness. This is the faith of Jesus Christ, and, by it, the righteousness of God was revealed falling in wrath upon him who bore the iniquities and sins of his people in the place of judgment.

This is the faith of Jesus Christ, and according to his faith it was done unto him. And when it was finished—for it was finished: he cried, saying, It is finished!—he gave up the ghost and died. And his faith was equal even to death itself, for, before he died, he prophesied, saying, 'The third day the Son of man shall rise again from the dead'. And the third day he did rise again from the dead.

This is the faith of Jesus Christ. And God honoured that wonderful, that unique faith, and gave him glory, having raised him from the dead. He was justly set on the highest throne of the uttermost glory that heaven could afford, and how could it be otherwise? This is called, the faith of Jesus Christ and 'out of' it, the righteousness of God is revealed from faith to faith, as it is written, The just shall live by faith.

The Apostle Paul declares, Rom. 3:21,22, 'But now the righteousness of God without the law is manifested.' If without the law, then without works. And if without works, then through grace. And if through grace, then by faith. 'Even the righteousness of God by faith of Jesus Christ.' That is how it was manifested, by faith of Jesus Christ.

Nothing to do with the law, or the works of the law, on the part of Jesus Christ, no, nothing to do with the law, because he brought it in by faith. That is, the righteousness of God was revealed 'out of' faith, namely, out of the faith of Jesus Christ. But what of believers? That is what they believe, and that, in the preaching of the gospel, is what is revealed to their faith. 'Even the righteousness of God, by faith of Jesus Christ, unto all and upon all them that believe.' Righteousness is revealed 'unto' faith: in a word, 'From faith to faith.'

'Not having mine own righteousness', confesses Paul, Phil. 3:9, 'which is of the law, but that which is through the faith of Jesus Christ.' Here the righteousness which is through faith of Jesus Christ is set in contrast with that which is of the law. Then the righteousness which is by faith of Jesus Christ is clearly not of the law, not wrought on a legal principle, not achieved by his keeping the law, or by his having to do with it. No, as opposed to the law, and the works of the law, it is by faith only.

What is by faith only? 'Even the righteousness which is of God by faith.' The faith of Jesus Christ, which is not of the law, brought in the righteousness of God which is in like manner received by faith only. It is to be believed, works are excluded. That is, it is a righteousness 'from—out of—faith, to faith'. From the faith of Jesus Christ, unto the faith of all believers.

This is precisely the doctrine of Galatians 2:16, 'Knowing that a man is not justified by the works of the law'—legal works as such; either his own, or another's, or those of Jesus Christ—'but by the faith of Jesus Christ'—as opposed to the legal works of Jesus Christ. That is the whole point of the doctrine.

The righteousness of God, by which God justifies the ungodly, did not come, it was not revealed, by the works of the law, or on the principle of the works of the law. It was revealed by faith, on the principle of faith as opposed to works. 'But', in contrast to the principle of works, 'by the faith of Jesus Christ'. His faith brought in the righteousness of God, it is 'from', or 'out of', his faith, as that principle upon which it was brought in and revealed, 'unto' the faith of all that believe.

This is made exceedingly clear by the great cloud of witnesses in Hebrews 12:1. What cloud of witnesses is this? It is the cloud of witnesses summoned to give their testimony in the eleventh chapter. And what is this testimony? That righteousness is by the works of the law? That the law was their rule of life? God forbid! If that were so, all would be disqualified, and half would be excluded.

Why? Because half the witnesses had rendered their testimony before the law was given, or was in the world at all! As to the other half, including Moses himself, who knew more of the law than any of its peevish modern advocates, here are the men of faith who did not look for righteousness by works of the law, or on a legal principle, nor did they walk by the law, or on a legal principle. Their righteousness, like Noah's, was 'the righteousness of faith', of which they became heirs.

Their principle was faith only, as Abraham testified, who 'believed God, and it was counted to him for righteousness.' As to their walk, they walked by faith. As to their life, they lived by faith. And as to their death, they died in faith. And where is the law, its principle, or its works, in that? They were all, every one of them, of the sort that the blind legalists, with their rotten lives but legal pretences, called antinomians. But the truth is, the legalists are the antinomians, because by faith, those that are of faith, and those only, 'establish the law'. The legalists, by their own confession, do nothing but break it. And what is the good of a rule like that?

As for us, with Abel, Enoch, Noah, Abraham, Sarah, Isaac, Jacob, Joseph, Moses, the people of God, Joshua, Rahab, Gideon, Barak, Samson, Jephthae, David, Samuel and the prophets, we will, Heb. 12:2, 'Look unto Jesus, the author and finisher of our faith'.

As to them, with Cain, Ishmael, Esau, Hagar, the Egyptians, the bondchildren, the children of Abraham after the flesh, Saul, the false prophets, Jezebel, Herodias, the Pharisees, the Sadducees, the elders and the chief priests, with Alexander the coppersmith, and every persecuting servant that ever there was, together with all that justify themselves, walking in self-will and self-righteousness, they may look unto Moses. But they will be disappointed, for, 'There is one that accuseth you, even Moses, in whom ye trust. For had ye believed Moses, ye would have believed me', Jn. 5:45,46.

Then whom shall God justify? He shall justify those whose faith is in Jesus Christ, 'The author and finisher of our faith', Heb. 12:2. For 'as he is, so are we in this world', who 'hath left us an example, that we should follow in his steps', which steps are called, The steps of faith. And those that are of faith do follow him, to whom the righteousness of God has been revealed, out of his faith, unto their faith, as it is written, The just shall live by faith.

V

The Just shall Live by Faith

HERE the Apostle Paul quotes from the prophet Habakkuk in order to confirm the doctrine, saying, 'as it is written, The just shall live by faith'. The doctrine which the apostle corroborates is that of the revelation of the righteousness of God 'from faith to faith'. The text from Habakkuk reinforces the teaching that evangelical righteousness has been brought in by the faith of Jesus Christ—from faith—and is to be appropriated by the faith of the believer—unto faith—showing that everything in the gospel is based on faith. Faith is the exclusive evangelical principle, it is all of faith, as it is written, The just shall live by faith.

Before we believed the gospel, it had been fully outwrought by the faith of Jesus Christ. There was nothing to be completed, everything had been done by the faith of Jesus Christ. Everything was 'out of' the faith of Jesus Christ, it was established on the basis of his faith. Moreover the sent ministry of the gospel was by faith: called by faith, taught by faith, ordered by faith, and kept by faith. And the gospel was received by faith, believers were justified by faith, made holy by faith, they walked by faith, and they died in faith. How appropriate, then, the confirmatory word of the prophet, 'As it is written, The just shall live by faith'.

Habakkuk prophesied something like one hundred years after the destruction and dispersion of the ten tribes of Israel in the north by the armies of the Assyrians. Little more than

59

twenty-five years were to pass before the two tribes faithful to the throne of David, Judah and Benjamin, would go into captivity at the destruction of Jerusalem by the Chaldeans. So that it was a time of sore trial for the faithful, made worse by the fact that 'the wicked walk on every side, when the vilest men are exalted'.

Hence the prophet, Hab. 1:1-4, on behalf of the faithful remnant, complains of the iniquity and apostasy of the city and of the land. 'O Lord, how long shall I cry, and thou wilt not hear! even cry out unto thee of violence, and thou wilt not save!' He complains about the state of religion in Jerusalem and in Judaea. His complaint is that there is no righteous judgment. The godly man ceased, the faithful failed, from among the children of men. Those that were left of the godly remnant were a standing rebuke to the empty profession of the vast majority, who detested them in consequence. The Lord's poor had good cause to grieve before God at the spoiling and violence to which they were subject. But God did not answer their cries. The strife of tongues, the contention of the persecutors, compassed about the righteous, and this was a burden to the faith of the prophet.

Moreover, because the wicked persecuted the righteous with impunity, because God took no vengeance, the persecutors no longer feared, they became bolder and bolder. Therefore the law was slacked, and no judgment went forth for the oppressed. 'For the wicked doth compass about the righteous, therefore wrong judgment proceedeth.' How could God endure such wickedness, such despising of his holy word? How could he be indifferent to the apostasy which had broken the hearts of the godly, causing weeping and lamentation to ascend continually from the remnant of the faithful? This was 'the burden which Habakkuk the prophet did see.'

In answer to his cry, the prophet was given to perceive beforehand the rising up of the Chaldeans, a vast multitude from the far northern countries gathering for war, Hab. 1:5-11. This mighty army should in the time appointed sweep down from the north, overflowing the whole earth, scourging the nations. The Chaldeans would descend upon Jerusalem, slaying and devouring all before them, overturning the false prophets, the wicked priests, the unjust judges together with the apostate people, destroying and carrying off all that remained into far distant captivity, leaving the land desolate and forsaken.

Far from being a consolation to Habakkuk, however, such a prophetic insight gave rise to the utmost alarm, Hab. 1:12-17. What Habakkuk foresaw far exceeded the judgment for which he had pleaded on behalf of the faithful. If such catastrophic things as this came to pass, what would happen to the remnant? Indeed, what would happen to the people and land of Israel? Surely this dreadful scourge could not be for the destruction of God's heritage? Surely it was but for correction? Surely 'we shall not die'?

Furthermore, if God's people were to be punished for iniquity, should it be by the hand of idolatrous heathen less righteous than they? Was this just? If so, then where was the Chaldeans' judgment? Must the Israel of God suffer such a humiliation at the hand of the uncircumcised? How would the faithful few, the poor remnant, be preserved amidst such terrible calamities? What would be the end of such things? When would judgment be established in the earth?

These were the bitter questionings that now became the cry of the prophet. Cast into confusion, he knew that he ought not to question, ought not to complain, but he could not help himself. Hence he makes his complaint, fully aware that he might be reproved, helpless under the weight of the burden that pressed upon him. 'I will stand upon my watch, and set me upon the tower, and will watch to see what he will say unto me, and what I shall answer when I am reproved', Hab. 2:1.

As the prophet waited, the Lord spoke. The reply, when it came, far from being a reproof, brought comfort and consolation that Habakkuk had never expected. This was given in a vision. The prophet received a vision of the coming of Christ and the bringing in of the New Testament. For this, both Habakkuk and the godly remnant must wait in faith. 'For the vision is yet for an appointed time, but at the end it shall speak, and not lie: though it tarry, wait for it; because it will surely come, it will not tarry.'

Until that time, though the Chaldean nation sent to destroy Israel was unrighteous: though the soul of the Chaldean king was lifted up in him: though the faithful remnant was to suffer the same judgment as the apostate people, yet that remnant should abide and endure by faith. This was the message to the godly before, during, and after the captivity, throughout all the perplexities of God's providence, until the fulfilment of 'the vision'.

Faith was to sustain the remnant according to the election of grace throughout the ages of God's dealing with Israel after the flesh, until the coming of Christ. Through the darkness and affliction, they, the just, must live by faith. The more especially when the vision seemed to tarry, and to tarry beyond their own generation. Nevertheless the prophet, together with the remnant, was to wait, and to wait patiently, through all the times, ways, and providences of God that seemed beyond resolution or understanding. Humbly the prophet— the guide and example of the remnant—was to submit. This was in contrast with the pride of the Chaldean king: 'Behold, his soul which is lifted up is not upright in him.' But what is that to the prophet? 'The just shall live by his faith.'

To the spiritual whose heart had perceived the heavenly vision described by the voice of the prophet there appeared a deeper meaning to his words. And since Habakkuk was to 'write the vision, and make it plain upon tables, that he may run that readeth it', we are not to suppose that this deeper meaning eluded the faithful of that day. For the 'vision' was not only a vision to sustain the remnant in their own time: it was also a revelation to them concerning the coming gospel times. But a revelation of what? A revelation of the truth that God's Just One should live by his faith. Now, this is the faith of Jesus Christ with a witness, and so Paul testifies.

The Just One, Jesus Christ the righteous, should bring in the gospel on a principle of faith. This was perfectly clear to Habakkuk, it was written upon tables, he that ran could read it. The New Testament should be 'out of' the faith of that Just One. If he lived by faith, how could his work be other than on the principle of faith? The life is that which brings forth the work. Well, God's Just One should live by his faith. Then, his work was the work of faith. That is, it was the work of faith with power.

It follows that those who were to believe the gospel should in like manner 'live by faith'. How otherwise could they live who received the gospel from him whose life was by faith, who wrought through faith, who died in faith, and who established the faith? Evidently the gospel was 'unto' faith, that is, from faith to faith: as it is written, 'The just shall live by faith.'

If this was the prophet's vision of the gospel day, a day made conspicuous by the faith which should bring in the gospel and receive the gospel, then the prophet himself ought to live by that faith, together with the believing remnant, whilst waiting for the coming vision. Whatever the circumstances, however long the delay, no matter how wicked the ungodly, nor how ill-disposed the one of whom it was said, 'his soul which is lifted up is not upright in him', still the unalterable truth should stand, 'the just shall live by his faith'.

Once seen in its true prophetic light, the passage quoted from Habakkuk 2:4 by the Apostle Paul in Romans 1:17, far from being obscure, could not be more apposite. No other quotation could have confirmed the apostle's doctrine with greater precision. The revelation given to the prophet Habakkuk abundantly illuminated the truth that faith, and faith only, provided the basis upon which Christ established the New Testament at the first, from which it was to be ministered by the apostles in consequence, and by which it should be received by every believer so long as the sun and moon endure. Indeed 'the just shall live by faith.'

And if by faith, then not by works. That is, men shall not live before God by their own works, which are nothing worth, as says the prophet Isaiah, 'All our righteousnesses are as filthy rags', Isa. 64:6; and Paul confirms, saying, 'Not by works of righteousness which we have done, but according to his mercy he saved us', Tit. 3:5. Neither shall men live before God by the works of others on their behalf, as the priests, vicars, and suchlike propose, working for reward, hiring out their labour. Nor yet shall men gain life by the works prescribed by and wrought in the temple, or what has become known as the church, with its vicarious sacrifices, ceremonies, and sacraments, as these superstitious inventions are called. No, not by works at all. But by 'his faith'.

And if by faith, then not by law. Not by the law of Moses, the ten commandments, the two commandments, or by the great commandment, because salvation is by grace alone, through faith only, as we have been taught. Neither is salvation or life to be obtained by perverting the gospel into a mixture of faith and works, law and grace, or by any suchlike perfidious confusion. Nor yet is righteousness or life gained before God by attempting to reach to moral perfection, to attain to the law of love, as they call it, labouring after an ideal of character, or working to maintain a code of ethics. Salvation is neither by a philosophy, nor by a method of moral excellence, it is by grace alone, through faith only. All the former things, though highly esteemed among men, are abomination in the sight of God, for, 'the just shall live by faith'.

And if by faith, then in the gospel. That is, faith in the doctrine of Christ in the New Testament, in the Person and work of Christ, in the Son of God and Son of man. In Jesus' perfect humanity, in his everlasting deity, in his sufferings, atonement, sacrifice, death and burial. In Christ's resurrection, ascension, in his reign, glory, and inheritance. In the ministration of the New Testament, in righteousness and life, in justification, sanctification and redemption. Salvation is by faith, that is, in the gospel of Christ. For faith comes by hearing, and hearing by the word of God. In this way it is clear that by believing, and by believing alone, shall be brought to pass the saying that is written, 'The just shall live by faith'.

The doctrine of the Epistle to the Galatians provides the Apostle Paul with a further occasion for quoting from Habakkuk 2:4. Here the text is used to demonstrate the immutable truth than no man is justified by the law in the sight of God. This is evident 'for'—because of the following demonstrable reason—'the just shall live by faith', Gal. 3:11.

Paul had shown previously, Gal. 3:6, that Abraham was accounted righteous some four hundred and thirty years before the law was given, and, moreover, that this was by faith alone: 'Abraham believed God, and it was accounted to him for righteousness.' It follows therefore that they only are Abraham's spiritual children—found in the character and walking in the steps of their father—who are of like precious faith. 'Know ye therefore that they which are of faith, the same are the children of Abraham.' But who are these children?

Not the Jews. The Jews went about to establish their own righteousness. This did not Abraham. Then, they were not his true children. Abraham submitted unto the righteousness of

God. But the Jews 'submitted not unto the righteousness of God.' Then, if they did not, how could they be Abraham's children? Had they been Abraham's children, doubtless they would have walked in his steps. But these, to Abraham, were strange, carnal children, as saith the apostle, 'Not the children of the flesh, but the children of the promise, are counted for the seed.' Then had Abraham no spiritual children? Yes, but, Gal. 3:8, they are of the heathen. That is, God would justify the heathen, and account them righteous, through faith alone, even as he justified Abraham. And if God would do so, then by so much are they Abraham's children by faith, and must and shall inherit the blessing, Gal. 3:9.

The opposite is the case with those under the law. They are, Gal. 3:10, under a curse. They work for life, not live by faith. These are Abraham's children after the flesh, but neither the God of Abraham nor Abraham himself owns or counts them for children. Why not? Because they are not, nor ever will they be, justified before God. 'For by the deeds of the law there shall no flesh be justified in his sight.'

Cursing and death are all that the fleshly seed can either earn or expect. For the wages of sin is death. And, under the law, such wages are all that ever can be earned. This is evident, Gal. 3:11, in that no man is justified by the law in the sight of God. Evident, saith the apostle, 'for, The just shall live by faith.' Here 'justified' and 'just', or having righteousness accounted to one, are the same thing. These live by faith because they have righteousness. First, they are just, or righteous, and have been justified; and last, they have life because of righteousness. For grace reigns through righteousness unto eternal life by Jesus Christ our Lord.

And what do those who are under the law of works know of that? Nothing at all. For the law requires works. It requires no faith. Then, those that are of works obtain no life, for, The just shall live by faith. The law, requiring works, can only bring forth fruit unto death. It cannot give life. Sin and death are all that the law can produce, under the curse and by wrath. This is the judgment already passed upon all that are under works, as saith the Apostle Paul, 'As many as are under the works of the law are under a curse: for it is written, Cursed is every one that continueth not in all things which are written in the book of the law to do them.'

The third and last quotation from Habakkuk 2:4 occurs in the Epistle to the Hebrews, Ch. 10:38. Here the context answers more to the primary meaning of the prophet Habakkuk, where the passage was intended for the comfort of the faithful remnant of Israel waiting in adversity for the coming of Christ. The godly that remained were suffering for the failure of Israel, for the general apostasy, which they lamented, and from which, morally, they withdrew. Yet they were required to endure the affliction and calamity that should fall upon Judah and Jerusalem under the Chaldeans sent of God to chastise the wicked falling away of the people.

So with the Hebrews—after such a bright and auspicious beginning—affliction and chastisement, confusion and darkness had come upon them, a falling away had begun, and the writer of the epistle speaks to the faithful in circumstances not dissimilar to Habakkuk. In such a context, the same consolatory passage is given, namely, 'The just shall live by faith'.

The former days of the Hebrew Christians, so noticeable in the early chapters of the Acts of the Apostles, were characterised by great illumination from the Lord of glory. God, who commanded the light to shine out of darkness, shone in their hearts to give the light of the knowledge of the glory of God in the face of Jesus Christ. The light had arisen upon them, they had come to the brightness of his rising, and this was the glory of his people Israel. Christ was their light, and by him they were illuminated within through the Holy Ghost from heaven. In his light they saw light, it was sown for the upright in heart, and they walked in it, the path of the just being as the shining light, shining more and more unto the perfect day of the inheritance of everlasting glory by the resurrection from the dead.

Inevitably this illumination was accompanied by a great fight of afflictions in this present world. Had it not been, the work would not have been genuine. But the Hebrew saints were compassed about with afflictions, and to endure them they must needs fight valiantly in the fight of faith. The tribulations which they endured came partly from a mocking world, joined together with the raging persecution of the self-righteous and self-justifying in religion: the world and the worldly religious. These, particularly the latter, made the saints to be a gazingstock, both by reproaches and afflictions.

Another part of their great fight of afflictions came from their whole-hearted unity with those who had been so persecuted. In the days when they first embraced the faith, and the church was first established on earth, they had to endure great derision as a result of receiving and obeying the ministers of the gospel. When they obeyed from the heart the form of doctrine delivered unto them, joyfully accepting those sent for the obedience of the faith among all nations, the reproaches and insults that fell upon such faithful ministers fell also upon them that received them. They became, Heb. 10:33, 'Companions of those that were so used.' Yet they were not ashamed, no, not even when the ministers of the gospel were falsely imprisoned, 'for ye had compassion on me in my bonds, and took joyfully the spoiling of your goods, knowing in yourselves that ye have in heaven a better and an enduring substance.'

Thus it began, but then outward conditions deteriorated; the circumstances became worse and worse. There were those who drew back, who cast away their first confidence. The work no longer grew apace as in the beginning: indeed, as more and more fell away, the work diminished. Questionings began, darkness and confusion came down, and doubting and reasoning rose up to assail the faith. If they were in the way, why was there such failure, why were so many going back? And why was there such unremitted persecution and evil speaking against the few faithful ministers, if God was with them? Hence the great urgency with which the writer admonishes the suffering people of God, enduring so great a fight of afflictions, 'Cast not away therefore your confidence', Heb. 10:35.

The writer exhorts the poor and tried remnant to hold fast to the end, assuring them of their need of patient continuance, Heb. 10:36. Patience was a quality necessarily associated with the passage of time under adversity. It was a quality needed in order to maintain what had been in the beginning, when the circumstances became adverse and drawn out. 'Ye have need of patience.' For bitter and protracted persecution would surely be their lot and portion. But having done the will of God, that is, having endured patiently by faith, they should receive the promise. 'For yet a little while, and he that shall come will come, and will not tarry.' This is exactly the same comfort given to the remnant under Habakkuk, waiting for the coming of Christ. Here that very word is administered to the afflicted saints, in strikingly parallel circumstances, waiting for the Lord's return from heaven.

Until then, 'The just shall live by faith.' The writer addresses the elect, exhorting them to walk by faith and not by sight, not to be moved by these afflictions, but to endure hardness and tribulation in this present world. They were to wait in faith, and to live by faith, for the fulfilment of the vision that tarried, for the return of Christ from heaven. To this end, the just shall live by faith. Not simply begin by faith: not live by faith only in the former days of glory. But live by faith in the latter days of adversity. Yes, and live by faith until Christ should come again from heaven. 'But if any man draw back, my soul shall have no pleasure in him', Heb. 10:38.

The importance given in the New Testament to the text from Habakkuk, 'The just shall live by faith', cannot be overestimated. This passage brings in the whole question of salvation, because it speaks of all that man lost in Adam, in the garden of Eden, just as it declares all that has been gained by Jesus Christ to secure an everlasting inheritance. What was lost by Adam in the garden was innocence, what lost it was sin, and what came in by sin was condemnation and death. What God brought in by Jesus Christ, the second man, the last Adam, was the gift of grace, what this brought in was the righteousness of faith, and what was brought in by the righteousness of faith was free justification, eternal life, and everlasting glory. Of these things Habakkuk speaks by the text in question.

Righteousness is spoken of in the Person referred to as 'the just' which is the same word as 'the righteous'. Righteousness pertains to this Person. But it also has application to all that believe in him. 'The just' therefore may refer to those justified by faith in Christ. Context will determine the application. Now, he who is righteous in the sight of God is not the man that worketh, but the man that believeth. Sinners, dead in trespasses and sins, cannot work. They may labour at the law, but they bring forth nothing but sin, the wages whereof is death. Then, who is the righteous, who is the just? The man that worketh not, but believeth on him that justifieth the ungodly. Such was Abraham. He 'believed God, and it was counted to him for righteousness.' Such a man is just, not by works, but by faith: that is, justification by faith.

This is the heritage of the servants of the Lord, 'and their righteousness is of me, saith the Lord.' God justifies, or reckons righteous, freely by grace, without works; nothing is earned, he accounts a man to be righteous because of Jesus Christ. The man's faith is reckoned to him for righteousness, and righteousness of God is imputed to his account. This is the righteous, or just, of whom the verse speaks, insofar as it speaks of the believer.

As to his living by faith, this manifests the folly of those who set the law before the man that is of faith. 'For the law is not of faith.' Then how can anyone in their right mind set the law as 'a rule of life' before him that is of faith? Immediately it negates believing, just as it negates that which is believed: because, of course, it requires works. 'A rule of life'? But the law cannot give life. 'For if there had been a law given which could have given life, verily righteousness should have been by the law. But the scripture hath concluded all under sin, that the promise by faith of Jesus Christ might be given to them that believe', Gal. 3:21,22. The law may have been ordained to life, but, saith Paul 'I found it to be unto death'. To set the law before those that have been justified by faith, as a rule of 'life', is nothing other than the error which Paul opposed so vehemently in the Epistle to the Galatians.

The truth for ever stands that faith is the rule of justification, and of course it must be the rule of life. Hence it is said, 'The just shall live by faith.' Whereas, if the law were the rule of life for the justified, of necessity the text would read 'The just shall live by works'.

The law requires no faith at all, works only, perfect works at that, and the man that doeth them shall live in them. Which is what no man ever did. But, like the Pharisees of old, who must boast in their self-righteousness, all who profess to set the law before the believer 'understand neither what they say nor whereof they affirm'.

Precisely because the believer is justified, or accounted righteous, he has life. 'He that believeth on the Son hath'—note the tense: hath—'everlasting life.' The life which he lives, he lives by the faith of the Son of God, who loved him, and gave himself for him. For just as sin earned death, so righteousness merits life. When Christ brought in everlasting righteousness to the account of every one that believeth, of necessity life became theirs by the gift of God. 'The gift of God is everlasting life.'

Because Christ is the King of righteousness, called Melchizedek in figurative language, and because through him righteousness reigns upon spiritual mount Zion, therefore God commanded the blessing upon the mountains of Zion, even life for evermore. Grace—which is upon mount Zion—reigns through righteousness—mark that, through righteousness—unto eternal life by Jesus Christ our Lord. As to that righteousness, it is from faith to faith. As to that eternal life, it is the life of faith, as it is written, The just shall live by faith. And by faith only.

Just as righteousness came in by the faith of Jesus Christ, and nothing else, so righteousness is received by the faith of all that believe, and by faith only. Likewise, since every one that believeth hath everlasting life, and none other, it follows of course from the nature both of life and of faith, that the life of the believer must be a life of faith alone. Which is what the prophet records and the apostle quotes, 'As it is written, The just shall live by faith.'

PART TWO
THE SUBSTANCE

THE SUBSTANCE

VI

Righteousness of God under Law

THE Apostle Paul introduces the substance of the gospel with the words 'But now', Rom. 3:21-26. This expression must not be dismissed as mere rhetoric. Failure to give due weight to the force of these words will lead to distortion in the doctrine, attenuation of the gospel, and infidelity to the scriptures.

The word 'but' is a word used to contrast one thing with another. It sets one state of affairs over against another. The second word, 'now', indicates a point in time. It is the time of writing, the present time. The two words together show that certain things and conditions prevailed up to the time of writing, but since that time other things and different conditions obtain.

From these observations two questions arise. What were the things that the Apostle Paul set in contrast one with the other? And when did the period of the former end and of the latter begin? The answer to the first question is that the apostle sets in contrast the revelation of the righteousness of God under the law with the revelation of the righteousness of God in the gospel. The answer to the second question is that the one came to an end and the other had a beginning when Christ cried from the cross at Golgotha, 'It is finished', and gave up the ghost.

The first of these things is indicated by the word 'but', and the second by the word 'now', in Rom. 3:21. The expression 'But now' therefore teaches that the exposition of the gospel does not commence at Romans 3:21, when the apostle first introduces the death of Christ, but that it commences at the beginning of the preceding context, that is, it goes back to the reason for the death of Christ. Any exposition that fails to observe this truth fails to present the whole and integrated context of the gospel, it has no foundation, and in consequence the root of the matter will be lacking in those who receive the truth of the work of Christ without any understanding of its ground and basis.

It is imperative to grasp that the Apostle Paul commenced the exposition of the doctrine of the gospel, the gospel of Christ, not in the third but in the first chapter. That is the proper commencement of the gospel. It follows therefore that there is a great body and weight of truth in the doctrine before the work of Christ itself is presented and explained. This is that body of truth introduced in Chapter 1:18 and continued until Chapter 3:20, the whole of which is in contrast with what follows thereafter.

It is the doctrine of Romans 1:18 to 3:20 in particular rather than that of Chapter 3:21-26 that men find offensive. For it is one thing to rejoice over the death of Christ, and to sing about the cross of Jesus, but quite another thing to sound forth the wrath of God against the sinfulness of man, and declare the judgment that is according to works to a guilty humanity found to be without excuse.

The use of the word 'but' in Romans 3:21 directs us in and of itself to that which preceded, and, if so, to the prior doctrine of the gospel. This word is used, as it were, at the centre of the exposition, when justification by faith is introduced. Therefore a great deal precedes the introduction of the work of Christ in the orderly and sound exposition of the gospel of God. In a word, we are directed to the revelation of the righteousness of God: how it appeared under the law and from creation. That is the truth to which the Apostle Paul addresses himself in Rom. 1:18, in the course of which he arrives at the central position of contrast indicated by the words 'But now', Rom. 3:21.

The revelation of the righteousness of God under the law, Romans 1:18 to 3:20, as opposed to the revelation of the righteousness of God without the law, Romans 3:21-26, appears in terms of wrathful vengeance against sinners. 'The wrath of God is revealed from heaven against all ungodliness and unrighteousness of men', Rom. 1:18; 'The judgment of God', Rom. 1:32, 2:2, 2:3; 'The righteous judgment of God', Rom. 2:5. This righteous judgment, or vengeance, under the law and from the creation, occupies the apostle throughout the passage. It is the righteousness of God, hidden from man by his own folly, revealed under the law, the first book of which accounts for the beginning of all things.

There is no excuse, though men, especially religious men, make inadmissible excuses: 'But if our unrighteousness commend the righteousness of God, what shall we say? Is God unrighteous who taketh vengeance? God forbid: for then how shall God judge the world?' Rom. 3:5,6. Such passages as this clearly establish, as does the tenor and context of the whole argument, that the apostle by the gospel reveals and brings to bear the righteousness of God against the sinfulness of the whole of humanity, and that no excuse is admissible.

This revelation of the righteousness of God is under the law. That is, it is how God appears to mankind under the

77

law. He will appear in terms of righteousness, and in no other terms. There are no other terms consistent with his nature. This is not arbitrary, nor is there any alternative, it is a divine necessity, consistent with the nature of goodness and love at its source and fountain-head in the deity.

As to the Gentile peoples of whom the first book of the law, Genesis, speaks, the heathen that received not the law of Moses, the apostle shows them to be accountable to law notwithstanding. 'For as many as have sinned without law shall also perish without law: and as many as have sinned in the law shall be judged by the law.' Sinned without law? 'The Gentiles, which have not the law, do by nature the things contained in the law; these, having not the law, are a law unto themselves: which show the work of the law written in their hearts', Rom. 2:12, 14, 15. Whence it appears that the righteousness of God revealed under the law, is in a manner a fuller and more formal statement of the work of the law in the heart of the Gentiles also.

That Romans 1:18 to 3:20 expounds the revelation of the righteousness of God is clear; that this revelation was manifested under the law is equally apparent. Just as emphatic however is the truth enforced by the apostle that the Gentiles are no more exempt from the rule of law than are the Jews. All alike are under obligation to the work of the law 'written in the heart'. But, as is stressed by Rom. 2:17, 18, 20, 23, 25, 26 and 27, the Jews have far greater responsibility—and in consequence worse culpability—than the Gentiles because that unto them were committed the oracles of God. 'What things soever the law saith, it saith to them who are under the law: that every mouth may be stopped, and all the world may become guilty before God', Rom. 3:19.

It is abundantly clear from the context that the revelation of the righteousness of God under the law and from the creation, a revelation manifesting the righteous judgment and

78

vengeance of God against all mankind, occupies the entire first part of the exposition of the gospel, Romans 1:18 to 3:20. After this, the righteousness of God without the law, apart from law, is expounded, and this unprecedented, unparalleled revelation is the subject of the continuation of the apostolic doctrine of the gospel from Chapter 3 and verse 21, 'But now'. It remains therefore at present to summarise the argument and context leading up to this place, this watershed of the evangel, before which the apostle had demonstrated the guilt of humanity and the judgment which men have brought upon themselves from the retributive justice of God in the day of wrath.

Romans 1:18 to 3:20 is concerned with the revelation of the wrath of God. In Ch. 1:18 the apostle lays down the proposition, the exposition of which occupies the remainder of the passage concluding at Ch. 3:20. In the proposition the apostle summarises that against which wrath is revealed from heaven. Firstly, it is against all ungodliness of men; in particular, the Gentiles. Secondly, it is against all unrighteousness of men who hold the truth in unrighteousness; that is, especially the Jews.

In the latter case the fact that men hold the truth is not denied. What is asserted is that this is irrelevant to the righteous judgment of God. It makes not the least difference to the wrath of God from heaven what the Jews professed when in reality what they practiced was unrighteousness.

The apostle commences to expound the proposition of Romans 1:18, in the first instance, by opening up the cause of the wrath of God being revealed from heaven against all ungodliness of men, Ch. 1:19-32. The justice of this indignation is clearly made manifest as the apostle declares by the Holy Ghost the light revealed to men inwardly, outwardly and variously. Such light being given, man is regarded as having ability, being accountable, and held responsible to live according to what had been manifest in him, and shown unto him. But man ignored this glorious light, and worse, perverted it. He is without excuse. Before God man is charged as having no excuse. And from the just judgment of God there can be no appeal, Ch. 1:19,20.

The open ungodliness of men against God is laid wholly at the door of mankind. The wilful change of mind and heart, the deliberate perversion of the true knowledge of God into a false representation of the deity, so as to justify disobedience, gendered the wrath of God, Ch. 1:21-23. The immediate consequence of this rebellion appeared in the visitation of God's swift vengeance, in which disobedient man was given over to his own will, without hindrance or restraint, bereft of either the entreaties or chastisement of God. Mankind sank into uncleanness and reprobation of heart, affection, and mind, given up of God, being filled with all conceivable forms of unrighteousness, beyond hope of human recovery, and under the sentence of condemnation from the righteous judgment of God, Ch. 1:24-32.

Here man is regarded as a kind of entity, a composite of each generation of all peoples from every age, as if all were alive at one and the same moment, with every lifetime co-extensive. Once and for all, time contracted to a single span, all humanity reduced to one generation, man is made to appear under responsibility, accountable, bathed in light within, without, above, and about. If so, man could not have requited his Maker more basely: he could not have reprobated himself more thoroughly. Hence, the wrath of God is revealed from heaven, and the sentence has gone forth from the righteousness of God in vengeance against humanity.

Next the apostle declares the revelation of God's righteous judgment, Ch. 2:1-11. The ungodliness before charged upon mankind was inexcusable. The ungodly themselves disapprove of it in others. They themselves bear witness to the righteous judgment of God upon each other. The judgment of God is according to truth: men should and must be punished for their ungodliness and ungodly deeds. According to truth: that is, according to what actually exists, according to the reality. The eyes of the judge, as a flame of fire, burn through all pretence and superfluous appearance, exposing the true state; the word of his mouth, which is as fire and a hammer, breaks the rock in pieces, bringing to light the hidden things within the interior. The sharp two edged sword, which is in his hand, cuts and pierces through soul and spirit, joints and marrow, revealing the thoughts and intents of the heart. This is judgment that is according to truth with a witness.

Here, following the assurance that none shall escape the judgment of God, three divine attributes are brought forward by the apostle in order to account for the fact that the day of wrath had not yet come, not for so long a time, though fore-told from ages and generations past.

The cause for this deferment of God's judgment lies in his goodness, his forbearance, and his longsuffering. He will delay the coming wrath till the very last day, holding back, suffering long, not rewarding the ungodly according to their iniquities. But the day shall and must come in which even the world itself cannot fail to see the hopeless incorrigibility of a wholly corrupt and irredeemable humanity. Then the righteous judgment will certainly fall. How can men despise such riches, such treasures, freely given to them of God? Are they not to lead mankind from hardness and impenitence to meltedness and repentance?

The day of wrath and revelation of the righteous judgment of God is that tremendous day on which he will render to every man according to his deeds, Rom. 2:5,6. It is called the day of the Lord, the last day, the day of judgment, the day of resurrection, the day of wrath, the day of vengeance, and the great day. It is the day appointed in the which God shall judge the world in righteousness by that man whom he hath ordained, whereof he hath given assurance unto all men, in that he hath raised him from the dead. Then, this is beyond the present life, after death, by resurrection, when the works and lives of men will be brought into judgment according to the righteousness of God, who will, as Judge, render unto men according to their deeds.

What men? What deeds? But two classes of men are acknowledged, each with their corresponding deeds. The judgment is without respect of persons. What God requires according to the righteousness of his own nature, what he requires as Judge, what he requires to uphold the law, what he requires according to the nature of man, is immutable. The life and work of men, of all men, religious or otherwise, by the resurrection from the dead, will and must come into judgment before God.

The word 'render' indicates that the judgment is not arbitrary. It is not a sentence that is beyond a sinner's comprehension. The judge does not conjure up a judgment: sinners themselves will have provided the cause of that judgment by their own lives on earth. The Judge assesses and weighs nothing other than that life against the rule of law, dispassionately passing the sentence accordingly. That is the function of the Judge. Not to have mercy, but to pass judgment. As to appeal, the time for appeal will have passed. Agreeable to what was sown, the sentence will be pronounced on what is raised up. In a figure, if men sowed grain, corn will arise, and the sentence shall be passed accordingly. If men sowed thorns or thistles, these shall rise up, and it shall be rendered to the sower according to his deeds. For whatsoever a man soweth, that shall he also reap.

The word 'render' means To give back, to requite; to repay a claim, to discharge an obligation. God gave to man his being: God maintains in man his breath. And shall men not requite him? Mankind would not own the knowledge of God, neither would render what was owed to him, nor requite his due. Now God is to judge in righteousness. Right, inherent in God's nature and attributes, requires that God should judge. His character obliges him to judge, and judge in righteousness. 'Shall not the Judge of all the earth do right?' Then, he will render to every man according to his deeds, without respect of persons. God shall requite them.

The righteous sentence of God, or the sentence of his righteousness, according to the requirement of the law, appears in Rom. 2:7,8. Firstly, upon the righteous, and lastly, upon the wicked. Paul commences with the case of the righteous, or just. The lives of the righteous are described by the apostle from their existence in this present world, as if reviewed in the resurrection at the day of judgment. Their life was one of patient continuance, an enduring whilst waiting. The words mean 'a remaining under anything'. The impression is one of a life of hope and patient waiting under present suffering. Their life appears to be a life of affliction whilst patiently continuing in hope. Why? Because this world to them was a place of pilgrimage: a wilderness to be endured. They looked for the world to come, and they lived for it. This is taken account of in the day of strict and impartial judgment.

Their patient continuance was in 'well doing'. That is, good works. What is profitable, virtuous, of goodness or excellence in the issue of their life. They continually acted in virtue, and with good will, in the tenor of their lives. This cut across the way of the world. Like Moses, they 'esteemed the reproach of Christ' in the promise, 'of greater riches than the treasures of Egypt'. Then, they were 'persecuted for righteousness' sake.' This caused much suffering, but they endured meekly, looking for a city and a country, that is, an heavenly, continuing in benevolence, good works of virtue, endeavouring to keep a conscience void of offence before God and men.

83

However such patient continuance in well doing could not be acceptable before the righteous judgment of God in and of itself: the spring and motive of such a life and pathway is to be examined. That is, the patient continuance in well doing acceptable to God must not be with an eye to man, or the praise of men, neither must it be with a view to this world, or to time. There must be a higher motive, a deeper purpose, than the thing in and of itself. It must be through 'seeking for glory and honour and immortality', Rom. 2:7. That is, the patient continuance in well doing acceptable before God must be in pursuit of a heavenly end, the motive must be to appear before the eye of God, to please him and to dwell before him in the world to come.

In that day it will be found that the righteous sought for glory. That is, in the land that is very far off. It is in the heavenly country, the holy city, having the glory of God. In new Jerusalem it shall be seen, wherein shall appear the brightness of God's outshining for ever in the world to come. They sought for it, they lived for it, and they continued patiently in good works with the eye of faith fixed upon that glory yet to be revealed.

The righteous sought for honour. That is, weightiness, worth. The very opposite to the vacant, brittle, light and empty religion of the fool. The righteous were sober, serious, weighty and earnest. They were deep, they were of the heart. And this depth and inwardness was what they sought all their lives, lamenting their relative shallowness, despising the honour that comes from man, that is of this world, seeking the honour that comes from God only.

The righteous sought for immortality. That is, for incorruption, which is what cannot be attained whilst in this present body. It is neither in life nor in death. For incorruption, for immortality, the language must be 'If by any means I might attain unto the resurrection of the dead.' It is the yearning to

84

put off mortality, negatively, and the seeking to put on immortality, positively. Then, it is to seek a better resurrection. The resurrection of the just.

For this character God's righteousness will seek in the day of judgment. For this is the character of the just. It is not a question of how they attained to this character. It is a question of the character to which they attained. It is not a matter of what they believed. It is a matter of what was effected by what they believed. The judgment is entirely on character, life and work, to the exclusion of all else. This divides mankind, as it justifies God in his judgments. The character approved by the righteous sentence of God in that day is one in which by patient continuance in well doing the just are found to have sought for glory, and honour, and immortality.

Their sentence follows, Rom. 2:7. It is the sentence of righteous judgment upon such character. Persons of this character can have but one sentence from the righteous judgment of God in that day: it is written: it is certain. The Judge does not view how such a character was developed, but that it was developed. Nor the means by which patient continuance in well doing was secured, but that it was secured. What is judged is not the cause of their seeking for glory, and honour, and immortality, but that they sought for glory, and honour, and immortality. The sentence, the righteous sentence, is pronounced, and must be pronounced, upon all possessed of such a character in the resurrection of the dead. And the sentence is, Eternal life, Rom. 2:7. Then, they will receive that for which they had sought. Those who suffered in this world, looking for the world to come, have the desires of their heart. What could be more just?

With equal justice appears the sentence of the righteousness of God upon the wicked. What is it that marks the wicked? The lives which they lived upon the earth before their death appear at the resurrection as lives precisely the opposite to those of the just. It is this that brings down condemnation upon the head of all whose portion was in this world, just as it is this that magnifies the impartiality of God's righteous sentence according to the law.

The character of the wicked is described, in the judgment of God, firstly, as contentious, Rom. 2:8. This characterises the wicked. Men might well think contentiousness a strange thing to select as that which distinguishes the wicked, but whatever men think, according to the apostles' doctrine it is so. Men would say, they were murderers, whoremongers, wastrels, and, indeed, some might well have been, but then again others might not. Irrespective of anything else, what God emphasises about the wicked is that they were contentious. This is stressed above all; whether they were outwardly corrupt or outwardly religious, what classed them as wicked or unjust, firstly, was that they were contentious. They contended against the word and truth of God. That was the worst sin. They despised the truth that inspired the just. Against promise and prophesy they wrangled, they argued, they debated, they opposed, and they strove. Every revelation of God must submit to them, rather than they to the revelation of God: in their own eyes they knew everything. Hence they contended every point of doctrine, and more especially that of the righteous judgment of God in the day of wrath. They were contentious.

Again, they 'obeyed not the truth.' Not 'they professed not the truth', but 'they obeyed not the truth'. What truth? Whatever truth God had revealed, that had inspired the just, that they contended. Truth within, truth without; truth from creation, truth from consciousness; truth by revelation, truth in scripture. Truth about glory, truth concerning honour, truth declaring immortality. They may have known it; they may have confessed it; but they did not obey it. Contentious persons, who obeyed not the truth, may well have contended for what they would not obey. They would argue for truths, contend for schools of thought, for interpretations, for traditions, for parties. They were intellectual, they would not just accept matters as did the ignorant and unlearned. No. They contended instead, and justified their contention. But God condemns it, and calls it disobedience to the truth in the resurrection from the dead.

What they actually obeyed was 'unrighteousness', Rom. 2:8. They contradicted revealed righteousness, whether that righteousness were revealed under the law or promised in the gospel. But God calls that unrighteousness, and they obeyed it, and now they are to account for it. They laid a crooked line to God's rectitude, and clave to their crookedness, and now the God of truth requires it of them in righteousness. They obeyed unrighteousness; had they owned and obeyed the revelation of God's righteous judgments, they would have fled from the wrath to come, as did the just. But, to the contrary, ignoring wrath they fled from righteousness, as do the wicked. And in the day of judgment, at the resurrection of the dead, God will call this 'obeying unrighteousness'.

That is the character, and the whole of the character, brought to light in the wicked in the day of wrath. That is how they will appear: they are contentious, they obey not the truth. This is the full description of those persons that bring forth such a sentence from the judgment of God as is now declared in the apostolic doctrine of the gospel. The sentence is 'Indignation and wrath', and, of course, in the resurrection, for ever and ever. Indignation, *thumos*, may be understood as 'fury'. Fury, that is, blazing forth from God, against such impenitent, contentious, and disobedient rebels. Where now will they appear? And wrath, *orgē*. This is a sustained, abiding anger. It is an inexorable wrath that cannot be changed, upon an immortal state that cannot be altered.

The everlasting judgment of God follows upon the sentence of righteousness, Rom. 2:9,10. The judgment of God, according to the law, falls first upon the evil. This judgment shows that the sentence of justice, after death, and in the resurrection, ushers in a fixed eternal state. The apostle here declares in the gospel the unending interior condition of the wicked. It is described first as tribulation, *thlipsis*, Rom. 2:9. This refers to pressure, as the corn under the millstone, the grapes in the winepress. Next it is defined as anguish, *stenos*, straitness. This shows constriction, pressing confinement, as when one is trapped in the narrowness of a dark underground tunnel.

The same words are used to describe the conditions on earth, and in time, of those who in their pilgrimage sought for glory, and honour, and immortality. They passed through the strait—*stenos*—gate. They walked in the narrow—*thlipsis*—way. Yet their light affliction, which was but for a moment, worked for them a far more exceeding and eternal weight of glory. But the pressure and confinement of the impenitent, who shunned the strait gate and the narrow way to enjoy the width and breadth of the world, and worldly religion, for a moment, shall now be exceedingly magnified, it shall last for ever, it is world without end. This is the judgment of the righteousness of God.

Likewise the judgment of God's righteousness upon the just shall stand for ever. This follows, Rom. 2:10. The sentence having been passed, the everlasting judgment commences in those who 'by patient continuance in well doing sought for glory, and honour, and immortality.' The glory which they sought is the glory that they are given. They are glorified, raised to glory, and they inherit a glorious possession. The God of glory appears unto them, they dwell in the house of the Lord for ever, and find in his presence fulness of joy, and at his right hand pleasures for evermore. This is their glorious portion, and, since it is given by the righteous judgment of God, it can never be taken away from them. Honour is theirs, and weightiness; dignity rests upon them. They are approved of God, they attain the resurrection: thus shall it be done unto the man whom the King delighteth to honour.

Furthermore the peace which they sought becomes theirs, and peace like a river flows over them. Their enemies have perished, their warfare is accomplished, nothing offends. Before they had striven to enter the strait gate, and with much affliction traversed the narrow way, it was a pilgrimage of great tribulation, the world was at enmity with them whilst it enjoyed its day of glory, and honour, and peace. Now, in the resurrection, in the world to come, all is reversed. What could be more just?

The apostle concludes the passage on the righteousness of God according to the law by showing the impartiality of his righteous judgment, Rom. 2:11. There is no respect of persons with God. Judgment is impartial. It is not an enquiry into the means by which the just were brought to the life and walk, the character and behaviour to which they attained, but into the result, into the character itself. Here there is no excuse, no claim, no difference. It is but a question of strict justice: 'That thou mightest be justified when thou speakest, and clear when thou judgest.'

None, not even the most wicked, could question God's judgment upon the righteous, or raise the least doubt as to its fairness. It is so impartial and just, relative to his judgment upon the evil: all can see that. They were righteous, just as these were evil. And so the judgment falls: 'Who will render to every man according to his deeds', Rom. 2:6. 'For there is no respect of persons with God', Rom. 2:11. And if it were not so, where were the righteousness of God under the law, and from the creation? Or what else doth the apostle mean by this holy doctrine of the gospel, Romans 1:18 to 3:20?

The judgment of God is enforced, and the retribution of God assured, against all ungodliness of men, irrespective of whether they had received the law in an exterior form or not, Rom. 2:12,13. Here the apostle teaches that receiving or not receiving the law makes no difference in principle to the righteous judgment of God according to men's deeds because 'As many as have sinned without law shall also perish without law: and as many as have sinned in the law shall be judged by the law.' Sinned in the law: judged by the law? Yes, For 'not the hearers of the law are just before God, but the doers of the law shall be justified.' That is the principle of God's impartial judgment.

But how shall God judge those 'without the law'? By what rule? In answer to this question God's judgment without the law against 'all ungodliness of men' is explained and vindicated by the apostle, Rom. 2:14,15. The answer resolves itself into a matter of standards. If 'without law', to what rule are the ungodly accountable, and by what standard shall they be judged? By that rule and standard declared in Rom. 1:19, which, as was observed, 1:20, left men without excuse. By 'the work of the law written in their hearts', by their conscience bearing witness to the light of their own consciousness, by their thoughts, reason, and judgment, Rom. 2:15, by 'that which may be known of God manifest in them', quite apart from what God hath 'shown unto them'. If these are not standards, what are standards? By these standards the righteousness of God shall judge the ungodly.

Returning again to the proposition of Romans 1:18, the apostle now shows cause why the wrath of God is upon all unrighteousness of men who hold the truth in unrighteousness. This takes up the remainder of the passage, firstly by exposing those that hold the truth in unrighteousness, Rom. 2:17-29, secondly, by refuting religious, or Jewish, objections to this exposure, Rom. 3:1-8, and lastly, in pressing home the truth by way of conclusion, Rom. 3:9-20. This concludes the revelation of the righteousness of God under the law.

The apostle exposes those who hold the truth in unrighteousness, exemplified by the religious Jews, first by enumerating five characteristics of such persons, next by listing five assumptions held by them, and last by asking five questions which bring to light their true state. The characteristics of these religious persons were, respectively, that they rested in the law: which is precisely what the law of works would never permit; that they boasted in the law: though boasting was excluded by that law which they broke continually; that they knew the will of God: but they did not perform the will of God; that they approved the things that are more excellent: yet they performed the things that were more base; that they were instructed out of the law: nonetheless neither the instructors nor the instructed had any more conception of the real meaning of the law than the Gentiles.

Such religious persons were full of assumptions obnoxious to the wrath of God. The Jew assumed that he was a guide to the blind, though he himself was without sight; that he was a light to them that were in darkness, though he himself dwelt in the black night of ignorance; that he was an instructor of the foolish, though he was the fool that cleansed the outside of the cup and platter and neglected the filth within; that he was a teacher of babes, though the things of God were hid from him, who was wise in his own eyes, and revealed unto the babes, whom he presumed to teach; that he possessed the form of knowledge and of the truth of the law, though he was void of the substance, empty of the reality, and destitute of the verity of that for which God looked in righteousness from those that were under the law.

Next, five questions are pressed home forcefully to the conscience of the religious. These questions are directed at those who trusted in themselves that they were righteous, who were sure of their own justification. Paul pointedly addresses himself to the individual Jew. He taught others: would he not teach himself? The Jew preached that others should not steal: did he steal? He said that others should not commit adultery: did he commit adultery? He abhorred idols: but did he not commit sacrilege? He boasted in the law: yet through breaking the law did he not dishonour God? Five questions.

The apostle enforces his penetrating exposure of false religion, standing in profession, opinion, repetition and ceremony, by insisting, from the figure of circumcision, that all such religion was vain in the sight of God. 'For he is not a Jew, which is one outwardly; neither is that circumcision, which is outward in the flesh.' No, the righteousness of God requires a deeper, more profound work before ever there can be approval from him. 'But he is a Jew, which is one inwardly; and circumcision is that of the heart, in the spirit, and not in the letter; whose praise is not of men, but of God', Rom. 2:28,29.

At this doctrine, there is much outrage and protestation from the religious, and the Jews have great reasoning among themselves. But it all amounts to no more than three objections against the righteousness of God by which he shall judge the world. Paul refutes and dismisses these objections with ease, showing the great impudence and daring of such groundless and unseemly questions, concluding of the questioner 'whose damnation is just', Rom. 3:1-8.

Here Paul reaches the culminating point of this part of the exposition. He asserts that he had 'before' proved both Jews and Gentiles that they are all under sin, Rom. 3:9. By the force of the revelation, by the weight of the truth the apostle had given ample evidence of man's being under the just judgment of the righteousness of God. This was not proof as the scientist regards proof. Only the judgment itself will provide that. But it is proof of overwhelming moral force, of unanswerable spiritual revelation, by which the Creator himself testifies to all whom he has created, that, irrespective of excuses or accusations, philosophies or religions, science or ignorance, all are ungodly, all the religious hold the truth in unrighteousness, and all mankind is proven to be under sin.

This is a most important statement. What the apostle had actually shown in his doctrine was that all 'had sinned'. All had light, if in varying degree, all were answerable to that light, all were held accountable to their Maker, all had sinned. That is, all had committed sin, and, in the sight of God, nothing but sin. So Rom. 2:12. This refers to wilful action. Not in deed alone, but in intention also. And not only in intention, but likewise in the ruling choice governing each intention, the ultimate resolution determining the direction of the life itself. Still, all was choice. Wilful, deliberate choice.

The resolutions which proceeded from this ruling intention of the will, as the streams from the fountain, took their character from their source, as did the outward actions resulting from these resolutions, irrespective of their specious appearance before men. 'All have sinned.' It is the deliberate wilful choice to sin, and, such is the nature of the will and its related actions, it is nothing but sin. All outward deeds, no matter how deceitful the appearance, as bestowing one's goods to feed the poor, or giving one's body to be burned, praying, fasting, preaching, all gain their character from the inward resolution, in turn determined by the ruling preference governing the life itself. If that is sinful, all is sinful. 'The light of the body is the eye: if therefore thine eye be single, thy whole body shall be full of light. But if thine eye be evil, thy whole body shall be full of darkness.' 'A good tree cannot bring forth evil fruit, neither can a corrupt tree bring forth good fruit.'

In the judgment of God's righteousness man's eye is evil, the tree of humanity is bad, and the stock is corrupt. Neither had revealed religion made the slightest difference: the darkness and rottenness lay within, and the law was incapable of providing salvation. The law compounded the error. And this error lay at the heart. It was in the ultimate intention of the will. Men would sin. It was the deliberate, wilful and set resolution of the whole race.

This the apostle had before 'proved'. Humanity chose to sin. The word 'sinned' occurs first in Rom. 2:12. Again it is found in Rom. 3:23. Next in Rom. 5:12,14 and 16. Then lastly in this epistle, Rom. 6:15. That is the verb. It is what is done. But it is not the form of word that Paul uses in Rom. 3:9, when he declares that all are 'under sin'.

Here 'sin', as such, occurs for the first time in the epistle. It is the noun form of the word. This does not denote action, moral or otherwise, but rather the thing itself. It may be 'a' sin, but the word has a far deeper meaning. Used in this place it refers neither to the deed, nor to the intention, but to the inbred state. However it is certainly not the case that the apostle introduces this revelation of man's condition in order to mitigate his inexcusable action of sinning, but rather to show that this exposes a far deeper and more serious inward state.

The action 'sinned' came before the state 'sin' in the revelation. Here, for the first time in Romans, the apostle shows the state of fallen man. However, he exposes it—and this must be observed—first by proving man's sinning disposition. What that reveals, what that wilful rebellion brings to light, what that disposition in the whole human race exposes is an inbred condition deeper in the life of man than the genesis of any one individual.

'They are all under sin', Rom. 3:9. 'Under' is the word that determines here the precise bearing of the noun *hamartia*, sin. The pronoun 'they' refers to the whole human race, Jew and Gentile, religious or irreligious. Humanity's wilful, inexcusable, sinning shows that in every nation, all generations, each condition, mankind is 'under' sin from the fall. Here this important truth is introduced to be taken up again and again in the epistle, Rom. 3:9,20; 4:8; 5:12,13,20,21; a further sixteen times in Ch. 6; twelve times in Ch. 7, and so on. This refers to the state of man in the fall, revealed by his deliberate sinning in life, the one in no way mitigating the other, but both alike meriting the just judgment of the righteousness of God in the day of wrath. It is this that the apostle had 'before proved'.

Finally the teaching is confirmed by a series of quotations from the scriptures. Albeit such moral weightiness and overwhelming force lay in the apostolic doctrine already revealed, such is Paul's reverence for holy scripture that he brings forth this, the strongest of testimonies, as the final and closing confirmation: 'As it is written'. Paul gives four quotations from the Psalms, one from the prophet Isaiah, and finally quotes again from the Psalms to press home the truth that had been taught.

The first quotation, Psalm 14:1-3 (53:1-3), is negative. It is what men are not. They are not righteous, neither have they any understanding, nor do they seek after God. As if that were not enough, the Holy Ghost testifies of man in respect of righteousness, prudence, and godliness, that there is not, and there never has been, one single human being with these qualities.

'No, not one.' The whole of humanity, all men, every nation, each generation, all classes and conditions, from the beginning of time to the end of it, appear in a state of total and wilful moral depravity, sold under sin, not an impulse of righteousness, not a glimmer of understanding, not a vestige of godliness, anywhere in the world.

Next three positive statements are made, drawn respectively from Psalms 5:9, 140:3 and 10:7. The first concerns the throat and tongue, the next the lips, and the last the mouth. This threefold testimony shows what proceeds from the inward parts, out of the heart of man. It commences at the throat, figuratively the entrance to the interior soul: 'their throat is an open sepulchre.' Then, within, they are full of dead men's bones, and all uncleanness. The soul is corrupt and dead. That is what is seen, morally, through the entrance to the inward parts. As to what comes forth by way of the throat to the tongue, it is deceit, an appearance that quite belies the reality. The poison of the adder is, in turn, under their lips. This poison appears in the saying of the serpent 'Thou shalt not surely die', which was gladly and freely received in the beginning. This is the lie denying God's righteous judgment that so readily springs to the lips of man. No wonder his mouth is full of cursing and bitterness.

Now the prophet Isaiah is brought to witness against the violence of man's heart in response to which his feet are swift to shed blood. Out of the heart proceed murders, and the ways of the heart are ways of destruction and misery. The way of peace is what men have never known. Finally the apostle quotes from Psalm 36:1 'There is no fear of God before their eyes.' Why not? Because men do not reckon on the judgment to come, according to the righteousness of God. They prefer to trust in the lie of the serpent, and to digest his venom. 'Thou shalt not surely die' is the poison in the life-blood, a venom in possession of the heart, deeper than any rational faculty, a pollution in the well spring of being. Against all reason, all righteousness, all divinity, the fool hath said in his heart, 'There is no God'. And, if not, then no accountability, no resurrection, no sentence, no judgment, no immortality, and nothing to fear but oblivion. 'There is no fear of God before their eyes.'

The nineteenth and twentieth verses of chapter three conclude the doctrine. These verses apply particularly to the Jews. Anticipating the accusations of the Jews against the Gentiles, the apostle directs the Jewish scriptures against their own consciences. The Jews knew that the law spake to those who were under it, not to the Gentiles with their vile and filthy works, walking after the lusts of their hearts and minds. But the scriptures which Paul quoted were not levelled at the lasciviousness and ungodliness of the Gentiles, but at the religion of the Jews. It was Israel under the law to whom the psalms and the prophets spake.

Therefore it is the Jews themselves who ought to be convicted. Far from this, however, they preferred to distract attention from their own condition by levelling accusations against the state of the Gentiles. But it is the Jews themselves that are brought in guilty by the law. It is to them and to their condition that David in the psalms, and Isaiah in the prophets, direct their stinging rebukes. Not the Gentiles but the Jews are those that have no fear of God before their eyes. If so, the Gentiles being self-condemned, then all the world becomes guilty before God.

Not the Gentile mouths only, but the mouth of every Jew shall be stopped before the tribunal of God's righteousness. The entire world, each generation, every age, all peoples, the whole of humanity shall be brought in guilty under the righteousness of the law, and the inward witness of the work of the law on the heart, according to the righteousness of God in the day of retribution and vengeance at the resurrection of the dead.

This is the guilt that brings down the wrath of God upon mankind. It was this that Paul proposed at the beginning of the doctrine, Rom. 1:18, saying, 'The wrath of God is revealed from heaven against all ungodliness and unrighteousness of men, who hold the truth in unrighteousness.' According to the righteousness of God, Paul had shown just cause and given sure testimony, proving both Jew and Gentile alike to be under sin. There can be no escape. God, the mighty God, hath spoken. From the rising of the sun unto the going down of the same hath he spoken. This speech is in the gospel of God concerning his Son, and it is given by the Holy Ghost sent down from heaven.

The apostle concludes that by the deeds of the law there shall no flesh be justified in his sight. No flesh at all, neither Jewish flesh, nor Gentile flesh. No flesh shall be justified. Not by the law as a rule of justification, which is what it is. Neither by the law as a rule of life, which is what it is not. Nor yet by the law as a rule of walk, because it is neither a guide nor is it advice: it is the law, with all its sanctions, all its dreadful force and majesty: it can never be anything else, and by the deeds of the law there shall no flesh be justified in his sight.

For by the law is the knowledge of sin. And of nothing else. The law gives no knowledge of God, neither of divinity, nor of worship. It gives the knowledge of sin, and sin alone. Anything else is mere intellectual presumption. The superficial, such as the scribes and Pharisees, may pretend to a knowledge of God by the law in order to support their system of self-justification, and to appear to establish their own righteousness, but this is not the law, it is a travesty of the law. All who submit to the law as it is in truth, and yield to its voice as it sounds in itself, are brought to the knowledge of sin, the curse, bondage and death. For by the law is the knowledge of sin.

By the law sin is awakened, and the motions of sin work in the members to bring forth fruit unto death. By the work of the law therefore it is not the seriousness of what it is to sin that is discovered, but rather what sin is in itself. By the work of the law the whole nature of man is found out to be corrupt and dead.

This is the whole of the work of the law, and the law was sent to do the whole of this work. When this is done, man is shut up to wrath by the righteousness of God revealed under the law, without a solitary door of hope, without a single avenue of escape, and without the least possibility of any redemption. And this experimental knowledge is called 'being shut up unto the faith which should afterwards be revealed', Gal. 3:22,23.

VII

Righteousness of God without Law

THE word 'But', Rom. 3:21, points back to the preceding and contrasting revelation of the wrath of God against the ungodliness of man, Rom. 1:18 to 3:20. This revelation lays the groundwork for the introduction of the work of Christ in the gospel. Here is a fulcrum, a kind of hinge, on which turns the doctrine: as if to say, That is the truth of man, yes, 'but' this is the truth of Christ. That is so of the darkness of nature, 'but' this is so in the light of the glory. Yet the whole is the gospel: what precedes the introduction to the work of Christ is as much a part of the gospel as that which follows.

If Paul preached faith in Christ, he preached also repentance towards God. If Paul persuaded concerning Christ and the kingdom, he reasoned likewise of righteousness, temperance, and judgment to come. If the apostolic teaching of the gospel expounds and opens the Person and work of Christ, similarly it reveals the state of man with or without the law under the wrath of God. The whole is the gospel. To neglect one part at the expense of the other is to ensure the collapse and ultimate ruin of the testimony rendered to Christ and his truth. The effect of this upon souls and upon the church will be disastrous.

The word, 'Now', acts in this context as an emphasis, an underlining, to the word 'But'. The first word indicates a contrast, and the next the immediacy of that contrast. This precise application of the word 'now' teaches that whatever had been revealed before, in times past, what was to come unveiled a glory eclipsing anything hitherto imaginable. Now, Christ had come, God was glorified, the gospel was established, justification by faith had been brought in, 'now' everything was completely different. The New Testament superseded the old, the heavenly the earthly, the church took the place of Israel, the gospel that of the law, mount Zion was exalted, Sinai depressed, in a word, the righteousness of God had been manifested by faith of Jesus Christ in the gospel, and everything was changed in consequence.

The expression 'But now the righteousness of God without the law', Rom. 3:21, evidently looks back upon a period with the law. This period in turn succeeded a time before the law was given, or was 'in the world'. Thus, two distinct eras appear: first from Adam to Moses, and next from Moses to Christ.

The period 'from Adam to Moses', Rom. 5:14, was one which commenced in the garden of Eden at the dawn of time. Adam in innocence 'heard the voice of the LORD God walking in the garden in the cool of the day.' Here was a communion that was intimate, but not interior. It was a communion that was vocal, but the text stops short of saying that Adam knew God by union. It was a case of a creature in innocence being visited at the time, in a voice, by his Creator. What is said is that man in the image of God heard his voice in the garden, 'in the cool of the day', namely, when the sun was down. Communion stood in communication.

There is no suggestion of God dwelling in man in the garden of Eden. With man, yes, but not in man. 'Whom no man'— mark that, no man—'hath seen, nor can see.' Saith Jesus, 'Ye have neither heard his voice nor seen his shape.' Though Adam in innocence heard his voice, which his posterity in guilt did not, at no time did he 'see his shape'. No man hath seen God at any time.

To have seen God, to have dwelt in him, would have necessitated the righteousness of God being put to the account of man in innocence, which is what never happened, albeit—together with the tree of the knowledge of good and evil—the tree of life was set before Adam as a figure of that which was to come. What was to come, alluded to in both figure and promise, did not come to pass until the gospel. 'But now the righteousness of God without the law is manifested.' Which it was not in the garden of Eden, no, not even to Adam in innocence. However, in the tree of life 'in the midst of the garden' was seen a sign and a promise of righteousness and life in him whom Adam himself typified, 'the figure of him that was to come', Rom. 5:14.

What actually characterised the period 'from Adam to Moses' was the reign of sin introduced by the transgression of the first man. 'Wherefore as by one man sin entered into the world, and death by sin; so death passed upon all men, for that all have sinned.' As by one man's offence death reigned by one, even so by one man's disobedience many were made sinners. It was a reign of sin: sin reigned unto death, that is, from conception to dissolution; sin reigned over all living, up to and until the grave. But how could sin be imputed where there was no law? Though sin was in the world from Adam until the law, nevertheless it was not imputed. But sins were, and although men did not sin in precisely the similitude of Adam's transgression, two things are certain. The first thing is that men were reigned over by sin whether it was imputed or not, and the second is that men were wholly accountable to light received both without and within, against which all had sinned and come short of the glory of God.

The law is said to have 'entered' when it came in by Moses, who received it by the disposition of angels. The law was given to man in Israel, who embraced it as glad tidings of great joy, offering remedy and hope in answer to the dreadful reign of sin and death that had preceded from Adam to Moses. By the law men would now aspire to attain to life because of righteousness. Their own righteousness. Through this they hoped for a rule of life by the law. Moreover, had there been a law given which could have given life, verily righteousness should have been by the law, Gal. 3:21. But there was no such law. Nor could man attain to righteousness by the law. It was this that the earnest Jew found out experimentally: 'The commandment, which was ordained to life, I found to be unto death', Rom. 7:10. Which is what the scripture confirms doctrinally, saying, 'Therefore by the deeds of the law shall no flesh be justified in his sight: for by the law is the knowledge of sin.' And of nothing else.

By the law is the knowledge of sin. It saith not, of sins, as of many, but as of one, sin, the thing itself. That is, the inward state. For the scripture hath concluded all under sin, the commandment finding out the carnal mind which is not subject to the law of God, neither indeed can be. The law said, This do and thou shalt live; and the Jew set to with a will. But how to perform that which he willed he found not, it was not present with him: what he discovered was the power, the inwardness, and the origin of sin in the flesh.

This discovery to those under the law showed the real state of man to be one of enmity against God, a state contrary to the righteousness required of God from man. It was not the law that was at fault, it was that the law discovered the interior state of man's heart to be throughly obnoxious to the wrath of God. Wherefore the law was holy, and just, and good: but man was discovered to be full of unrighteousness, under sin, with the sentence of death passed already in his mortal body. The law was spiritual, yes, but man was not. What therefore the law exposed was the carnality of man, sold under sin. Thus, 'The law entered, that the offence might abound', Rom. 5:20. And abound it did, shutting man up to the faith that should afterward be revealed.

But now, Rom. 3:21, the righteousness of God without the law is manifested. And, if so, despite the giving of the law. For if the law could have brought in righteousness, or given life, then afterwards there had been found no place for the bringing in of the gospel. But the gospel has been brought in, showing the weakness and unprofitableness of the commandment which went before. Indeed, so weak and unprofitable was the law, from Moses to Christ, that when righteousness of God came in by the gospel it was altogether 'without the law'. The law itself made nothing perfect, and therefore it would have been meaningless for a law previously shown to be ineffectual to be added in any way to that gospel which by itself brought in perfection. Hence, the gospel is 'without the law'.

As to the period before the law was given, from Adam to Moses, the need of salvation was as apparent then as it was from Moses to Christ. From Adam to Moses sin was in the world, imputed or not, and all sinned, law or not. Then, sin created an insurmountable barrier between God and man. That it was not imputed to men, could not alter its offensiveness to God, and the impossibility of approach in consequence. As to sins, they were imputed, they were debts, humanity was bankrupt, man was insolvent by his own profligacy, and he should answer for it to the Judge before the Creditor in the last day: 'Every one of us shall give account of himself to God.' Then, with or without law, the words 'but now' look back to a time which in itself demonstrated the need of salvation and the inadequacy of everything that went before to provide it, up to and until the time of the coming of the gospel.

The need of salvation therefore goes back to the fall of Adam, and continues unfulfilled without interruption until the coming of Christ, the entrance of the law making no difference whatever. As to the law, far from bringing any hope of salvation its coming was for the worse, 'That the offence might abound.' How then could it add to the gospel, be a basis for the gospel, or become a partner with the gospel in that salvation concerning which it was not only irrelevant but a hindrance and a further liability? But now the righteousness of God without the law—apart from it—is manifested, and it is this, and this alone, that provides the ground and hope of salvation, a salvation that stands solely in Christ, alone through grace, and only by faith.

The enormity of the fall of Adam and its momentous significance to humanity cannot be overstated. All nations, every generation, the whole of mankind fetch their origins, trace their blood, and discover their destiny in that one man from whom all flesh was begotten and whence every soul was drawn. The truth that so much of the narrative of the fall is couched in mystical language and allegorical form, the fact that this requires such a high degree of spiritual discernment to determine figure from reality, substance from shadow, type from antitype, can neither alter nor diminish the immensity, the universality, or the severity of the fall of man.

The incalculable worth of what was set forth by the tree of life in the midst of the garden, the concealed and deep meaning of the tree of the knowledge of good and evil, the spiritual interpretation of the serpent and of his speech: all these are truths of immense value. But it is the fall itself, the wilful disobedience of the first man, the violation of the prohibition, that must grip the attention. Man was cast out of the presence of God, a flaming sword turned every way to keep the way to the tree of life, venom had come in, sin had been conceived, moral darkness had fallen, and corruption had entered into the constitution and life-blood of a humanity now to be born outside of the presence of God, outside of paradise, and outside of the blessing. By one man sin entered into the world, and death by sin. As in Adam all die, so sin and death must pass by natural generation to all the seed till the end of the world. Henceforward the race must be conceived in sin, shapen in iniquity, and estranged from the womb: that is to say, the state of man had become irrevocably altered from the original.

The farther mankind removes in time from the beginning the more he is under necessity to stand back from his generation, to trace from the utmost branches down to the deepest root, to come to the very end of the line of humanity, to find the first man Adam at the genesis of all things. Here are the origins. Man must, in a figure, look at the brass of which the serpent is made, as well as the serpent made of brass, that he may discover the origin and nature of the plague from which he stands in such desperate need of salvation.

It was not only man who was affected to such depths by the fall, equally profound was the effect upon God. Although the world had been committed to the hand of man and to his dominion, nevertheless the earth was the Lord's, and the fulness thereof, and the heavens were the work of his hands: and what had man brought to pass? Cursed was the ground for his sake, the creation had become subject to vanity; man had done this, with things not his own, things entrusted to him. As to his own fallen condition, what prospect now was opened for a Creator who had delighted in a creation at once 'very good'? What offence, what wrath, what indignation, must be gendered, how greatly, by such a transgression, was the glory of God despoiled, his holiness violated, his righteousness outraged, and his justice offended? He himself was of purer eyes than to behold iniquity, yea, the heavens being not clean in his sight, at what distance should he now stand from fallen man? At infinite distance.

Instead of paradise with man in innocence and God his conversant visitor in the cool of the day, the earth was cursed, man had been cast out, the serpent had come in, inbred sin had polluted the creature, the sentence of death had been passed, the great transgression found no answering atonement, and God was removed to an infinite distance. Besides all this a great gulf appeared, and no man could pass over from this side to that, neither could a holy God draw nigh to pass from that side to this. The gulf was fixed, and the great issue of unatoned sin stood betwixt the two sides of the yawning chasm that had opened between God and man.

Before man could be just with God—for there could never be recovery of innocence—atonement must be made, transgressions must be forgiven, sins must be covered, and iniquity must no longer be accounted. But how could these things be? Not only must a sacrifice be found commensurate with the nature both of the transgression and of the transgressor, but that sacrifice must be perfect. Furthermore man must find a redeemer of sufficient willingness, substance, and power, a redeemer able to draw him back from the infinite distance of his own removal by the fall, by guilt, by Satan, and by inbred corruption. Then, and only then, will man be found, reconciled and cleansed, at the edge of the gulf on the earthly side, his own side, of the great divide between God and man. Yet far beyond all these things, across the vast abyss, on the distant heavenly side, still the forbidding ramparts of wrath soar above the plunging chasm, marking the place of God's departure in offended holiness. Removed to an unmeasurable heavenly distance beyond this place, God must be reached, God must be propitiated, God's wrath must be appeased, God's holiness must be satisfied, the justice of God must be requited, the truth of God must be vindicated, and God's righteousness must be fulfilled. When all these things can be accomplished, then man may be just with God.

Moreover, saith the apostle, the 'law entered'. Entered what? Entered where? Entered the distance between the throne of the eternal God and the divine, the heavenly side of the vast abyss brought in by the fall? By no means. Entered the great fixed gulf betwixt God and man, from the extremities of which both God and man had long departed? Not at all. The law entered between the brink of the gulf on the earthy, manward side, and the incalculable distance that man has travelled from that place by his sins and transgressions. But the law, delivered to man's side of the gulf, with man at infinite remove from the brink of the vast abyss, in darkness, bondage, corruption and guilt, the law could do nothing, nothing but bring down curses, nothing but thunder condemnation, nothing but dispense a ministration of death. Then the offence abounded. Hence the question of salvation raised in the garden of Eden by the fall of man remained not only unanswered but rather aggravated by the entrance of that law which came in 'by the bye', Rom. 5:20.

The law came by Moses, under the administration of angels. It was ordained by angels in the hands of a mediator. Then, the law came in to show man his distance not simply from God—that was veiled—but from the place from whence he fell. After the fall, after the opening of the great gulf of unatoned sin, man removed to an immense distance, carried down the slopes of ungodliness and unrighteousness, far off from the place at which the first man transgressed. In the deception of the fall, in the darkness, in the power of the god of this world, man is born, marries, gives in marriage, begets and dies, generation after generation. Between the place that mankind had reached in his subsequent decline and the place of the fall of the first man, that is, the distance between fallen Adam and the generation of Moses, there the law entered. Then, the law was delivered between the point at which Adam first transgressed and the point to which fallen generations of humanity had descended, 'added because of transgressions'.

The law prescribed a rule of righteousness for man. If this rule were kept man should live. Yes, but such a rule of righteousness assumed in itself four things calculated to bring man to the conviction that it could avail him nothing at all. The first assumption was that the man who would attain to the righteousness of the law must never have sinned. The commandments are not addressed to the guilty that they might obtain mercy. They are addressed to the guiltless that they might maintain righteousness. The law has nothing to do with mercy for past transgressions: its role is that of justice alone, demanding that every transgression and disobedience receive a just recompense of reward. Then he only may address himself to the law who is without sin, who is not guilty: otherwise, though he should attain to the righteousness of the law, the attainment would be upon a rotten and unjust foundation that would altogether fail him at the last. The guiltless therefore may attempt the task, but none other. As to sacrifices, they are not for those who answer to the commandments of the law, they are pure gospel in a figure. The commandments themselves speak of nothing but law, not at all of mercy.

Next, he that goes to the work of attaining righteousness by the law must assume that he has sufficient strength for the task. Now strength is the energy of life: it is the life force. But the law was given on the assumption that man needed life, not that he had it, that he must earn it, saying, 'This do and thou shalt live'. Therefore life is conditional upon doing. But the man needs life for the doing: from whence then shall he obtain strength to labour for life? Not from the law. Then the commandment, which was ordained to life, proved to be unto death, because it revealed man's bankruptcy in relation to what was essential to commence the work: life itself. That was what was lost in the garden. 'In the day that thou eatest thereof thou shalt surely die.'

The third assumption in the giving of the law is that the man who would keep it must be free from inbred sin, he must be void of interior corruption. For the law is not carnal and outward, it is inward and spiritual. It is not merely to regulate outward conduct, but interior conditions. 'For we know that the law is spiritual, but I am carnal, sold under sin', Rom. 7:14.

Of this carnal, interior bankruptcy and pollution man is naturally oblivious, he is quite dead and insensitive to his condition. But by the law he is awakened to the knowledge of it: 'I was alive without the law once: but when the commandment came, sin revived, and I died', Rom. 7:9. 'For without the law sin was dead.' Then the coming of law, which man took to be the occasion to work righteousness, as if he were guiltless, or already had life, was in reality the cause of the awakening, reviving and exposing of man's true inward condition: in bondage to sin in the flesh from the fall.

Lastly, the life held out in the commandment is conditional upon uninterrupted future sinlessness. That is to say, the law requires absolute—absolute—obedience: the least transgression, and the whole is lost. Every least one of the commandments, inwardly and outwardly, must be rendered entire and whole-hearted obedience continually, otherwise the law serves no purpose. The law is right, it is spiritual, and the commandment holy, and just and good; but man must never have sinned, he must find life to earn it, he must be void of inbred sin, and he must be completely sinless at any given instant. Else, if he keep not this whole righteousness of the law at any one and every single moment, he shall surely die. All his righteousnesses shall be remembered no more, as it is written, 'Cursed is every one that continueth not in all things that are written in the book of the law to do them.'

Were these four assumptions ignored, and it should for a moment be considered what would be the effect if the law were kept, even then no remedy to man's perdition would appear. The law could not bring man back over the distance between godless, corrupted humanity and the place where Adam fell, the brink from which the immense and unbridged gulf stretches out to eternity. Where Adam fell? Where is the garden? Where the tree of life? Where the flaming sword turning every way to keep the way to the tree of life? All perished in the flood, all obliterated, because of the degeneracy of mankind since the fall. Then where will the law bring man?

The law can never bring man over the distance to the place of the fall, the precipitous edge of the gulf: could it, what of the gulf itself, fixed, immense, bottomless, infinite? What of the atonement, the sacrifice, the only possible bridge?

When all this has been considered, still the greatest of difficulties in the way of salvation lies upon the other, the heavenly side, infinitely far beyond what eye may behold, or the mind conceive. For God is as much removed in distance from the great gulf of the fall upon the divine and heavenly side, as is man upon the human and earthy side. However, the law was given to man and entered into the world long after the fall of Adam, addressing itself to none of the insuperable heavenly difficulties whatsoever. Wherefore then serveth the law? It was added because of transgressions. And because of nothing, absolutely nothing else.

The law condemned transgressions, it made known those transgressions to which blind, fallen and depraved man was otherwise oblivious. The law revealed sin, dormant within man, utterly obnoxious to the holiness of God. Deluded men were unconscious of the filthy fountain, the spring of corruption which polluted all that came from within, that lay hidden and unsuspected in the inward parts. But God knew, angels saw, and the judgment anticipated the state concerning which ungodly and unfeeling men without the law were wilfully ignorant. Again, the law brought in the knowledge of judgment. It alerted men to the wrath to come, as well as to the curse and sentence of condemnation now present. This service of the law proved invaluable in the awakening and convicting of sinners, shutting them up to the coming of Christ and the bringing in of the righteousness of faith by the gospel when the fulness of time should come.

Wherefore serveth the law? Its invaluable service teaches how deep is the need of salvation. It teaches that the need of salvation goes back to the fall, though the law itself went back no further than Moses. The law was for Israel but salvation is for the world. The world is that which springs from Adam, but Israel sprang from Jacob. Salvation goes to the beginning of things, it goes back to the origins, it roots all up, sweeps all aside, and brings the bottom of the matter to light: 'Then the channels of waters were seen, and the foundations of the world were discovered at thy rebuke, O LORD, at the blast of the breath of thy nostrils.' As to man, he walks on in darkness, and knoweth not that all the foundations of the earth are out of course.

Then what is required? What is required first of all is that one be found who can traverse the vast distance between the place to which corrupt, deceived, and ungodly mankind has descended, and the edge of that great gulf which opened when Adam fell. This distance, measured by the law, appears as the unrighteousness of man. What is required next is a sacrifice beyond conception, a substitutionary sacrifice that can make atonement, an offering that will fully answer to the great transgression, and, if so, take away the sin of the world. What is required withal is a bridge of sprinkled blood, of a body condemned and judged in death, of an acceptable oblation able in itself to span the great abyss, reaching both sides of the great fixed gulf. What is required lastly is one who can cross that great divide, and answer to God in his own nature, passing into the mists of obscurity shrouding so much as the ramparts the far side of the abyss, one who can enter into that thick darkness veiling the other, the heavenly, the eternal, the divine side, traversing unknown infinite realms and coming even to where his seat is. Such an inconceivable, incalculable distance is measured by the divine nature, and manifested in terms of the righteousness of God.

This shows that the law could never bring in salvation, any more than it could provide a means of justification. Justification cannot, simply cannot, be on a legal basis, nor can it be on a principle of law. Salvation can have nothing to do with law, save to satisy it, magnify it, and make it honourable, for that must be done. But that done, there remains the atonement, there remains the great transgression, the fixed gulf, there remains an offended God of purer eyes than to behold iniquity, there remains the infinite distance of the righteousness of God. There remains the immeasurable, the inconceivable remoteness of the throne above the heaven of heavens. In a word, there remains the gospel. That is the power of God unto salvation, and that alone. Why? Because therein the righteousness of God is revealed from faith to faith, as it is written, the just shall live by faith.

As to the law, it came in 'by the bye', it 'entered', it came ages and generations after Adam, at the hand of Moses, and with it came the figures and types of the gospel, the shadows and forms of salvation. These were seen in the tabernacle in the wilderness. Within the hangings of the great outer court, as the worshippers entered past the curtain at the gate, appeared first the brazen altar. Thus far the worshippers might approach with the ordained offering: they might pass only from the entrance to the place of sacrifice, the altar of brass. Further, only the priests might proceed. First to the laver of brass, at which the priests washed their hands and their feet, and thereafter to the tabernacle itself. Passing through the hanging of the entrance into the sanctuary, the service was accomplished about the candlestick and the table of shewbread, and, centrally, about the golden altar of incense.

Beyond this point no priest might proceed under any circumstances. For here was the holy of holies, after the second veil, wherein was the ark of the covenant overshadowed by the cherubim of glory. In the Holiest of all went the high priest alone, not without blood, which he offering both for himself and for the people, having laid aside his own priestly garments, clothed to represent another yet to come. This was the service that was accomplished once a year on the day of atonement.

These things were called 'a pattern of things in the heavens', a figure of things spiritual, divine and heavenly. The people were habitually outside the courtyard, setting forth how far man had departed from the place of the fall, departing by iniquity to the darkness, deception and corruption in which humanity is found at this present. The distance between the people and the courtyard shows man's departure, and the distance from the courtyard to the brazen altar shows the righteousness required of man or ever he can reach the place of sacrifice, that is, the place of the original transgression.

But the sacrifice, the outpouring of the blood, the taking of the life of the substitute, the fiery judgment upon the choice inward parts, the burning to ashes of the body of the offering in a clean place outside: all this shows what is required by retributive justice if ever the great transgression were to find a suited atonement. Only thus could the gulf be bridged, the great divide closed. Then the long journey might begin, bearing the precious blood of the sacrifice made on earth across the abyss into the heavenly regions where all that is human and finite staggers and fails at the immensity of things divine and infinite, absolute and eternal. Nevertheless when the blood of the sacrifice made on earth is sprinkled seven times upon the propitiatory made higher than the heavens before the God of glory, then, and not until then, may the distance be said to have been closed between the heavenly extremity of the vast abyss and the infinite remove from thence of the dwelling place of the eternal and Almighty God. When all these things are accomplished, then salvation may be said to have been effected.

As for the law, prescribing righteousness for man, this came in, or entered, not on the heavenly, the divine side, with its infinite distance reaching from the heavens to the excellent glory: the law has no place there. To those vast heavenly tracts pertains the righteousness of God. Neither has the law any say as pertaining to the great gulf between God and man, opened when Adam fell. The law has to do with demanding righteousness from man under pain of a curse, and came in by Moses. But the vast gulf between God and man has to do with the fall, and came in by Adam.

Between the place of the fall of Adam, and that to which mankind degenerated as a race before and after the flood, there the law came in by Moses. That is, the law 'entered' because of transgressions. And by it transgressions increased, offences abounded, wrath kindled, rebellion rose, the curse fell, and condemnation sounded. By the law sin revived, death reigned, and judgment thundered. By the law deceit spread, self-righteousness prospered, self-justification increased, hypocrisy flourished, and hatred, enmity and persecution multiplied.

But now the righteousness of God without the law is manifested. O, thank God for that, the righteousness of God by faith of Jesus Christ, unto all and upon all them that believe. In his own Person he came to humanity in the place of degeneration, and, without sin, was born of a woman, made under the law. In the perfection of his manhood he reached to the very brink from which man fell, and, in the offering up of himself as a substitutionary sacrifice in the place of sin, and for sin, he glorified God in every divine attribute, closed the gap, bridged the gulf, having received in his spotless, unblemished humanity the due reward and just punishment of the transgressors.

In the perfection of his deity he carried up into heaven all the value of his sacrifice, all the worth of his blood, traversing the vast reaches of infinity, ascending above the heaven of heavens, into the excellent glory, there to show forth the blood-sprinkled propitiatory. 'Whom God hath set forth a propitiation through faith in his blood.' There is one God, and one Mediator between God and men, the man Christ Jesus. This Mediator answers to God in his divine nature, to man in his human nature, and to the depths of the fall in his sacrifice. So that by him reconciliation is effected and ever-lasting righteousness brought in, world without end, Amen.

This wonderful Person by that gracious work alone accomplished eternal redemption. By himself, not by Moses: by the righteousness of God, not by the righteousness of the law: by the grace of God, not by the legal rule: by faith, not by works: once and for all, not repetitively or uncertainly: without the law, not on a principle of law. By himself he did the work. Alone. He 'by himself' purged our sins, and, having done so, sat down on the right hand of the Majesty on high, being made so much better than the angels, as he hath by inherit-ance obtained a more excellent name than they.

VIII

Righteousness of God apart from Law

WHEN the Apostle Paul states that righteousness of God is manifested in the gospel 'without the law', Rom. 3:21, the meaning is that this evangelical manifestation is apart from law altogether. Not only is it apart from law regarding the faith of the believer in receiving the gospel, it is apart from law in respect of the faith of Jesus Christ in bringing in the gospel. That is what the apostle is emphasising: Christ brought in the gospel 'without the law'. Then the righteousness which Christ brought in by the gospel could not be a legal righteousness, it was not wrought by the law, or on a legal principle, it was 'apart from law'. It is nothing to do with law. It is to do with grace. It is to do with the Father and the Son. Christ brought this in by faith alone.

Evangelical righteousness could not be wrought by legal obedience. The righteousness of God brought in by Jesus Christ was not brought in by the works of Jesus Christ. It was brought in by the faith of Jesus Christ. Then it was not a legal righteousness. It was a divine righteousness. It was wrought without the law, and without the works of the law. It was not that Christ kept the law throughout his lifetime as a substitutionary law-keeper on behalf of believers. Had this been the case, of necessity it would have been called 'The righteousness of Christ with the law'. But it is not called that. It is called, 'The righteousness of God without the law', Rom. 3:21.

Again, had Christ been a substitutionary law-keeper on behalf of believers in his lifetime, then—because the law is not

116

of faith—righteousness would have been by 'the works of Jesus Christ'. That is, the righteousness of Christ through the law would have been by the works of Jesus Christ. But the apostle teaches us in holy scripture that the righteousness of God is by faith of Jesus Christ.

Justifying righteousness was not wrought by Jesus Christ through the law. Had it been, it would have read, 'But now the righteousness of Christ with the law is manifested.' But the scripture reads in fact 'But now the righteousness of God without the law is manifested', clearly teaching that God wrought the righteousness of faith by Jesus Christ without the works of the law. The law was not involved. It had nothing to do with the way in which the righteousness was wrought. How could it? It is called 'The righteousness of God apart from law.'

This is not to say that Christ did not magnify the law, and make it honourable: he did. It is not to say that he did not fulfil the law, and establish it: he did. It is not to say that he did not bear the curse of the law and deliver lawfully from its bondage: he did. But none of these things is in question. What is in question is this: How was the righteousness of God brought to light by Jesus Christ in the gospel? And the answer is 'apart from law', or, 'without the law'. Then, neither through its rule nor by its works.

The gospel did not utilise the law as a basis on which to bring in justifying righteousness. Christ was not the pupil and subject of Moses in order to accomplish evangelical justification. Righteousness came in 'apart from law' in the gospel. It was not as if a legal foundation had been laid beforehand by Moses setting out the rule by which in due time the Son should build up the house of God. The truth is that Christ had no need of the law in order to bring in that full, perfect and finished righteousness which is preached in the gospel.

117

The essence of the gospel is the manifestation of the righteousness of God by faith of Jesus Christ. And if by faith, then not by works. Consequently, not by the law.

What was brought in by Jesus Christ came down from God out of heaven. This neither took occasion from nor did it owe anything to that law which had been ordained by angels in the hand of a mediator, save to deliver from its dreadful condemnation. Therefore in the gospel a free righteousness is preached which has nothing to do with the legal rule, for the simple reason that justifying righteousness was not accomplished by the works of the law but by the grace of God. That is why it is called the righteousness of faith, why it came by the faith of Jesus Christ, and why it answers to the grace purposed by the Father and the Son before the world was formed or earth's foundations stood.

However, the law came by Moses in the midst of time, 'by the bye'. The law entered because of transgressions, made the offence to abound, brought down the curse, ministered death, increased the condemnation, and worked wrath. And shall that be either mentor or dictator to the everlasting gospel of the grace of God? It shall not. By the works of the law there shall no flesh be justified in his sight, either by one's own works, or by the works of another keeping it on one's behalf. Hence the words 'apart from law' do not mean without the law in those receiving the gospel, they mean without the law in the bringing in of the gospel.

The righteousness of God manifested by Jesus Christ in the gospel was not achieved by his keeping the law for others, but by his delivering others from the law. It is not a legal righteousness, it is a divine righteousness. It is not a righteousness of works, it is a righteousness of faith. It is not called the righteousness of Christ, it is called the righteousness of God. 'But now the righteousness of God without the law is manifested.' 'Even the righteousness of God which is by faith of Jesus Christ', Rom. 3:21,22.

Notwithstanding all these things, there has arisen, and presently exists, a certain school which holds that 'the believer stands before God on the footing of one who has rendered, by proxy, a perfect obedience to the law, under the legal covenant, Do this and live.' This is called 'legal innocency (sic) or positive obedience, through his imputed righteousness', and stands in 'Christ in his human nature, and as a normal man among men, rendering perfect obedience to the moral law by living a sinless life during the thirty-three years of his earthly career.' This is a notion which has had a considerable following, especially among schoolmen and academics, who mistake it for orthodoxy. Therefore they may say, 'Thou seest, brother, how many thousands of Jews there are which believe; and they are all zealous of the law', Acts 21:20. But Paul was zealous for the gospel. He could say, 'I through the law am dead to the law, that I might live unto God.'

The words 'without the law' or 'apart from law', χωρὶς νόμου *chōris nomou*, Rom. 3:21, are exceedingly strong. The Greek *chōris* has been rendered in English, Apart, apart from, parted from; Alien from; On a distinct footing from. Independent of; Without the agency or employment of; Irrespective of. In Rom. 3:21, what is 'Alien, apart from, on a distinct footing from, irrespective of' what? Why, justifying righteousness is 'Apart from, without the agency or employment of, independent of, parted from' the law. Then how on earth, or in heaven, or under the earth, could it have been wrought by the law? If that is not a contradiction in terms, what is? What, justifying righteousness—apart from, irrespective of, on a different footing from law—wrought by law? Christ keeping the law without the agency or employment of the law?

Given that the law is a rule of righteousness for man, how is it that the apostle calls it 'the righteousness of God'? Will they tell us it is a rule of righteousness for God? To do no murder, not to steal, neither to commit adultery, nor to covet? But, they say, justifying righteousness was wrought by the law; yet, saith Paul, it is called the righteousness of God. Will they run in desperation to the truth that Christ was divine? But they told us that 'Christ in his human nature, and as a normal man, rendered perfect obedience (on our behalf) to the moral law.' Then how can it be called, for it is called, The righteousness of God? Why is it not called The righteousness of the law? Then it would read 'But now the righteousness of the law without the law has been manifested.'

Why is it not called The righteousness of Christ? And why is it not called The righteousness of Christ at any time or in any place throughout the whole New Testament? Why? because justifying righteousness is always and in all places referred to in the apostolic doctrine of the gospel as 'The righteousness of God', that is why. And, as to that, it is said with constancy to be 'without the law', not on a principle of law, not wrought by the law, either on one's own part or that of another acting on one's behalf: it is *chōris nomou*.

The use of the word *chōris* in the New Testament is unequivocal. Occurring forty times in all, three times it has been translated Beside; once, By itself; and thirty-six times, Without; (Margin: Severed from, once). In John 20:7 the napkin is referred to as not lying with the linen clothes, but wrapped together in a place 'by itself'. So is the righteousness of God in relation to the law. Rom. 3:28 states that 'A man is justified by faith without the deeds of the law.' As justification is 'without' the deeds of the law pertaining to the believer, so the bringing in of justifying righteousness is 'without' the deeds of the law pertaining to Jesus Christ. That is, in the same manner, and with the same force, that Christ brought in the righteousness of God 'apart' from law, so the believer is justified 'apart' from law.

Likewise, 'Without' shedding of blood is no remission, Heb. 9:22; 'Without' him was not any thing made that was made, John 1:3; 'Without' faith it is impossible to please him,

Heb. 11:6; 'Without' a parable spake he not unto them, Mt. 13:34; Unto whom God imputeth righteousness 'without' works, Rom. 4:6. Such references demonstrating that the use of the word *chōris* places the matter on an independent footing, make it to be without the agency or employment of anything else. It is without or apart from any other factor. In this case, 'without' the law.

The law, says Paul, Rom. 5:20, 'entered', παρεισῆλθεν, *pareisēlthen*. That is, having traced all things down from two Heads, Adam and Christ, and having brought his argument to a conclusion, the apostle adds, 'Moreover' the law entered: it came in 'by the bye'. The word is taken from παρεισέρχομαι, *pareiserchomai*, meaning, To go or come in, enter; To enter by force. Begin to exist; Come into existence; To make one's appearance on earth. Literally, To go or come in beside. Medically, it is used of fingers or instruments to be inserted. In Rom. 5:20, *pareisēlthen* actually means, To come into sideways; To be introduced, of a side issue; To come in from the side to a state of things already existing.

In Gal. 2:4, the only other occurrence of *pareiserchomai* in the New Testament, the word has been translated 'Came in privily'. Literally this means, To come in alongside by stealth. Sneak in. It is used of those who would have brought in the law, unlawfully and unevangelically, to have a place with and in the gospel. But the gospel of Christ is God's salvation from the fall of Adam; the law merely 'came in sideways' long afterwards, compounding the error by making the offence to abound until the coming of Christ. As to gospel righteousness, it can have nothing to do with legal righteousness, which entered 'by the bye': gospel righteousness is 'apart from law'.

The false assumption that evangelical or justifying righteousness came by Jesus Christ on a basis of law proposes two things. The first proposition is that Christ addressed himself to the legal rule throughout his lifetime on behalf of believers, to keep the law for them as their substitute. This substitutionary life of righteousness by the law is then supposed to have been imputed to all that believe. The next proposition is not disputed: it is that Christ bore the curse or penalty of the law in his own body on the tree. Here there is no disagreement whatsoever. The first proposition is referred to as Christ's 'Active' obedience, the latter as his 'Passive' obedience.

Issue is taken with the former assumption, that of 'Active' obedience, on a great number of points. Immediately I assert that justifying righteousness did not come by the law; it was 'apart from law'. Christ did not keep the law vicariously as a substitute, hence the righteousness of faith is never called the righteousness of the law, neither is it referred to as the righteousness of works, nor is it said to be the righteousness of Christ, all of which would be the case if this assumption were correct. Legal righteousness wrought by the works of Jesus Christ according to the law is not imputed to believers, neither indeed could it be, what is imputed to believers is the righteousness of God by faith of Jesus Christ, Rom. 3:22, Phil. 3:9.

The notion that Christ kept the law in his lifetime as the substitute or vicarious law-keeper of believers, so that his righteous law-keeping provided works of supererogation afterwards to be put to their account is as demonstrably false as it is palpably absurd. It is not what the apostles taught about Christ's bringing in justifying righteousness, neither is it what the scriptures teach about the imputing of that righteousness, nor is it what is revealed by the Holy Ghost about justification. It is a legal error, dangerous in its ramifications, foisted upon Christ and his apostles in the name of tradition since the close of scripture. The fact that such views were held by revered, evangelically canonised figures, doctors, professors, reverends, academics, highly honoured by the world, and likewise acclaimed by the adulation of their followers, is nothing to point, it is nothing but the very popery that such people profess to abjure. The truth is—as shall be set forth in order—that this is a system at once illegal, irrational, unevangelical, unsafe, unscriptural, inconsistent, and unreformed. On every count of truth this assumption, this invention, once examined, straightway collapses. This is about to be demonstrated.

The assumption that Christ kept the law throughout his lifetime as the substitutionary law-keeper of his people—afterwards bearing their penalty at the cross—so that his perfect lawkeeping was accounted to believers as their own completed righteousness is demonstrably false. It requires that the price should be paid twice over for the same error. Either Christ's law-keeping was in the stead of the believers' law-breaking or it was not. If it was, then that law-breaking is covered. It cannot be accounted. It cannot be seen. It is superseded by substitutionary law-keeping. If so, the believer is reckoned to have kept the law. Then why must Christ die under the penalty imposed for breaking it?

Christ having kept the law for him, observe the position and standing of the believer. He is entirely covered by the robe woven through the vicarious life and substitutionary legal obedience of Christ. This, complete, is put upon him. Beneath it, his own real life cannot possibly be seen. Of what then has the law to accuse him, that the penalty should be exacted at the cross? If Christ kept the law for him, then the believer is reckoned to have kept the law. And shall such a man die, however vicariously? What law is this, that demands payment twice over for the same offence? What law, that condemns a man for things which it does not reckon him to have done?

Is this magnifying the law, and making it honourable, when the law is made to curse the guiltless? Is it revering the Judge, to oblige him to condemn the man who is reckoned to be without offence? Is it glorifying God, to require him to punish the substitutionary life of perfection of his own Son, in order to get at the transgressor after all? Is it exalting the cross, to make its work unnecessary, righteousness already having been fully outwrought before its advent?

The notion that Christ kept the law for his people, making such a substitutionary law-keeping their righteousness, really undermines the atonement. Because then that people would have possessed righteousness, it would have been to their account, by virtue of the work of Christ before the cross. Christ's perfect life of legal righteousness, imputed to them, would have perfected the people of God. By this they would have been righteous in the eyes of the law, legally it would have secured righteousness for them. It would also have made the cross superfluous.

But what saith the scripture? As to perfection, that it came not by vicarious law-keeping in life, but by a substitutionary offering in death, for, 'By one offering he hath perfected for ever them that are sanctified', Heb. 10:14. As to justifying righteousness, the scriptures teach that it was not by Christ's lifetime, but by his death, 'Being now justified by his blood', Rom. 5:9. As to the covering of sin, scripture teaches that it was not by Christ's righteous life but by his sacrificial death, 'He put away sin by the sacrifice of himself', Heb. 9:26; and again, He offered one sacrifice for sins for ever, Heb. 10:12. So that in the Bible it appears clearly that through death, and death alone, the work of righteousness was wrought once and for all. How dare they undermine that?

From the sacrifices of the Old Testament nothing is more clear than that, however perfect and unblemished the life of the substitutionary sacrifice, substitution commenced only with the laying on of the hands on the part of the offerer. That is, at death. It must be so. The truth is that there can be no substitute of one for another in terms of obligation to obey the law. It is entirely illegal. If a hardened criminal were brought before the judge, having been witnessed in the commission of a crime at a certain time, of what worth would be the plea that on that day the criminal had commissioned a man of exceptional integrity to perform on his behalf outstanding works of charity, over and above all that could be expected of him, so that these works of supererogation might count, at the very hour in question, as his own substitutionary behaviour? What would the judge say?

No man may be the substitute of another in terms of obligation before the law. Legally it is not acceptable. But if a judge should sentence a convicted criminal to a fine, another may certainly pay that penalty for him: that is a different, and lawful, matter. One may pay the penalty of the broken law for a convicted person, but none may take on the obligation to the law itself, for another. Now, Christ bore the penalty, but he did not, for he could not, take on the lawful obligations of others. He took on their lawful punishment. A substitutionary life instead of another is downright illegal: but a vicarious death on behalf of others is altogether gracious. In Christ the former would have been absolutely unlawful: but in truth the latter brought in everlasting righteousness.

The context of salvation must always be kept in mind. With the fall of Adam, sin entered into the world, and death by sin. A great gulf opened, on the one side of which God removed to an infinite distance in offended holiness, and on the other man descended to an immeasurable depth by ungodliness and unrighteousness. Salvation must resolve this calamity in its entirety. Now the law came in by the bye, between the edge of the gulf and the place to which man has descended since the fall by iniquity. The law could not make men righteous, it could not make amends for the fall, it could not close the gulf, it could not atone for sin, and it could not reach to God in his holiness.

Even supposing the unlawful notion of a substitutionary legal righteousness, such a thing could take men no further than to the place from which Adam fell. But the righteousness of God, infinitely removed across the divide, could never be met by a legal righteousness incalculably short of the divine measure. Such a legal righteousness would only leave men with the law, without an antidote, the sanctuary immeasurably distant, the veil unrent, and with the righteousness of God, and God in righteousness, utterly inaccessible. And—were it not illegal—what kind of a salvation is that?

How can anyone possibly contend for justifying righteousness being the righteousness of Christ with the law, when the apostle declares expressly that it is the righteousness of God without the law? Consider Rom. 1:17; 'For therein'—that is, in the gospel of Christ—'is the righteousness of God revealed from faith to faith'; then, evangelical or justifying righteousness, the righteousness in question, the righteousness revealed in the gospel, is not the righteousness of Christ, but the righteousness of God by faith of Christ. Likewise, Rom. 3:21, 'But now the righteousness of God without the law is manifested'; not the righteousness of Christ with it. Again, Rom. 3:22, 'Even the righteousness of God by faith of Jesus Christ'; not the righteousness of Christ by works of Jesus Christ, which is what it would have to read if the legal rule were the rule by which Christ should bring in justifying righteousness. But that is not gospel righteousness, nor can it be, because it is illegal. But the righteousness of God by faith of Jesus Christ is not illegal, it is evangelical, and, moreover, it establishes the law.

Once more, Rom. 3:25,26, God hath set forth Jesus Christ 'to declare his righteousness'; Not Christ's righteousness: God sets forth Christ to declare his own righteousness. Then, God's righteousness in Christ is justifying righteousness. Likewise, Rom. 10:3,4, The Jews 'have not submitted themselves unto the righteousness of God' in the gospel. As to that righteousness, 'Christ is the end of the law for righteousness to every one that believeth': where gospel righteousness is the righteousness of God by Jesus Christ. Also II Cor. 5:21, God 'hath made him—Christ—to be sin for us, who knew no sin;

that we might be made the righteousness of God in him';
here, without doubt, evangelical righteousness is that of God
in Christ through his death, not of Christ through the law in
his life. Finally, Phil. 3:9, renouncing the righteousness which
is of the law, any righteousness which is of the law, Paul
wholly and heartily embraces the righteousness which is in
the gospel, that which is through the faith of Jesus Christ,
even the righteousness which is of God by faith.

These passages declare beyond all reasonable doubt that
justifying righteousness is revealed to be the righteousness of
God, that it came by faith of Jesus Christ, and that it is
without the law. All of which is in the very teeth of the notion
that Christ kept the law in his lifetime as the substitute of
believers, and that this legal righteousness of Christ is that
which is revealed in the gospel. Such a notion is at once illegal,
unevangelical, irrational and unscriptural.

It is very clear that the righteousness imputed to believers in
the gospel is the righteousness of God. It is equally clear that
the rectitude of Christ is not and cannot be so imputed.
However the scripture strongly upholds the righteousness of
Christ, or rather, that Christ is the Righteous One. Jesus
Christ the Righteous is said to be the Advocate with the
Father, I Jn. 2:1, pleading the cause of a child of God fallen
into sin: too guilty, confused, and under obscurity to pray for
himself. But this is a case of describing the upright character
of Jesus Christ before the Father: his unchangeable rectitude,
his constant access to the Father's ear, his eminent suitability
and title to plead for those who have fallen.

Peter in Acts 3:14 describes the Lord Jesus as the Holy One
and Just—Just being the same word as Righteous, *dikaios*—as
opposed to Barabbas, who was a murderer. It is a question of
the contrast in character between Jesus and Barabbas, in
which Peter cuts at the conscience of the Jews for their evil
choice before Pilate. Stephen also, Acts 7:52, rebukes the

stiffnecked Jews, uncircumcised in heart and ears, whose fathers had rejected the holy prophets, and who, themselves, had despised the unparalleled virtue of the Just One, persecuting the former and betraying and murdering the latter. Why? Because all those sent of God to the Jews had exposed their rotten religion, and none more than Jesus Christ the Righteous.

This was he, so worthy in his manhood, whom the Father had raised to glory. From thence, before the Father in heaven, Paul was given to know his will, Acts 22:14, was chosen to see that Just One, and was enabled to hear the voice of his mouth. This text in Acts likewise speaks of the worthy character of the Man at God's right hand. But none of these passages has anything to do with imputed righteousness.

How excellent is the worth of Jesus Christ the Righteous! This is he who went about doing good, Acts 10:38; who knew no sin, II Cor. 5:21; who was without sin, Heb. 4:15; and who did no sin, I Pet. 2:22. He was holy, harmless, undefiled, and separate from sinners, Heb. 7:26. Thus at the cross appeared the perfection, the absolute suitability, of the Substitute of sinners. Then and there the work began. Not before. Prior to the place of judgment, previous to the cross, his eminent fitness had appeared. Now at the cross, at the place of judgment, his substitutionary work should have its commencement.

The words 'substitutionary' and 'sacrifice' go together. Of necessity therefore it was at the cross, the place of atonement, that the substitutionary work began. The Old Testament sacrifices illustrate this truth beyond a shadow of doubt. Their substitutionary function began at the altar. It could not begin before it: that would have been as meaningless as it would have been illegal. The altar was the place of sacrifice, and the place of sacrifice was the place of substitution. Hence the work is called 'Substitutionary atonement'. It was of this, and of the suitability of the One destined to be the substitute at the place of atonement, where the blood was shed, that Peter wrote, saying, Ye were redeemed with the precious blood of Christ, as of a lamb without blemish and without spot, I Pet. 1:19.

Those who claim that imputed righteousness is the legal righteousness of Christ wrought through his supposed substitutionary lifetime, and not the righteousness of God wrought through Christ's actual substitutionary death, appeal sometimes to certain prophetic Old Testament passages in which the LORD is said to be the righteousness of his people Israel. But the fact that the LORD is our righteousness, rather serves to demolish than to help the argument of those who would bring this forth to support the illegal notion of substitutionary law-keeping. The LORD is JEHOVAH, the covenant name of God given to Israel under the Old Testament. JEHOVAH was unknown beyond the unrent veil. He dwelt behind thick darkness. Nothing was revealed of divine Persons. What was revealed in prophecy of the coming evangelical righteousness was that it was divine: JEHOVAH himself should be their righteousness. In other words, it was the righteousness of God that Messiah should bring to light. But that is exactly what we are saying, and they are denying. Then it would have been better for them not to have meddled with this passage, any more than with the other places which they contort.

By such texts as Jeremiah 23:6, 'THE LORD OUR RIGHTEOUSNESS'; or Jeremiah 33:16, 'The LORD our righteousness'—and, for example, Isaiah 45:25 and 61:10—they propose to validate their theory of the imputed substitutionary legal righteousness of Christ. But such references contradict what they wish to assert. The righteousness of Christ, properly so-called, is his righteousness as Man. Whereas JEHOVAH OUR RIGHTEOUSNESS is without doubt the righteousness of God. It is this name whereby the Branch, or King, Christ himself, shall be called, 'He shall be called, THE LORD OUR RIGHTEOUSNESS', Jer. 23:6. It is also the name by which Judah and Jerusalem shall be

called, Jer. 33:16, 'She shall be called The LORD our righteousness'. That is, the Branch, or King, Christ himself, shall
bring forth a righteousness from JEHOVAH God by which both
he and all his people are to be named thereafter.

The meaning is that Christ shall be called JEHOVAH OUR
RIGHTEOUSNESS, when by substitutionary atonement he brings
in the righteousness of God by faith of Jesus Christ, Rom. 3:22.
Again, the people subject to the Branch, or King, a people
called in the feminine Judah and Jerusalem, shall also be
called by this name, for, Jer. 33:16, 'This is the name where-
with she shall be called, The LORD our righteousness'. In fine,
they are the righteousness of God in him, II Cor. 5:21. All
this establishes our case, but demolishes theirs who were foolish enough to draw attention to these texts.

The other passage—and the only passage—to which the
proponents of this illegal fabrication can retreat for apparent
support is Rom. 5:18. Having devised their scheme between the
cloisters, the common-room, and the lecture hall, belatedly
they find themselves obliged to go to the Bible for a text or two
to buttress this preconceived philosophy. So to Romans five
they repair: not, observe, on the subject of justification as
such, but of the righteousness by which we are justified. If so,
why start at Romans chapter five? Why not chapter three,
where Paul commenced?

Why not? Because chapter three does not once mention the
notion of the legal substitutionary righteousness of Christ: it
consistently speaks of the righteousness of God by faith of
Jesus Christ. Why not go to chapter four? After all, that is the
chapter dealing with imputation. But they must avoid that,
because the righteousness imputed is always that of the
righteousness of God, never the substitutionary righteousness
of Christ. But they can assault the context, wrench the text,
twist the words of Romans chapter five, forcing it to mean
what was never intended by the writer. And, shamelessly, that
is exactly what they do.

All this is in the teeth of everything that has been taught for five chapters: for craftily they set the thin end of the wedge of their philosophy half way into the fifth chapter, slamming it home with heavy blows from their theological traditions and clerical authoritarianism contrary to the doctrine of Christ. The fifth chapter? After having consistently taught the righteousness of God as that by which believers are justified in Christ, the fifth chapter informs us that we are justified by his blood, Rom. 5:9. It is this that brought in the righteousness of God to the account of all for whom it was shed. But these defiant inventors tell us that, contrary to Paul, the righteousness of God has not been brought in at all, no, the substitutionary law-keeping of Christ is put in its place, and, without the shedding of blood, counted to believers for righteousness.

Romans 5:12-21, which is really about the reconciliation, or substitution, contrasts Adam and Christ, two men, their acts, the judgment of God upon those acts, and the consequences of this to their respective posterity. As such, justification figures prominently, not to explain the doctrine —that explanation was given in the preceding chapters—but rather to enlarge on the blessing that flows from Christ's Headship. Here justification, its meaning taken for granted, appears as the consequence of the judgment of God in righteousness upon the obedience of Christ in death, made good to all the seed, with the issue everlasting life through Jesus Christ our Lord.

The point in dispute is whether or not the substitutionary righteousness of Christ in his lifetime, according to the law, is that righteousness referred to in Rom. 5:16-19. Not in verse 16: All that is said here is that the free gift is of many offences unto justification. Nor in verse 17: This states that they which receive abundance of grace and of the gift of righteousness shall reign in life by one, Jesus Christ. Thus far we read that the free gift is unto justification, and that the gift is in fact righteousness. But whose righteousness, and how was it wrought? That is the question.

The translation of the next verse, Rom. 5:18, must be clarified before exposition can be attempted. What does the verse read? This is a question that must precede the query, What does the verse mean? The reading is marred, and there is an alternative version in the margin. The marring is due to the italics, showing that the parts of the verse italicised are not in the original Greek, but are the interpolation of the translators in order to give their view of the meaning. The nature and extent of the italics in verse 18 shows that the translators laboured to give a meaning not conveyed by the Greek words of Paul. The additional fact of an alternative marginal reading—one that gives yet another, and quite different, sense to the verse—shows that the translators were divided in their judgment.

The verse appears as follows: 'Therefore as by the offence of one *judgment came* upon all men to condemnation: even so by the righteousness of one *the free gift came* upon all men unto justification of life.' But the translators have strained the text to meet their interpolation. Leaving out the italics the verse reads, 'Therefore as by the offence of one upon all men to condemnation: even so by the righteousness of one upon all men unto justification of life.' Yet even with the italicised bias omitted, the translators' rendering still forces an interpretation upon the text. Not so, however, the margin: 'Therefore as by one offence upon all men to condemnation: even so by one righteousness upon all men unto justification of life.' This marginal reading is an excellent and accurate rendering of the Greek.

By changing the meaning of the original from 'one offence' to 'the offence of one' the translators have radically altered the meaning. The fact that they cover themselves in so doing by giving the correct—and contradictory—reading in the margin is no excuse for obfuscating so vital and important a verse. However all this is as nothing compared with the enormity of changing 'one righteousness' to 'the righteousness of one'. By doing that they have forced the scripture to give support to a notion altogether foreign to text, context, and Holy Writ: the notion which we are opposing. Their contradiction of themselves in the margin reveals a struggle between tradition and scripture only resolved by the compromise of mutually exclusive renderings paying court to both. Either it is 'one righteousness', and, if so, the righteousness of God; or it is 'the righteousness of one', in which case it must be the righteousness of Christ, and, by implication, according to the law. But it cannot be both. The Greek, *dikaiōmatos*, is 'accomplished righteousness', or 'one accomplished righteousness'. The literal rendering of the text reads 'So then by one offence unto all men to condemnation: so also by one accomplished righteousness unto all men to justification of life.' This is more or less what the translators have put in the margin.

Then, the reader must choose: either the text—for all the italics—is correct, or the margin is correct. Let the Greek be studied, or an interlinear Greek-English text be consulted, and the question is resolved: the margin is correct. Now, if the margin is correct, scripture is consistent with itself, Romans is consistent with itself, and the one accomplished righteousness is the righteousness of God by faith of Jesus Christ. But if the italicised text is correct then 'the righteousness of one' would appear to be the righteousness of Christ, and hence according to the law. Then scripture is made to be inconsistent with itself, and Paul overthrows all that he had laboured to establish. Let the reader choose. It is not a question of interpretation. It is a question of the reading of the text. According to the text, or the margin, which are mutually exclusive, so the interpretation follows of course.

There is no dispute over the Greek: all relevant editions have ' καὶ δι ἑνὸς δικαιώματος '. Then all read 'through one

133

accomplished righteousness', or 'one righteous act', or 'one righteousness'. It follows that this refers to the one righteous act of God in which he poured out his wrath against sinners upon the Saviour on the tree, whereby, through the shedding of his blood, Jesus Christ brought in everlasting righteousness, even the righteousness of God by faith of Jesus Christ. And there is no doubt but that this is the exact meaning of the text.

The nineteenth verse follows: 'For as by one man's disobedience many were made sinners, so by the obedience of one shall many be made righteous.' Those who hold that Christ kept the law throughout his lifetime on behalf of others, thereafter to be reckoned to them as their righteousness, suppose that the obedience of Rom. 5:19 is this same substitutionary obedience to the law. They think therefore that the righteousness of this verse is Christ's righteousness in keeping the law on their behalf. But the obedience required in such a case as they presume is legal obedience. It is obedience to the law. Now, it is everywhere granted, that obedience to the law is the obedience of works. 'This do, and thou shalt live.' 'For to him that worketh is the reward not reckoned of grace but of debt.' It is the works of the law, by doing, by labouring, that must be kept, if legal obedience is to be realised. But the word obedience in Rom. 5:19 is nothing to do with works. It is to do with hearing. The word is ὑπακοῆς, *hupakoēs*, To hearken submissively.

Now, however submissively one hearkens to the law, hearkening will never bring forth any good works: the law does not require hearing, it requires doing. But faith requires hearing. And the obedience of Jesus Christ is the obedience of the faith of the gospel. 'Received ye the Spirit by the works of the law, or by the hearing of faith?' Without faith it is impossible to please God. But Jesus Christ, by the obedience of faith, pleased the Father. Everlasting righteousness was brought in by the faith of Jesus Christ. Thus many sons were brought to glory. Then, the obedience referred to in Rom. 5:19 cannot be the obedience of doing, that is, of works; it must be the obedience of hearing, namely, of faith. That being so, the righteousness referred to cannot be that wrought by the works of Jesus Christ, which would be the works of the law; it must be that brought in by the faith of Jesus Christ, that is, the righteousness which is of God by faith.

It is illustrative of the delusion and blindness of all legalists that the advocates of this preposterous scheme which abuses and makes void the law with a witness, nevertheless shrill 'Antinomian!' at those who honour the law with the true gospel. Did Christ keep the law for others by works of super-erogation? Then righteousness comes by the law. But Paul does not frustrate the grace of God by such a legal fiction: his language is 'If righteousness come by the law, then Christ is dead in vain.' Clearly righteousness does not come on a legal principle, and certainly not that of Christ being the legal substitute of believers: it does not come by the law at all, under any circumstances. No, it comes by the gospel, it stands exclusively in the death of Christ, and it is the righteousness of God without the law. If not, Paul protests, 'Christ is dead in vain', Gal. 2:21.

They are the antinomians. They overturn the law. They make void the legal rule. In the nature of the law, there can be no termination of obligation for the doer other than death. 'Cursed is every one that continueth not in all things that are written in the book of the law to do them.' The law requires all, mark that all, and it requires all continually, throughout the unfolding lifetime. Allow that Christ 'kept the law as our proxy', as they call it, giving all as a substitute in legal obedience for others throughout his years. What then? Then the question is, What do they mean by a substitutionary lifetime? The law does not deal in generalities, it knows no generalities, it deals in exactitudes, in 'all things' and that 'continually'.

The fact is that the legal rule will and must measure the life of the law-breaker precisely, so long as 'continually' and 'all' exist. If such a fantasy as proxy law-keeping for a given life-span were legal, then the judge would consider substitution in relation to that span, and nothing other than that span. The worth of the proposed substitutionary life, the excellence of its quality, would not be the point: that may well fulfil the 'all' at any given moment; but it could not possibly cover the 'continually' in the case of a life longer than that of the Proxy. For what we are being asked to consider is the legal implication of the life cover of a Substitute cut off out of the land of the living after thirty-three years.

If allowed, the scheme might then be considered for the first thirty-three years, the period during which the Substitute may be supposed to have rendered 'all'—nothing extraneous—'continually'—no remaining period: but what then? He died, but they continue—for whom he had lived some thirty-three years—until they themselves pass away, say, in old age. But what of the intervening period between the respective deaths? Since 'all' is required 'continually', not just for the first thirty or so years but for the entire life-span of the law-breaker, the advocates of this scheme need not think to escape the implications of legal exactitude by expressions of exasperation. What is to cover the lives of the law-breakers after the first thirty-three years and until their own death?

However rich and full of virtue the life of the Proxy, 'all' had been given. More could neither be demanded nor rendered. Then there could be no excess. The law had required 'all', and, they say, 'all' had been received by way of full substi-tutionary measure. Of necessity, and by law, this could be for no longer than the precise period of thirty-three years, eye for eye, tooth for tooth, year for year. After this period, where is the cover? The way in which those who embrace such notions ignore the rigour of the law, and its inexorable demands, is nothing other than blatant antinomianism. And this is not to mention the even more flagrant abuse of the law, in which thereafter they leave the believer under a legal rule divested through their antinomian scheme of its proper sanctions. O, tell it not in Gath, publish it not in the streets of Askelon; lest the daughters of the Philistines rejoice, lest the daughters of the uncircumcised triumph!

The devotees of this confused philosophy really think that their system is Reformed, but it is not Reformed. Many statements of the reformers were vague and unclear, and the consequence of this lack of definition has been that anyone with a bee in his bonnet can, if desired, clearly trace the buzzing to the Reformation. The reformers undoubtedly taught that Christ 'fulfilled the law for us' as may be seen from several places. As early as 1532, Tyndale in an exposition upon the fifth, sixth and seventh chapters of Matthew speaks of Christ's 'fulfilling the law for us'. Joye repeats this against Gardiner in 1543. The Homilies of the Church of England, in the Homily of Salvation, 1547, follow the wording of Tyndale, saying, 'God sent his only Son our Saviour, Christ, into this world, to fulfil the law for us, and, by shedding of his most precious blood, to make a sacrifice and satisfaction, or, as it may be called, amends to his Father for our sins.' Again, 'He provided a ransom for us, that was, the most precious body and blood of his own most dear and best beloved Son Jesus Christ, who besides this ransom fulfilled the law for us perfectly.' Once more, 'Christ is now the righteousness of all them that truly do believe in him. He for them paid their ransom by his death. He for them fulfilled the law in his life.'

On face value these quotations would seem to offer support to those who advocate that the believer stands before God on the footing of a substitute who has rendered, by proxy, a perfect obedience to the law. According to C. Hodge, Owen thought so, the Puritan doctor—he says—claiming to have derived his position from the Homilies of 1547: 'the Church of England is in her doctrine express as to the imputation of the righteousness of Christ, both active and passive, as it is usually distinguished. This has been of late so fully manifested out of her authentic writings, that is, the Articles of Religion and Books of Homilies.' However, this statement is a presumptuous deduction which does not confine itself to the meaning or intention of the reformers.

It must be said that the position of the reformers themselves was that there should be no presumption, everything must be based on Holy Scripture, tradition was notoriously unsafe, they themselves recognising their own weakness, who only lately had been delivered from the very priesthood and ignorance against which now they inveighed. This was very far from being the case with Dr. Owen. He appealed to the tradition of the reformers, and read into their writings to justify a system the ramifications of which extended far beyond what they would have tolerated.

It is clear that the consistent, but unelaborated, language of the Homilies has reference to Tyndale's 'Christ fulfilled the law for us'. The reformers repeated this wording several times over, without explaining what they meant in precise terms. Tyndale was commenting on the words, 'Think not that I am come to destroy the law, or the prophets: I am not come to destroy, but to fulfil. For verily I say unto you, Till heaven and earth pass, one jot or one tittle shall in no wise pass from the law, till all be fulfilled', Mt. 5:17,18. From this came Tyndale's, Joye's, and Cranmer's 'Christ fulfilled the law for us'. But we look in vain for the words 'for us', in Matthew 5:17,18. Equally significant is the omission of the words 'the prophets', from the gloss 'Christ fulfilled the law for us'. They say, 'Christ fulfilled the law for us', but Matthew quotes Jesus as saying, of both law and prophets, as such, 'I am not come to destroy, but to fulfil'. Which is precisely what he did. There is no mention of 'for us'.

The reformers understood the righteousness imputed to the believer to have been called, The righteousness of Christ. They also understood that the King of England was a better, or more practical, substitute for the Pope than the Lord Jesus Christ in glory. They understood, after they had browbeaten Hooper, that vestments were essential to consecrate the bishops, as they called them, of a quaintly robed clergy, distinguished from the laity by a popish collar, gown and title. They understood that buildings of bricks, stones, old rubble and mortar, facing east, by a process of incantation constituted none other than the 'dreadful house of God'. They understood that a drop of plain water made 'this child regenerate, and grafted into the body of Christ', seeing that thereby 'it hath pleased Thee to regenerate this infant.' And they came perilously near to implying that the bread and wine were not far different from a spiritual Mass, declaring, after some equivocation, 'Thou dost vouchsafe to feed us, who have duly received these heavenly mysteries, with the spiritual food of the most precious Body and Blood of thy Son our Saviour Jesus Christ.' But charity believeth all things, hopeth all things, beareth all things, and hence desires neither to read into nor enlarge upon the failings of otherwise excellent men at a time when they had just emerged from darkness, and, in many cases, were just about to be martyred.

The reformers were by no means clear in everything. The Homilies state that Christ fulfilled the law for us in his life. But to say, as did Owen, that this statement supports the preposterous and dangerous notion that Christ's so-called legal obedience procured our justification, or righteousness, whereas his death provided for our pardon, or forgiveness, is to assert what never entered into the mind of any reformer. Owen had no right to foist such views upon men who could no longer speak for themselves. What they had written, they had written. Far from suggesting that Christ obeyed the law as a substitute in order to procure our justification before his death, the Homily on Salvation states categorically 'Every man of necessity is constrained to seek for another righteousness, or justification, to be received at God's own hands; that is to say, the forgiveness of sins and trespasses.' Here justification and forgiveness of sins are the same thing. Again, 'To have ... by him remission of our sins, or justification.' Hence, contrary to the notion that Christ's life as a legal proxy secured justification in and of itself, without his death, the Homily states that justification is 'The forgiveness of sins and trespasses', and that 'the remission of sins' is another way of saying 'justification'. That is, justification, or righteousness, is in and by Christ's death alone.

Calvin taught the same thing, saying, 'To justify, therefore, is nothing else than to acquit from the charge of guilt.' Once more, 'But in Romans 4:6-8 he first calls it imputation of righteousness, nor doubts to place that in remission of sins.' Again, 'God by pardoning justifies.' In another place he says 'Certainly he does not cite the prophet as a witness, as if he taught that the pardon of sins were a part of righteousness, or that it contributed to his justifying a man, but includes the whole righteousness in gratuitous remission.' Calvin excludes the very idea of Christ's procuring a substitutionary righteousness for believers by keeping the law as their proxy. 'He is justified by faith who is purged before God by the gratuitous remission of sins.' For Calvin, as for the Homilies, remission of sins is justification, and justification is remission of sins.

Just as was the Lord Jesus, and particularly the Apostle Paul, so were the reformers charged with setting aside the law. But it was their accusers who did that. The gospel, however, establishes the law. Luther thunders against these legalists, 'Leave Moses and his people together; it is finished with them, it does not concern me. I have the word which regards me—we have the gospel.' Again, 'The law is a light which makes plain and clear, not grace, also not righteousness whereby man obtains life, but sin, death—Gods wrath and judgment. That is the proper and right work of the law, in which it should remain, and not take a step further.' He declares the law to have ceased when Christ came, having nothing to say to the Gentiles. 'Those who are already righteous—by faith in

Christ—are far outside and above all laws. Therefore the law should be laid alone on those who are not yet righteous ... until the righteousness which is by faith come; not that such righteousness be obtained by law ... but that they may, alarmed and humbled, flee to Christ, who is the end of the law for righteousness to all those who believe.' (Gal. 3:19-23.)

The notion that Christ brought in righteousness, or justification, by acting as a proxy under the law before his death, whereas pardon or forgiveness was to be secured afterwards by his death, is in the very teeth of Holy Scripture. The idea that believers can have the one, pardon, without the other, justification, is revolting. This novel conception, conjured up after the Reformation, is denied by the Homilies, by Calvin, and by Luther. Withal, it is correct to say that the reformers were vague, perhaps deliberately vague, concerning not the fact but the mode of deliverance from the law, about which they were conscious of not yet having been fully taught of God. No such humility hinders the proponents of this harmful fantasy, however. The reformers called justifying righteousness, The righteousness of Christ, they taught that Christ fulfilled the law for us, but that said, for them all, justification was in the death of Christ, and righteousness by his blood alone. As to making a difference between remission, or pardon, and justification, or righteousness, this is clean contrary to Luther, Calvin, the Homilies, the Thirty-nine Articles, and the entire doctrine of the Reformation.

The acolytes of this neo-legal system, who would put salvation on a basis of Christ making void the law, say this: 'The believer stands before God on a footing of One (Jesus Christ) having rendered, by proxy, a perfect obedience to the law, and can claim its rewards in heaven itself, under the terms of the legal covenant, Do this and live.' They consider that Christ, having lawfully lived their lives for them by proxy, has secured thereby a substitutionary righteousness, a full justification, which entitles them to everlasting life in heaven, without his having died and without his blood having been shed. And yet, quite apart from this complete righteousness and absolute justification, Christ is said by them to have died to secure their pardon, and to have shed his blood to obtain their ransom.

Their view is illegal, irrational, unevangelical, inconsistent, antinomian, and unscriptural. First, it is illegal. Those who hold this notion would force both legislature and Judge to rule and ratify what is manifestly unlawful. They grasp the legal maxim that what a man does by another he does by himself. But then they wrest this maxim to the advantage of their contrived scheme by proclaiming that the law regards Christ's obedience as ours, on the assumption that it was lawful for him to have obeyed for us. That is a *non sequitur*. It does not follow at all. This legal maxim does not apply and cannot be accepted as lawful by a judge, unless one acts in behalf of another by his own prior appointment. The proxy must be duly and legally appointed by the person on whose behalf he is to act, for the purpose of that act.

In no circumstances can a proxy appoint himself. Imagine the law justifying one appointing himself proxy to some substantial person without his awareness and liquidating his assets accordingly! Neither can a third party appoint a proxy for another without the knowledge and consent of the person concerned. Not in law. But we are considering the law. We are considering what is lawful, and what is not lawful.

Quite apart from this consideration, the extent of that to which one may appoint a proxy is severely limited at law to specific actions such as signature, conveyance, voting, marriage, meetings and the like. All these matters require a due legal authority from the appointee to the proxy prior to the event. To suppose from this maxim of convenience that the law would accept a proxy—and at that, without the appointee's knowledge—concerning obligations of obedience to

142

universal precepts the very pillars of civilized society, and, at that, for an entire lifetime, *carte blanche*, reveals a singular lack of grey matter on the part of those advocating such a preposterous notion. But to make the law, and the judge, wink at this deliberate contrivance permitting the habitual law-breaker to go scot-free, nay, to claim the right by proxy to the State's noblest honours, is contempt of the highest order. It is not merely lawless, it is anarchistic, it overturns the whole judicial structure.

It is irrational. The view that Christ's obedience to the law was accounted as our obedience, rests upon the fallacious and irrational concept that Christ, made of a woman, made under the law, owed no obedience to the law on his own behalf. Then, because Christ need not obey for himself, any obedience rendered was of necessity a work of supererogation, and thus might be considered as a substitutionary life of obedience in place of lives of lawlessness. But what a nonsensical conception!

Was Christ under no obligation to the law, as made under the law? If he was, then what was that obligation, that they should say, There was sufficient virtue in excess of his personal obedience to the law that it could be spread and multiplied to cover countless lives of disobedience from the beginning of the world to the end of it? If they think this, then let them tell us what obligation was due from him to the law for himself? But we know the answer. It was precisely the same obligation as that demanded from any other Jew under the law. He was equally bound to love God with all the heart, and all the soul, and with all the mind. Then, if all means all, it was impossible for him, even were it legal, to perform a work of supererogation, that is, to be more righteous than the law required.

Notwithstanding that his deity was united with his humanity through the mystery of his incarnation, however wondrously his divine nature was joined with or was indivisible from his human nature, all, mark that, all was demanded by the law of that human nature. All the heart, all the soul, all the mind. However unique that heart, soul, or mind. The obedience demanded of and rendered by Christ according to the law could do no more than render the righteousness required of his own manhood in the sight of the law. That could not possibly be imputed to others. He stood under the same obligation as others, however vast his capacity.

He was as obliged as his contemporaries to love God with all his heart, and soul, and mind, and strength, and his neighbour as himself. How could there be superfluous virtue or righteousness when such an 'all' had been rendered? All was demanded—unique as he was—and all was rendered. He could render no more. Than 'all', there is no more. It was therefore impossible—as it is irrational—for him to obey in behalf of others that which required everything on his own account.

This scheme is unevangelical. In the gospel the glory of God is revealed, the veil is rent, God is glorified, and the deity made known in Christ, magnified in all his attributes. But how does their fable make him known? As One who required his Son to satisfy justice by an exact substitutionary life of obedience to the law for his people, so as to procure for them a perfect righteousness, a full justification. Then why should Christ suffer, and why should his sufferings be counted to them, in addition? Justice cannot require the imputation of his perfect obedience to them, so that they are accounted in law to be perfectly righteous, and then demand Christ to suffer for them, and those sufferings to be put to their account, as if he had not obeyed for them. What kind of a Judge does such a doctrine as this reveal? Is God first to exact from his Son on their behalf a full and perfect obedience, and then demand the equivalent amount of penal suffering as if there had been no obedience? What does such a 'gospel' predicate of God? It is downright unevangelical.

144

It is this that makes such a view inconsistent with itself. It is inconsistent. By no stretch of the imagination is it possible to grant pardon or bestow remission upon persons accounted to be perfectly righteous and absolutely justified in the eyes of both law and justice. Remission from what? Pardon for what? Perfect righteousness? If such persons are justified by an imputed righteousness it is wholly inconsistent to speak of remission. Why pardon those whom the law accounts to be absolutely just? Pardon implies previous condemnation, not prior justification. Forgiveness stands in setting aside the execution of the penalty of the broken law, not setting aside a perfect righteousness. It is the height of inconsistency to justify a people on the ground of the obedience of their substitute, and at the same time pardon them when they are regarded as having perfect righteousness.

This scheme is antinomian. Not only does such a fiction bring the law into contempt by requiring the penalty of the broken law to be exacted upon those who are counted as never having broken it, but it treats the law with derision in that it holds believers to be under the law, whilst making the law that they are under a feeble mockery of itself. According to them believers in Christ enter into a relationship with the law in which it is to be their rule, but in which its penalty is for ever set aside.

The fact that believers are said not to be under the law, that they are dead to the law, that they are delivered from the law, that they are redeemed from the law, that the law has no more dominion over them, that they are free from the law, makes no difference to people as blindly prejudiced as this. No, their scheme is all, and if the scriptures contradict it, then they must be wrested: whatever the scriptures would say, they must be forced to confess that believers are under the law, and that such a law has no penalty. But a precept without a penalty is no law. If the penalty is set aside, and they say that it is set aside, then of necessity the law is made void. The dismissal of the penalty is a repeal of the precept, it is a setting aside of the law in fact, it is a making void the law. A precept or a law without a penalty is no law at all: it is nothing but advice. And they are nothing but antinomians.

Their fabrication is unscriptural. We are justified by faith without the works of the law, not by the works of the law without faith. However they may twist and turn, they hold to justification by works of the law, that is, by Christ's works of the law, which is what scripture never teaches.

They hold that the righteousness of Christ came by the law, but the apostle teaches that the righteousness of God came without the law. They pontificate that the law is eternal, but the apostle declares that it came in by the bye. They maintain that the law came by Moses, and that the works of the law were wrought by Jesus Christ: the gospel affirms that the law was given by Moses, but grace and truth came by Jesus Christ. They suppose that Christ was a schoolmaster to lead us to Moses, but Paul believed that Moses was a schoolmaster to lead us to Christ. They say that they are under the law, but the apostle asserts that we are not under the law. They testify that they are alive to the law, but the Holy Ghost witnesses that we are dead to the law. So the scriptures teach one thing, and they teach another.

The scriptures teach that now the righteousness of God without the law is manifested, even the righteousness of God which is by faith of Jesus Christ, unto all, and upon all, them that believe. The scriptures teach that in the gospel the righteousness of God is revealed from faith to faith, as it is written, the just shall live by faith. The scriptures teach that we are justified by Christ's blood. The scriptures teach that God hath made him to be sin for us, who knew no sin; that we might be made the righteousness of God in him.

The scriptures teach that Paul did not, could not, and would not have a righteousness which was of the law, but that which

146

is through the faith of Jesus Christ, even the righteousness which is of God by faith. The scriptures teach that if righteousness comes by the law, then Christ is dead in vain. And if the scriptures teach that, then this scheme and all its advocates are thoroughly and fundamentally unscriptural, whosoever they are, or were, it maketh no matter to me: God accepteth no man's person.

IX

Righteousness of God by Faith of Jesus Christ

JUSTIFICATION is laid upon the foundation of the righteousness of God by faith of Jesus Christ. Righteousness is the basis already established on account of which afterwards God justifies the ungodly. It follows that before justification could take place, righteousness must have been secured. It was secured. It was secured by Jesus Christ. It was secured by the faith of Jesus Christ. And it is called the righteousness of God. That is what the scripture teaches, Rom. 3:22, 'Even the righteousness of God which is by faith of Jesus Christ.'

The Apostle Paul states seven things about the righteousness of God by faith of Jesus Christ in this context. It is without the law; it is by faith of Jesus Christ; it is unto all that believe; it is upon all that believe; it is free; it is by grace; and it is through redemption. This describes that perfect righteousness on the ground of which God would proceed to justify the ungodly. The subsequent divine act of accounting sinners righteous is called justification; it is by faith; faith is counted to them for righteousness; and their righteousness is called The righteousness of faith. However, before justification can be comprehended, righteousness, its basis, must be clearly understood.

The first thing to grasp in order to understand righteousness is that it is not of the law, neither is it by the law, either on the part of the sinner or on the part of Jesus Christ. It is the righteousness of God by faith of Jesus Christ, not the righteousness of the law by works of Jesus Christ. What could the law do? It could work wrath, gender sin, bring forth despair, and minister condemnation. It could make nothing perfect, it could not atone, neither could it justify, nor could it rend the veil. It was a dead letter, a killing ministry, and an administration without light, life, love, grace, faith, justification or hope. It obscured the nature, promises, purpose, counsel and oath of God. It was made for sinners, the lawless, and the disobedient, and its voice was the voice of cursing. But now, thanks be to God, the righteousness of God without the law is manifested, and that law which came in 'by the bye' has given place to the faith of Jesus Christ to every one that believeth. This is the voice of justification, a gospel voice, the voice of grace, mercy, and peace from God our Father, and the Lord Jesus Christ.

The divine revelation of justification is enshrined in its essence in Romans 3:19-28. This, together with the entire New Testament, was translated by Tyndale into English in 1525. He rendered Romans 3:22, the first part, 'The rightewesnes no dout which is good before God, commeth by the fayth of Jesus Christ.' Tyndale was followed by the Great Bible, 1539, 'The ryghtewesnes of God, commeth by the fayth of Jesus Christ.' Next the Geneva Bible of 1560, '(To wit,) the righteousnes of God by the faith of Jesus Christ.' The Bishops' Bible, 1568, put it thus, 'The righteousnes of God *commeth* by the faith of Jesus Christ.' The Roman Catholic Rheims version, 1582, has this to say, 'And the justice of God by faith of JESUS CHRIST.' The King James, 1611, of course gives us, 'Even the righteousness of God *which is* by faith of Jesus Christ.'

Then comes the Revision, 1881. But it was not a revision. It ought to have been a revision. The Committee was instructed to undertake 'A Revision of the Authorised Version' with a view to 'the removal of plain and clear errors', and, with this primary rule, 'To introduce as few alterations as possible into the text of the Authorized'. The Revisers introduced thirty-six thousand alterations. Is that as few as possible? Drs. Westcott and Hort, having prepared their own Greek text with the avowed purpose of overthrowing the *Textus Receptus*, the original Greek text from which the Authorised Version was translated, at the first meeting of the Revisers, distributed the page-proofs of their novel text under the pledge of secrecy, with the design of supplanting the ancient Greek *Textus Receptus*.

That is no revision of the English. It is a supplanting of the Greek, and by a text based on a hypothetical, unproven, and untenable theory. But it was their hour, Christendom's judgment, and the power of darkness. They succeeded, thereafter providing the basis of the modern translations which have forsaken the old Greek text, the old but more accurate English, the old paths, and the old landmarks. Westcott and Hort really hated both ancient Greek and old Bible, and were set upon their overthrow down to the foundations: 'the villainous *Textus Receptus*'. 'That vile *Textus Receptus*'; so wrote Hort in 1851. In place not only of the edifice of the Authorised Version, but of the foundation of the *Textus Receptus*, he was to insinuate a new Greek text, which was to become the basis from which future English versions should follow.

Observe the difference: Revised Version, 1881, 'Even the righteousness of God through faith in (*sic*) Jesus Christ.' Here it is man's faith, not the faith of Jesus Christ. This is the beginning. Next, the Revised Standard Version, 1946, followed the Revised in the wording of Westcott and Hort's Committee, 'The righteousness of God through faith in (*sic*) Jesus Christ.' No apparent change, rather the slow establishing of a position fundamentally destructive of the gospel. And, yes, the dropping out of the vital footnotes grudgingly included in 1881. After this, the New English Bible, 1961. Here appears the reason for the supplanting of the ancient Greek text in the so-called 'Revision' of 1881: a complete destruction of the English by which the words of the gospel are conveyed.

First, 'the faith of Christ' is left out, 1881 and 1946. But it is a small thing, and we must not be uncharitable. Our charity mellowed over the years, at last the reason for the change appears without shame, New English Bible, 1961, 'It is God's way of righting wrong, effective through faith in Christ.' Now, that is not the gospel. But then, nor is it the Bible. There exists no Greek text for this language. And since faith comes by hearing, and hearing by the word of God, under such a deception, none can be saved. After the New English Bible, there has been sheer wild chaos. Though, of course, lucrative chaos to those who publish at such a price to the souls of men.

Then the faithful will stand by the Greek text of our Authorised Version, the *Textus Receptus*, Δικαιοσύνη δὲ θεοῦ διὰ πίστεως Ἰησοῦ χριστοῦ: 'Righteousness of God through faith of Jesus Christ.' Upon this only sure and stable basis, that of ages and generations, the doctrine of the gospel has been translated into English, and in that English the faithful intend to continue, for, 'the just shall live by faith', Rom. 1:17.

Quite properly the Authorised translators have rendered the Greek 'faith *of* Jesus Christ'. The original cannot be made to mean 'faith *in* Jesus Christ'. It is genitive. It is his faith. And that is what all the translators have rendered until Westcott and Hort changed the Greek text and altered the English meaning under the guise of Revision. Then the faith of Christ was dropped, and the 'faith' of man was preferred. After that, the faith itself was dropped, witness the New English Bible, 1961, 'It is God's way of righting wrong, effective through faith in Christ', a blatant exhibition of misconstruction shamelessly and arrogantly ignoring even so much as their own Greek text.

'The faith of Jesus Christ', Rom. 3:22, is that which is said to manifest the righteousness of God 'from', or 'out of' faith, Rom. 1:17. That is, 'out of' the faith of Jesus Christ by which he glorified God in righteousness at the cross. This brought in that everlasting righteousness on the basis of which God could justify sinners. The reference in Rom. 3:22 could not allude to the faith of the believer in Christ for justification, because it speaks of what necessarily preceded justification: that is, the manifestation of the righteousness of God. That righteousness came by the faith of Jesus Christ. It is the foundation of justification by faith.

The first part of Rom. 3:22, 'The faith of Jesus Christ', therefore does not speak of our believing in Christ, but of his believing in God and the Father. Not of our being justified, but of his bringing in that righteousness by which we should be justified. To justify sinners is one thing. To secure the righteousness by which they could be justified is another. It is of the righteousness which God wrought by the faith of Jesus Christ enabling him justly to justify sinners that the apostle speaks in this place. Not of justification itself: but of a righteousness prior to justification by which God would afterwards justify the ungodly. Such a righteousness, insists the apostle, was secured 'without the law' on the one hand, and 'by faith of Jesus Christ' on the other.

Justifying righteousness was brought in by faith. Therefore, not by the law. The law requires works and not faith. Had Jesus Christ brought in righteousness by the law, the word 'works' would have been in place of the word 'faith'. However the words 'righteousness of God by faith of Jesus Christ' assure us that righteousness did not come by the law, because we know that the law is not of faith, Gal. 3:12. As to the works of the law, 'The man that doeth them shall live in them.' But Christ, the Just, lived by faith; and by his faith alone, without works, that righteousness was wrought and established through which thereafter men should be justified by faith.

Therefore it is of faith, that it might be by grace. Not by law. By grace. For the promise was not through the law, or through

Christ's keeping the law, but through the righteousness of faith, and through Christ's believing God and the Father, as opposed to the law and all its works.

If they which are of the law be heirs, then faith is made void, and the promise of none effect, Rom. 4:14. The promise, which pertained to justification, was given four hundred and thirty years before the law was in the world. Then it did not, and it could not, come by the law. It came by grace. And if by grace, then through faith. And if through faith, then through the faith of Jesus Christ. That is what brought in justifying righteousness, according to promise: 'Therefore it is of faith, that it might be by grace', Rom. 4:16.

All is of grace. We are justified by grace. Grace wrought righteousness through the faith of Jesus Christ. Grace imputes righteousness through the faith of the believer. All is of grace, and everything is by faith. Otherwise all would be of law, and everything would be by works. Because grace and faith, law and works, are mutually exclusive. 'If by grace then it is no more of works': either our works, or Christ's for us. Not of Christ's legal works of supererogation for us? No, for, 'If it be of works, then it is no more grace.' But it is by grace: 'By grace are ye saved through faith.' 'Being justified freely by his grace.' Either it is of the law, therefore of Christ's keeping the legal rule, and hence of works; or it is of grace, therefore of Christ's obedience unto death, and hence of faith. But it cannot be both. 'Otherwise grace is no more grace.' Conversely, 'Otherwise work is no more work', Rom. 11:6.

Romans 3:22 speaks expressly, justifying righteousness came by 'the faith of Jesus Christ'. 'Faith' is in the genitive, 'Jesus' is in the genitive, and 'Christ' is in the genitive. It is possessive: it is his faith. No amount of juggling with Greek grammar or exceptional instances can alter the normal rule, or what a common Greek would have understood by the words in Rom. 3:22, 'Even the righteousness of God which is by faith of Jesus Christ.'

153

No ordinary, or for that matter extraordinary, contemporary of the writer of this epistle would have understood anything but what the translators have rendered, namely, 'The faith *of* Jesus Christ'. Never faith *in* Jesus Christ. The preposition is not ἐν, but διά. The case is genitive. It is perverse to read anything other than 'of'. Not, therefore, our believing in him after his faith had brought in justifying righteousness: that may follow. But, his believing in God in order that justifying righteousness might be brought in: that must precede. And that is the clear and plain meaning in this place.

Exactly the same thing occurs with the parallel expression in Galatians 2:16, 'The faith of Jesus Christ'; and, again in the same verse, 'by the faith of Christ'. As they have done to Romans, so these Revisers of the gospel have done to Galatians. If 'evangelicals' neither knew nor cherished their holy places, these have known them, and hated them, yes, and torn them down unnoticed and unmolested. Thus they have robbed us of our heritage without a finger being raised, save for those few counted as 'troublers of Israel'. From Tyndale in 1525 through six versions in the English tongue—including the Roman Catholic Rheims version—until almost the beginning of the twentieth century, the wording has stood unchanged in faithful answer to the Greek, 'The faith of Jesus Christ'.

Then came Westcott and Hort, with their pliant Revisers. It is not even as if they had the excuse of a different reading in their own Greek text for changing the English. Here their Greek is the same as the *Textus Receptus*. Then why change the correctly translated English? The phrase, 'by the faith of Jesus Christ', Gal. 2:16, is exactly the same in the Greek as that in Rom. 3:22. Neither is the next phrase, 'by the faith of Christ', Gal. 2:16, materially different, despite the change of the preceding preposition from διά to ἐκ. Then, if the Greek is the same, and the English needed no revision, why did Westcott and Hort's Revisers alter 'the faith of Jesus Christ', and 'the faith of Christ' to 'faith in Jesus Christ', and 'faith in Christ'?

And why did they do exactly the same thing in Rom. 3:22? Without any sound reason? In respect of what is foundational to justification by faith?

There can be only one reason for changing what refers to the objective truth of the gospel into what points to the subjective response of man. Particularly when there is no ambiguity in the Greek, grammar or text; the precedent is established and uncontested; the Revisers knew that the expression that they changed three times over was perfectly correct as it was; and the small alteration to 'in' from 'of' completely overturned the vital truth of justification dependent for clarity on these very places.

So small, they hoped it would not be noticed. But they knew perfectly well how disastrous would be the damage caused by their knowingly and deliberately tampering with the scripture, without even the excuse that they were following their novel Greek text. As in the case of Rom. 3:22, after the Revisers had done their damage, the Revised Standard, the New English Bible, and all the train of lucrative 'modern versions' have followed suit. Now there can be no pretence of 'Scholarship' or new Greek manuscript discoveries in this case. The Greek is the same. Only the English is worsened to cause intolerable abuse of the text.

The Greek text compounded by Westcott and Hort, with which they effectively dazzled the eyes of the Revisers, was based upon the Vaticanus, Sinaiticus and Bezae codices. These two men had turned from the *Textus Receptus*, the Greek text of the Authorised Version, with abhorrence, in favour of promoting their own alternative. Dean Burgon, a painstaking and orthodox scholar, considered 'their cherished codices as the depositories of the largest amount of fabricated readings, ancient blunders, and intentional perversions in any known manuscripts.' Like many scholars before him, he was convinced that these manuscripts had survived—

one in a monastery waste paper basket, the other on a forgotten Vatican shelf—only because they were full of mistakes
and little used.

'Shame, yes, shame on the learning', protested Burgon,
'shame on the learning which comes abroad only to perplex
the weak, and to unsettle the doubting, and to mislead the
blind. Shame, yes, shame on the two-thirds majority of well-
intentioned, but most incompetent men, who—finding
themselves (in an evil hour) appointed to correct 'Plain and
clear errors' in the English Authorised Version—occupied
themselves instead with falsifying the inspired Greek text in
countless places, and branding suspicion on some of the most
precious utterances of the Spirit. Shame, yes, shame upon
them.' Thus Dean Burgon. And as if well over five thousand
changes in the Greek text were not enough, these 'Revisers'
added thirty-six thousand alterations to the English, some of
them exceedingly subtle, to the great detriment of the word of
God in our mother tongue.

Nowhere is this detriment greater or more subtle than in
Romans 3:22 and Galatians 2:16. But to those who seemed to
be somewhat then, and to others who have something in
which to glory now, the faithful will give the same response as
did the Lord Jesus, the disciples, the holy apostles, and all the
saints, to the scribes, Pharisees, priests, doctors, elders, wise
and prudent of their day. Like those at the beginning, to our
generation of imperious priests, haughty scholars, and learned
scribes we will 'give place by subjection, no, not for an hour,
that the truth of the gospel might continue with you',
Gal. 2:4,5. As to that truth of the gospel, it is summed up in
this word, justification by faith. As to justification by faith, it
is founded upon the righteousness of God. As to the righteousness of God, it is by faith of Jesus Christ. For thus saith
the Spirit, and hence writes the apostle, and therefore appears
the Greek, and so the translation is rendered in English, 'The
righteousness of God by faith of Jesus Christ', Rom. 3:22. And

again, 'Knowing that a man is not justified by the works of the law, but by the faith of Jesus Christ, even we have believed in Jesus Christ, that we might be justified by the faith of Christ, and not by the works of the law', Gal. 2:16.

Observe that a man is not justified by the works of the law. Whether he should seek to keep the law for himself, if that were possible, or whether another should keep it for him, if such a thing were legal, justification is not on that principle. By whatever scheme or method, saith the apostle, 'A man is not justified by the works of the law.' Not by the works of Jesus Christ according to the law? No, by no means. By what then is a man justified? 'By the faith of Jesus Christ', Gal. 2:16. As opposed to the works of the law.

But how is a man justified by the faith of Jesus Christ? In that Jesus Christ 'Shall see of the travail of his soul, and shall be satisfied.' For 'by his knowledge shall my righteous servant justify many; for he shall bear their iniquities', Isa. 53:11. The knowledge of which the prophet speaks is that possessed by Christ, God's righteous servant, concerning the way in which many should be justified. It is by way of the cross. 'For' he shall bear their iniquities. Then, justification stands exclusively in the bearing of iniquities. If so, justification is in the death of Christ, which brought in everlasting righteousness freely to the account of every one that believeth. Christ knew that by dying he would achieve their justification. By faith he died, according to that knowledge. And by his knowledge, through faith, he justified many, for he bore their iniquities. Then, they were justified by the faith of Christ.

A similar passage occurs later in the same chapter, Galatians 2:20, 'I am crucified with Christ: nevertheless I live; yet not I, but Christ liveth in me: and the life which I now live in the flesh I live by the faith of the Son of God, who loved me, and gave himself for me.' By now we have learned three things. We have learned the places that the enemies of the gospel will attack. We have learned that they will always attack these places. And we have learned that if they cannot attack by their spurious Greek text then they will do so by blatantly overturning the correct translation.

Therefore it should not surprise us that, perceiving the beauty of holiness through justifying righteousness in this passage, 'I live by the faith of the Son of God', immediately we discover that the enemies of the gospel have been here before us with their evil meddling. By following the apostles' doctrine concerning the faith of Jesus Christ through each consecutive passage, inadvertently we have found that we were tracing the semi-obscured footsteps of those of a previous century who with diabolical mischief have deceived the English speaking peoples in the matter of salvation by confounding the truths of justification in their Bible.

Galatians 2:20 is, like Romans 3:22, a text vital to the knowledge of justification by faith. Then the Revisers must alter it. Inconveniently, however, the Greek of Westcott and Hort and that of the *Textus Receptus* proved to be identical. Failing, therefore, to find cause for alteration from the Greek, the Revisers were forced to bend their critically destructive faculties against the perfectly satisfactory English of the Authorised Version. Because it followed that, since the text concerned vital justifying doctrine, it was not a question of whether, but of how, Galatians 2:20 was to be mutilated.

From 1525 to 1568, through three versions, 'the faith of the Son of God' stood untouched in Gal. 2:20. The exception to this rule was the Geneva Bible of 1560 which, curiously, rendered the passage 'the faith in the Sonne of God', a strange outburst of interpolation. In 1582 the Roman Catholic Rheims Bible, having stated 'I live in the faith'—rather than 'by the faith'—returned to the original translation, 'the faith of the Son of God'. Likewise from 1611 it was 'the faith of the Son of God' and remained so until the Revision of 1881. Once again the unaltered testimony of over two and a half centuries was overthrown for the worse by the Revisers when without the least warrant 'the faith of the Son of God' became 'faith which is in the Son of God', Revised Version, 1881.

This mistranslation was in the teeth of the language, grammar, and wording of the Greek text. Save for one single exception it was in defiance of the unanimous agreement in translation of version after version from 1525 until the 'Revision'. Since that 'Revision', 1881, there has been no attempt to correct this perversion of the text. Far from it. With a kind of inevitability the mistranslation was perpetuated in the Revised Standard Version 1946, in the New English Bible 1961, and in the host of more recent versions. Remark that there was no question of a different Greek reading; only of the translation of the same Greek into the English. But the Authorised was perfectly accurate: 'The faith of the Son of God'. Then what explanation for the alteration can there be other than enmity against justification by faith?

Galatians 2:20 commences, 'I am crucified with Christ.' This is not an explanation of a subjective attainment peculiar to the apostle. It is a personal affirmation of the objective doctrine common to all. It is not the experimental state reached by a few. It is the positional standing gained for everyone. That is, all have been crucified with Christ: 'Our old man is crucified with him', Rom. 6:6. 'For ye are dead', Col. 3:3. In the counsels of God, when Christ died, we died. 'If one died for all, then were all dead', II Cor. 5:14. 'We be dead with Christ', Rom. 6:8. That is the position through substitution, not the sensation by holiness. His death is counted before God as our death.

That may be so, but our experience is not one of death but of life. 'Nevertheless I live; Yet not I, but Christ liveth in me.' Whence comes this life? 'The life which I now live in the flesh I live by the faith of the Son of God.' Live by the faith of the

Son of God? But his faith is spoken of in relation to his death. Yes, because his death is the source of our life. Why? Because his death brought in righteousness to the account of those for whom he died. But how does righteousness being to our account give us life? In that the Spirit is life because of righteousness, Rom. 8:10.

Just as it was sin that brought forth death, so it is righteousness that brings forth life. 'That as sin hath reigned unto death, even so might grace reign through righteousness unto eternal life by Jesus Christ our Lord', Rom. 5:21. So that when Paul says he lives by the faith of the Son of God, he means that the faith of the Son of God brought righteousness freely to the account of all believers through his death, and that the consequence of this righteousness is everlasting life. That is the life which he lived, for, 'They which receive abundance of grace and of the gift of righteousness shall reign in life by one, Jesus Christ', Rom. 5:17. Then the faith of the Son of God, the source of the apostle's life, to which he alludes, is that which respected the salvation of his people through the death of the cross.

This is confirmed by the following clause in the verse, 'Who loved me, and gave himself for me.' Just as the faith of the Son of God respected his death, so his love drew him to die for his people. The everlasting love which he bore for his people, in the nature of love, could have but one conclusion. He loved them before the foundation of the world. He loved them through the ages of time. He loved them when he came into the world. But the issue of all this love was to the end that his people might be saved: 'for this cause came I into the world.' For what cause? The cause of dying for his people. 'What shall I say? Father, save me from this hour: but for this cause came I unto this hour.' That was the hour of death, the hour of glorifying God, the hour of saving his people from their sins. 'He loved me' said Paul; yes, but the consequence, the issue of that love follows immediately, 'And gave himself for me'. Then the faith of the Son of God, the bringing in of righteousness, and the giving of everlasting life, all centre upon his death, confirming the comfortable doctrine of justification by faith.

Reference is also made to the faith of Jesus Christ in Philippians 3:9, 'Not having mine own righteousness, which is of the law, but that which is through the faith of Christ, the righteousness which is of God by faith.' The fact that the rejected and obsolete manuscripts favoured by Westcott and Hort agreed in this place with the *Textus Receptus* must have been annoying to the Revisers, because it robbed them of the obvious excuse for changing the English. But the lack of excuse was no deterrent. They changed the English anyway. Nor were they hindered by the existence of a perfectly satisfactory English translation in the Authorised Version. Determined to undermine the gospel at its most vital point, justification by faith, the Revisers set about the task of misrepresenting even their own Greek text, dismissing the correct Authorised Version, and providing a deceitfully false translation of words which the Holy Ghost gave by the pen of the apostle for the salvation of men.

What was their motive? The same motive as the leaders of the Oxford Movement and their present-day heirs of the Anglican-Roman Catholic Commission on Justification, ARCIC II*. They were resolved to undo the division caused by the Reformation. Since that division occurred through justification by faith, then at all costs such a doctrine, if it cannot at once be destroyed, must be steadily eroded generation by generation. No greater erosion occurred at any one time, nor was any less noticed, than when the Revisers changed the word 'of' to 'in', Romans 3:22, Galatians 2:16, again Galatians 2:16, Galatians 2:20, and Philippians 3:9.

*See 'The Elect undeceived', A reply to the C. of E.-R.C. Agreement on Justification by Faith (ARCIC II), John Metcalfe Publishing Trust.

This did not merely strike at justification by faith. It struck at the foundation of justification by faith.

Spurning the faithful testimony of centuries, the Revisers of 1881 in effect set about dismantling the bulwarks of salvation. They really were Edom's spiritual children, who in the day of Jerusalem said, Raze it, raze it, even to the foundation thereof. They were of spiritual Babel, witness the confusion of tongues which they sowed, Psalm 137. They did their work with guile, pretending to bring to the people an Authorised Version corrected from any errors or inconsistencies that remained. But they changed the Greek text. Secretly. And they changed the version. Deceitfully. Their appearance to the public was like that of the accomplice of a thief who makes a great ado over the wonderful quality of the worthless trinkets he has brought to sell to the jeweller, gaining attention by crying his wares to both staff and public. Meanwhile under the cover of this noise and bluster, privately the thief himself lifts every tray of precious stones and priceless jewellery, quietly making off with all the stock. And so it was.

In Phil. 3:9 the Revisers altered the reading 'That which is through the faith of Christ, the righteousness which is of God by faith', to 'that which is through faith in Christ, the righteousness which is from God by faith', but this sly manipulation had no basis whatever in the text: the former was indisputably the more correct translation. Next the Revised Standard Version, 1946, 'That which is through faith in Christ, the righteousness from God that depends on faith.' Afterwards the New English Bible, 1961, 'The righteousness which comes from faith in Christ, given by God in response to faith.' What they all mean—and over the years express more and more clearly—is that righteousness comes by man, not God; that it is of persuasion, not faith; that it is subjective, not objective; that it is self-justification, not justification by faith; that self-righteousness is imparted, not that divine righteousness is imputed; and that salvation is under papal authority in the

Roman church by priestly sacraments, not in the Lord Jesus through the Holy Ghost by the word of God.

The meaning of Phil. 3:9 is that any and all righteousness which is 'of the law', that is, wrought through the legal rule, of necessity must be contrary to and on a different principle from that wrought through the faith of Jesus Christ. By definition the righteousness of faith could neither be 'of the law', nor wrought through the law. The faith of Jesus Christ stood in his belief that by the grace of God he should be made the sin-offering of his people at the cross, and that God should pour out upon him the just judgment against them both of the law and of the divine nature. This he did, and it brought in the righteousness of God by faith of Jesus Christ to their account.

Thus his people became the righteousness of God in him, and that righteousness was called, The righteousness of faith. That they were justified was therefore due to the shedding of his blood; 'Being now justified by his blood', Rom. 5:9. The righteousness which was the basis of their being justified by faith was wrought on a principle of faith, by grace; not on a principle of works, by law. It is called, Τὴν ἐκ θεοῦ δικαιοσύνην ἐπὶ τῇ πίστει, 'The righteousness which is of God upon'— the basis of—'faith', Phil. 3:9. The meaning is that the righteousness by which the ungodly are freely justified rests upon—ἐπὶ—the ground or principle of faith, even the faith of Jesus Christ. If not, why do the enemies of the gospel, both ancient and modern, rage so against it?

In the book of the Revelation, Ch. 2:13, Jesus Christ declares unto the angel of the church in Pergamos, Thou holdest fast my name, and hast not denied my faith. But what shall Jesus Christ say to those who have deliberately obliterated all reference to his faith, from Romans, Galatians and Philippians, in the Revised Version, the Revised Standard Version, the New English Bible, and their succeeding volumes? I say, what shall he say to those who deny the existence of 'the faith of Jesus Christ' in Holy Scripture, against the testimony of centuries, of the original Greek, of grammatical usage, of plain honest translation, yes, and of the testimony of the Holy Ghost?

Unlike those who disobediently refused to translate the words 'the faith of Jesus Christ' and 'the faith of Christ', the Holy Ghost greatly honours the faith of Jesus Christ, bearing witness to the same several times over through the writings of the holy apostles. By these references to his faith in scripture, the Holy Ghost takes the things of Christ and shows them unto us, so glorifying Christ. But these Revisers and their followers are different. They do the contrary. They rob Christ of his things and hide them from us, so debasing Christ. And in that day when God makes inquisition for iniquity, what excuse shall be offered by these blind leaders of the blind who have added to and taken from the words of this book at their own will?

The saints therefore stand under great need of patience, to endure unmoved through all the swirling mists of the present mystery of iniquity. Still, 'Here is the patience of the saints: here are they that keep the commandments of God, and the faith of Jesus', Rev. 14:12. The commandments of God in the New Testament were given to Jesus Christ by the Father: 'The Father which sent me, he gave me a commandment, what I should say, and what I should speak', Jn. 12:49. 'I have kept my Father's commandments, and abide in his love', Jn. 15:10. The Father's commandments to the Son were several. Particularly, What Jesus should say, Jn. 12:49. How he should die, Jn. 10:18. And that he should give everlasting life to as many as the Father had given him, Jn. 12:50; 10:27,28. But when did Moses ever require a servant under the law to give blessing to the worthless, blood for sinners, and life to the ungodly? For that was what the Father required of the Son.

164

As to the faith of Jesus, Rev. 14:12, the simplicity of the name Jesus directs us to the record of the four gospels. The faith of Jesus, the faith of the Son with the Father, was evident from the beginning. This was the Just One who should live by his faith. But the law is not of faith, Gal. 3:12, neither could it give life. Those under the law had no Spirit of life, for the servant must labour for life: 'This do, and thou shalt live.' However the Spirit was seen visibly to descend upon the Son, abiding upon him, and the voice of the Father was heard to say from heaven, 'This is my beloved Son, in whom I am well pleased.' Thus it became Jesus by faith to fulfil all righteousness, not only that of the law on earth, but also that of God in heaven, as he was plunged, submissive, beneath the waters of death in the figure of baptism.

By faith Jesus was led up of the Spirit into the wilderness; by faith he commenced his ministry; and by faith he gave to the people on earth the words which he had heard of his Father in heaven. By the ministration of the Spirit he unfolded words that were divine and heavenly, and all the people said, Never man spake like this man. For the doctrine was not his, but the Father's which had sent him. Therefore he spake as one having authority, and not as the scribes. And the common people heard him gladly. The rulers, however, protested, saying, 'Whence hath this man letters, never having learned?' But the Father who had opened his ears in secret now opened his mouth in public, and, like David, he could say, I believed, and therefore I spake. Said Jesus, 'I speak that which I have seen with my Father.' 'The words which I speak unto you, they are spirit; they are life. I speak not of myself; but the Father, that dwelleth in me, he doeth the work.'

By faith he cursed the fig tree, 'Have faith in God', said he. By faith he said to the mountain, 'Be thou removed, and be thou cast into the sea.' And thus it came to pass, for, 'Thou wilt cast all their sins into the depths of the sea', Mic. 7:19. Jesus could say, Thy faith hath saved thee, and, Thy faith hath made thee whole, and again, I have not found so great faith, no, not in Israel: because faith was that for which he looked. Faith marked out the Son, and faith marked out those children taught of the Father, 'Every man that hath heard, and hath learned of the Father, cometh unto me.' By faith they came, for, He that believeth on the Son hath everlasting life, and, He that believeth on him, out of his belly shall flow rivers of living water: this spake he of the Spirit. And it is evident that the adoption should receive of that same Spirit, for it is written, 'We having the same spirit of faith', II Cor. 4:13.

By faith he wrought miracles. 'He therefore that ministereth to you the Spirit, and worketh miracles among you, doeth he it by the works of the law, or by the hearing of faith?' By faith he set his face as a flint to go to Jerusalem; by faith he made clay of spittle; by faith he put his fingers into the ears of the deaf. By faith he cleansed the lepers, healed the sick, and cast out demons. By faith he made the dumb to speak, the deaf to hear, and the lame to walk. By faith he made the blind to see, and the dead to live. By faith he lived, by faith he died. By faith he pleased God: 'This is my beloved Son, in whom I am well pleased.' But without faith it is impossible to please him. But Jesus pleased him, for he was the Son of his love, the Just One who should live by his faith.

The obedience of faith distinguished Jesus' life, and it was magnified in his death. This is called the hearing of faith. This was the obedience of Jesus Christ, 'the obedience of one', Rom. 5:19. Here the word 'obedience' is a compound, ὑπακοή, *hupakoē*, made up of two Greek words. The main word is ἀκούω, To hear, hearken, listen. It is the word from which we get 'acoustics'. To this has been added the prefix ὑπό, 'under', giving the compound meaning, To hear under, to hearken submissively. And that was how Jesus obeyed. By the hearing of faith. Virtually the same word is used in Phil. 2:8, 'He humbled himself, and became obedient'— ὑπήκοος, *hupēkoos*, a variant of the same word—'unto death, even the death of the cross.'

How can anyone possibly confound that 'obedience', unto death, called 'hearkening submissively', with the doing of the works of the law? Such things are set in contrast: 'Received ye the Spirit by the works of the law, or'—mark that, or—'the hearing of faith?' Gal. 3:2. Again, 'He therefore that minis-tereth to you the Spirit, and worketh miracles among you, doeth he it by the works of the law, or'—it is either the one or the other, observe—'or by the hearing of faith?' Gal. 3:5. Jesus 'hearkened submissively'. Even unto death. Even the death of the cross. What law required such a death, the just for the unjust? It is grace, not law. Faith, not works. Hearing, not doing. It is an obedience in total contrast with that of the law. It is the obedience of faith.

If by definition Jesus' obedience, the obedience of faith, was that of 'hearkening submissively', then to what did he listen? To the word of God. For faith comes by hearing, and hearing by the word of God. 'Mine ears hast thou bored', he could say, as he listened always to the word of God. The Jews went about to kill him, but he was 'A man that hath told you the truth, which I have heard of God', Jn. 8:40. God spoke; he listened. What did the Jews know of this? Nothing. They knew of reading the dead letter, hearing the scriptures recited, and seeing the books, but nothing else. 'Ye have neither heard his voice at any time, nor seen his shape', Jn. 5:37. But Jesus had heard his voice, he heard it constantly, and had seen his shape.

Their presumption stood in the dead outward letter, his faith stood in the words of the living God: 'He that is of God heareth God's words: ye therefore hear them not, because ye are not of God', Jn. 8:47. But he was of God, he heard God's words, and listening, submitted. This is the very opposite to the works of the law, it is the hearing of faith. It is called, The faith of Jesus. He could say 'He that sent me is true; and I speak to the world those things which I have heard of him', Jn. 8:26. He walked by faith, they walked by works. He heard the God of all grace, they read the law of Moses. He was alive to God, they were dead in sins. He heard the Father, they were of their father the devil, who abode not in the truth. 'They understood not that he spake unto them of the Father', Jn. 8:27.

His language was consistently the language of faith. 'Verily, verily, I say unto you, the Son can do nothing of himself, but what he seeth the Father do', Jn. 5:19. But the law required a servant to do everything for himself, irrespective of what the Father did: 'This do, and thou shalt live.' Jesus walked by a totally different rule, his language was, I speak not of myself: but the Father that dwelleth in me, he doeth the works, Jn. 14:10. Again, 'I can of mine own self do nothing: as I hear, I judge: and my judgment is just; because I seek not mine own will, but the will of the Father which hath sent me', Jn. 5:30. And the will of the Father was, that he should give his life for the sheep.

The living Father had sent him: he lived by the Father. But what had that to do with the law, by the keeping of which one might earn life? He lived by the Father. As to the law, far from owning it as his rule, he said, 'It is written in your law', Jn. 8:17; 10:34. And again, Jn. 15:25, 'It is written in their law'. As to his rule, he lived by the Father, Jn. 6:57. For the Father had given to the Son that he should have life in himself. If men had known him, they should have known his Father also. He and his Father were one: he dwelt in the Father, and the Father in him. This was the life by which, in all the perfection of his manhood, he walked. And walked by faith. For the just shall live by faith.

What obedience was it, and to which law, when Jesus kneeled down, and prayed, saying, Father, if thou be willing, remove this cup from me: nevertheless not my will, but thine, be done; and being in an agony, he prayed more earnestly: and his sweat was as it were great drops of blood falling to the ground? Was that threefold agony, and casting himself down on the ground, offering up prayers and supplications with strong crying and tears, in anticipation of bearing sin, and being made sin, was it, I say, obedience to the law of Moses? It was not. The law of Moses required no such thing. But the will of the Father required it. And how should he know that will? By faith. And how should he have faith? By hearing. And how should he hear? By the word of God. That was the obedience of faith, the obedience of faith unto death, even the death of the cross.

This was seen in Abraham four hundred and thirty years before the law was given. 'And Abraham took the wood of the burnt offering, and laid it upon Isaac his son; and he took the fire in his hand, and a knife; and they went both of them together. And Isaac spake unto Abraham his father, and said, My father: and he said, Here am I, my son. And he said, Behold the fire and the wood: but where is the lamb for a burnt offering? And Abraham said, My son, God will provide himself a lamb for a burnt offering: so they went both of them together. And they came to the place which God had told him of; and Abraham built an altar there, and laid the wood in order, and bound Isaac his son, and laid him on the altar upon the wood. And Abraham stretched forth his hand, and took the knife to slay his son. And the angel of the Lord called unto him out of heaven, and said, Abraham, Abraham.' By faith Abraham, when he was tried, offered up Isaac: and he that had received the promises offered up his only begotten son, accounting that God was able to raise him up. And by faith Isaac submitted. By what law? Of works? Nay: but by the law of faith. And so it was with the faith of Jesus Christ.

Likewise Elijah, upon mount Carmel, when the impotence of man and his religion had been exposed, by faith set the

169

matter as far outside the realm of normality, and the help of natural law, as was possible. With the twelve stones he built an altar in the name of the LORD: and he made a trench about the altar, even a great trench. Why? To fill it with water. What for? Because God was to answer faith by fire, and the arm of the flesh, the assistance of man, as well as the aid of nature were all excluded by pouring water, barrel after barrel, over the burnt sacrifice, and over the wood.

How will that burn? How indeed. For Elijah said, 'Do it the second time. And they did it the second time. And he said, Do it the third time. And they did it the third time.' And the sacrifice was awash, and the wood sodden, and the trench brimming over with water. But Elijah prayed, by faith he prayed, and the fire of the LORD fell, and consumed the burnt sacrifice, and the wood, and the stones, and the dust, and licked up the water that was in the trench. So it was with the sacrifice of the Lord Jesus. Against every hope, contrary to all law, with the whole world, religious and secular, against him, he was crucified in weakness. But he believed God. And according to his faith it was done unto him. Our sins were laid upon him. He was made sin. And the fire of the righteousness of God fell from heaven and consumed the sacrifice below. This is called, the faith of Jesus Christ.

Through the offering up of the body of Jesus once and for all, God procured a complete and free righteousness to the account of all that should believe from the beginning of the world to the end of it. In the figure of the sacrifice upon mount Carmel, the law, epitomised by Elijah, slew the sacrifice on earth. But it was the fire of the wrath of God falling from heaven above that consumed the pieces, that made the sacrifice complete, and that consummated the offering. The one was the righteousness of the law on earth; the other the righteousness of God from heaven. The body of Jesus, made sin and bearing sins by the divine and supernatural work of God, hanging between heaven and earth, therefore became that substitutionary sacrifice, that vicarious atonement, in which all righteousness was fulfilled. And so the saying of Jesus came to pass, 'Thus it becometh us'—us: John and Jesus, law and grace, God and man, the legal and the divine—'to fulfil all righteousness.' For as the law in a figure submerged him beneath the waters of death, so the heavens opened, and the righteousness of God from heaven was manifested by the faith of Jesus Christ.

How perfect was the sacrifice offered up on the cross at Golgotha: as of a lamb without blemish and without spot. How suited to bear away iniquity was that sinless humanity: a humanity indissolubly united with deity in one divine Person. Jesus the Righteous One, the spotless Lamb, the sinless Surety: without fault, throughout his impeccable life, in the eyes of the law. And in his believing manhood, in the sight of God, of a morality and perfection transcending all that the law could demand or envisage of human nature.

He was led as a lamb to the slaughter, and as a sheep before her shearers is dumb, so he opened not his mouth. At Golgotha he stood on the brink of the abyss opened by the fall, possessed of a humanity baffling to the legal rule, a quality of manhood beyond its scope or comprehension. He stood, I say, at the brink of the abyss of the fall, truly man, really possessed of the divine nature, equal to divine righteousness, able to meet the incalculable distance between heaven and earth, God and man, stretching away over the gulf into the uttermost reaches of infinity. Behold the Lamb of God, which taketh away the sin of the world!

Imperfectly set forth by the richness of the fat and of the blood in the sacrifices under the Old Covenant, the worth of the offering up of the body of Jesus, and of the shedding of his blood, could know no measure. His death would meet the curse of the law, his blood would cover the sins of his people, his sacrifice would take away the sin of the world, his oblation

171

would answer God in his righteousness, and his condemnation would quench the avenging wrath of everlasting fire. Behold the Lamb of God!

Immoveable, transfixed upon the tree, yet there by faith he would travel untold spiritual distances, past all imagination, beyond the mind to conceive. Not only would he go in the strength of the meat of his faith through all that waste howling wilderness to Horeb, ascending all the weary steps to mount Sinai, to bear the curse of the law, but he would climb the infinite steeps of heaven, the immeasurable distance to the glory, to tread out the fierceness of the wrath and indignation of Almighty God. Men below, and God above, should look upon him whom they had pierced, as, by faith, all his garments stained with blood, the obedient Sufferer should finish the work which the Father had given him to do.

It was all faith. Jesus believed that he would be made the Substitute of his people before the law of God, on the accursed tree. Jesus, the Righteous, who owed nothing to the law, believed that God would execute upon his Person the sentence of offended justice against all those in whose place he stood as Surety. He knew that in submitting to the cross he must suffer the penalty of the broken law for countless multitudes. Though he hung inert, he knew in spirit that he should step out over the abyss, being made an offering upon the brazen lattice of the altar of God, to bear sin in his own body on the tree. And it was so.

He gave his back to the smiters, his cheeks to them that plucked out the hair; he was stricken, smitten of God, and afflicted; for the rod, the legal rod, was not spared. He was bruised beyond measure for the chastisement of our peace; the penalties of the law were laid to the charge of the Accursed on the tree. Of old the legal curse was put upon mount Ebal, Deut. 11:29. Six tribes climbed to the top of Ebal, the bare mountain, and the Levites spake to the men of Israel with a loud voice the curses of the book of the law. The tens of thousands of Israel, standing high upon the barren rock, roared out in response to the Levitical curse: 'Amen'. Twelve times over the mighty shout sounded, echoing and re-echoing from mountain to mountain, ringing again and again across the valley floor. Yet for all the dreadful cursing, an altar was raised on this mountain of barrenness and death: twelve great stones were plastered, the law clearly written in Hebrew letters upon the paleness of the plaster. Yes, but blood ran over the dark characters on the whitened stones, and the sacrifice was laid upon that altar in his pieces, and burned with fire.

By faith Jesus was laid upon the altar of God, the commandments written upon tables of stone, testifying against the Surety, as the fire was kindled below, and the curse sounded above. Vengeance rose up from beneath, and out of the throne proceeded lightnings, and thunders, and voices. The curse sounded loud and long from heaven, and again and again the great 'Amen' sounded and echoed over the lonely Sufferer who absorbed every curse, every sanction, every recompense of reward, until none remained. Christ in his death met all the legal penalties for his people, at once discharging the transgressors from all debt for ever, and the Judge from all vengeance world without end. He blotted out the handwriting of ordinances that was against us, which was contrary to us, and took it out of the way, nailing it to his cross. The ashes of cancelled transgressions fell away as dust through the grating of the altar of judgment, drifting pale into the great void to be remembered no more for ever.

By the obedience of faith, in the one great act of obedience, Jesus justified the Judge in discharging the lawless. He magnified the law and made it honourable. He delivered the transgressors under the first testament. Truly he fulfilled the righteousness of the law. Therefore God could say, 'As for thee also, by the blood of thy covenant I have sent forth thy prisoners out of the pit wherein is no water', Zech. 9:11. O, but it was not to bring us to law that he suffered by faith; neither to bring us to an unrent veil, an unrevealed Jehovah; nor to an earthly tabernacle with carnal service, and a prospect of death: but to bring us to God, as sons to the Father, with an inheritance of everlasting glory in the kingdom, world without end. Then, he must meet divine righteousness: he must fulfil all righteousness: he must fulfil the righteousness of God.

And Jesus lifted up his eyes to heaven, and said, Father, the hour is come; glorify thy Son, that thy Son also may glorify thee. Father, glorify thy name. Then came there a voice from heaven, saying, I have both glorified it, and will glorify it again, Jn. 12:28. For this cause Jesus came unto this hour, that he might glorify God, and render satisfaction to divine righteousness on behalf of all those for whom he died.

If so, he must, in his own Person, bring man back to the place from which Adam fell. He must, through the eternal Spirit, offer himself without spot to God, a sacrifice suited to make atonement for the great transgression of the fall of man. He must, by that offering, bridge the immeasurable gulf between God and man. He must, having bridged that vast abyss by the acceptance of his oblation, himself bear its worth into the presence of God. He must, on behalf of all those for whom he died, carry manhood up each massive steep of holiness, up to the heavenly heights of glory, into the light unapproachable, to enter that radiance which no man hath seen, nor can see. He must take that manhood up into infinity, up into eternity, up into deity, there to present humanity, a new humanity, before the glorious presence of the everlasting God.

Under the Old Covenant the sacrifice was made at the brazen altar, in the courts of Israel. The blood was shed at the foot of the altar. There the people were accepted. But what of the distance to the laver? To the holy place? What of the distance to the unrent veil? To the Holiest of all? And beyond the unrent veil, what shall be said of that distance which defies all imagination, the greatest distance in heaven and earth, time and eternity, the distance between the mysterious veil and the ark of the covenant overlaid round about with gold?

Whatever the figure of the high priest depicted, in garments not his own, but once a year, in the pattern of things in the heavens, no mortal flesh might ever traverse that distance. But now a second Man appears, having a visage marred more than any man, and his form more than the sons of men: a last Adam, of manhood immortal, incorruptible, heavenly. He shall traverse the distance. He shall enter into the very presence of God's glory. And he shall bring with him, in himself, that people for whom he died, and with whom he is united. Because on their behalf he brought in everlasting righteousness, putting it to their account; for both he that sanctifieth and they that are sanctified are all of one. In their place, united with them, through death he met and brought in divine righteousness. He went to prepare a place for them. The distance between where they were, and that place, is the distance between the sin of man and the righteousness of God. It is precisely that immeasurable distance which Jesus closed vicariously for his people, when he hung silent and unmoving upon the cross. Of this his blood is witness.

Jesus Christ, having gone by faith to the cross as the Surety and Substitute of all who believe, on their behalf met the righteousness of God without the law at the place of atonement. The seven vials full of the wrath of God which liveth for ever and ever, were poured out from the highest heaven upon the poor Sufferer hanging between heaven and earth below. All the waves and billows of God's almighty indignation and wrath broke upon the head of him who hung in the place of sin for the sinful people before the righteousness of God.

Here, absolutes are reached. God and man meet together in the place of vengeance. Eternity and time, heaven and earth, join issue in the day of the Lord. Infinity and the finite converge at the place where the ends of the earth bow together, where the ends of all the world are met. The prince of this world is judged: the judgment of this world is come. The frame of nature shakes. The rocks break asunder. The sun turns to darkness at noonday. The earth convulses. The graves are opened. The tomb gives forth the dead. And the veil of the temple is rent in twain from the top to the bottom. Because, through the suffering of death, the righteousness of God has been brought in, by the faith of Jesus Christ, to the account of every last one of his people, world without end, Amen.

X

Righteousness of God unto All and upon All

THE phrase 'Unto all and upon all' them that believe, Romans 3:22, has been contested by those who reject the Received Greek text. But if the facts are examined, and they must be examined, it will be seen that there is no just contest. There is an attack, because the words 'Unto all and upon all' respect the righteousness of God by faith of Jesus Christ, and are at the heart of justification by faith. Then, the enemies of justification, under whatever pretext, textual or otherwise, must surely oppose them. And they have opposed them. But there is no justice in this opposition.

These words came down from the Father in heaven to the holiest of men on earth. They have been cherished from ages and generations by the innumerable company of the faithful. They are inestimable in worth, words which the Holy Ghost gave. Invaluable, divine, the gift of God. 'I have given unto them', said Jesus to the Father, referring to the apostles, 'the words which thou gavest me; and they have received them.' But Westcott and Hort, their Greek text, and the new Versions, have not received them, they have cast them out.

Why have they cast them out? Because these are words essential to elucidate the truth of justification, without which that truth cannot be properly understood. Rightly appreciated, these are among the most priceless words of the gospel. They are at the heart of justification. If any man comprehends the spiritual meaning here, then he has grasped the meaning of justification by faith everywhere.

To those who were so bitterly opposed to justification, because it stood in the way of the slow and painstaking realisation of their long cherished dream of universal reunification with Rome, such a phrase must be contested. It was contested. The textual question ought to be seen in this context. It served a purpose. That purpose was to put out the light of the Reformation, namely, justification by faith, in order to remove the greatest single barrier to the dismantling of Protestantism. No better occasion presented itself than the Revision of 1881. Here was the opportunity not to oppose the truths of the Bible but to alter them. And to do so in such a way that the general public would think that they had a more accurate version in the issue.

It is essential to keep in mind the fact that when the Apostle Paul uses the words 'Unto all and upon all them that believe', he is referring to the righteousness of God by faith of Jesus Christ. It is the righteousness of God that is unto all them that believe. And it is the same righteousness that is upon all them that believe. Whatever may be the meaning of the phrase 'unto all and upon all', it is the righteousness of God by faith of Jesus Christ that is unto all and upon all. And whatever may be the meaning of the expression 'by faith of Jesus Christ', it is the righteousness of God that is by faith of Jesus Christ. It follows therefore that nothing is more fundamental to the understanding of the apostle in this place than a clear and distinct knowledge of what is intended by the words 'the righteousness of God'.

The faith of Jesus Christ referred to in Romans 3:22 is not that seen generally throughout his unique and peerless lifetime; neither is it that faith which, because of his perfect suitability, anticipated his becoming the Sin-bearer of his people in death. It is his faith specifically during the hours of vicarious atonement. It is his faith whilst actually bearing the sin of his people upon the cross. It is his faith as Substitute at Golgotha, from the time that he began to bear sin and wrath

178

until the moment that there was no more sin and wrath to bear. That is the faith of Jesus Christ to which Paul refers. That is the faith which manifested the righteousness of God. 'But now the righteousness of God without the law is manifested: even the righteousness of God by faith of Jesus Christ.'

The faith of Jesus Christ here is specific. Just as the righteousness of God here is specific. It is his faith as the substitutionary Sin-bearer, during the whole period of the atonement, whilst he was exposed to the righteousness of God in the position that he had taken for his people. That faith took away sin and wrath during that period. And during that period the same faith brought in righteousness of God.

When his blood was shed in death, God's righteousness could find absolutely nothing in him against those in whose place he had died. Then, divine righteousness was fully satisfied, completely at rest, in respect of their persons. That is, righteousness of God was now to their account because of him who died for them, and as them. In death, their death in him, and his death for them, God's righteousness could find nothing at issue between himself and them. They answered to his righteousness, and his righteousness answered to them, in their Substitute. The witness of this was in the blood. 'Being now justified by his blood', Rom. 5:9.

The distance between God and the sinful people was what was measured in the Sin-bearer on the tree. The measure was the righteousness of God. The intensity of the meeting of sin and of divine righteousness, as the distance contracted and was absorbed in the Person of the Substitute, was fathomed in the hours upon the cross until he cried, 'It is finished'. It was not only the distance between the sinner and the law that was measured by the righteousness of God, though that distance was measured. The righteous Judge according to the law measured the distance of the sinner from that law, bringing in condemnation and executing judgment so as fully to satisfy the legal rule. This answered to the distance between the people and the brazen altar.

Immeasurably beyond the law, however, lay the righteousness of God's own nature, of his intrinsic Being, of the character proper to the divine Person. Then it was not by some external measure, but from within himself, that there came forth the righteousness which was meted out and executed upon the Saviour of sinners. Here was a distance infinitely beyond the finite space between the transgressor and the law. It was a distance that was incalculable, a distance inconceivable, beyond time, unfathomable, outside of creation, pertaining to eternity, within the deity. Here was the unbounded distance between God's ineffable Being and character, and corruptible man. This infinitude between Almighty God in his own dwelling and sinful man in a fallen world finds its answer in the measure between the brazen altar and the Holiest of all beyond the veil. It was this entire distance that was compassed in and by the substitutionary offering of the Son of man upon the tree.

It follows therefore that righteousness of God has been brought in for all those for whom Christ died as Substitute; and that this righteousness was effected by the faith of Jesus Christ specifically during the hours of substitution. It also follows that this is a righteousness which, having been wrought by God through Jesus Christ during the time on the cross, must be external both to himself and to the sinner as an objective verity thereafter. It is as distinctive as it is historical. Righteousness of God, not abstractly, but in relation to particular sinners, was brought in at that time. This was an accomplished fact that took place neither before nor after the event of the crucifixion.

When the faith of Jesus Christ looked up to God in the hour that he was lifted up upon the tree, what he believed was that he should bear the curse, meet the condemnation of the law, be made sin, bear sins, endure wrath, and suffer the righteousness of God in judgment against an innumerable company of ungodly and condemned sinners, until, in the absolute judgment of that righteousness, absolutely nothing remained to be judged. Righteousness of God was divinely satisfied, and everlastingly at rest in respect of that entire company in the one great Substitute. That is the righteousness which was wrought at the cross.

It is not as if that was the righteousness in terms of the negative condemnation of sin but that there remained some further positive expression of righteousness, say, in the resurrection, afterwards to be put to the account of forgiven sinners. All the righteousness was in the death of Christ. That was the righteousness that was to be accounted to all them that believe. 'Being justified by his blood', Rom. 5:9.

It is therefore a fallacy to suppose a negative, condemnatory righteousness at the cross, and a positive, justifying righteousness in the resurrection. This is an erroneous view perhaps owing its origin to the Active—or positive—and Passive—or negative—legal obedience theory, as if the idea of positive and negative righteousness were, *per se*, a verity. Another influence to the same effect was the view of justification held by J.N. Darby, who, whilst being alert to the folly of the legal system of Active and Passive obedience, fell into the trap of a 'negative' righteousness at the cross, and a 'positive' righteousness in the glory, meanwhile negating the idea of 'imputation' in the accepted sense altogether. This is to be examined in its place; what is now being observed is the contribution of such a view to the idea that there must be a positive as distinct from a negative expression of justifying righteousness.

Many have been confused because of this. They acknowledge what is patent, namely, that in the death of Christ the righteous judgment of God was manifested in condemnation against all coming short of the righteousness of the law on the part of the sinner, and, more, against all shortcoming between fallen man and the righteousness of God in himself. They own also that righteousness of God according to his own nature measured the distance between God and sinful men, and judged that distance in the Substitute. Yet their preconceptions oblige them to look for what they think of as a 'positive vindication' of righteousness, because they regard what took place on the cross as no more than a 'negative condemnation'.

Like Mr. Darby, they are clear as to their views on the cross, and equally definite in their teaching concerning Christ's glorifying God, and he, himself, being glorified in consequence. But they are left with the problem of explaining just what is the righteousness that is to be accounted to the believer. Having developed a system which owns that God has judged sin righteously at the cross, yet finding that there is such a thing as righteousness imputed, they are obliged to look for a 'positive' righteousness in the resurrection. In consequence of this they have great difficulty in distinguishing the justifying righteousness of God—whence it came, what it is, how it is effected, and how it is to be imputed—because they cannot identify a 'positive' vindicating righteousness, as opposed to that negative condemnatory judgment which they freely confess to be a truth from many places in scripture.

Their difficulty lies in the fact that what is tantamount to a further, or second, manifestation of the righteousness of God is not to be found in the gospel. The idea is wrong. The very idea of two manifestations of divine righteousness, one in condemnation, the other in justification, one negative, the other positive, indicates a fundamentally false notion, and for the same reason as that which has been exposed in the Active and Passive obedience theory: it would require the identical work to be done twice over. Save that in the Active and Passive system the first, 'active', justification would precede the second, 'passive', condemnation; whereas in the view of Mr. Darby, and other teachers, 'negative' condemnation precedes 'positive' justification.

The first of these theories postulates a legal righteousness before the cross, and a removal of unrighteousness (*sic*) at the cross. The second predicates a condemnatory righteousness at the cross and a justifying righteousness in the glory. But the truth is otherwise, and places justification, and justifying righteousness, entirely in the death of Christ as a substitutionary sacrifice on behalf of sinners.

The righteousness of God in condemning evil was met by the blood of Jesus, and fully met by that blood. If one enquires, But where is the righteousness of God which is positively accounted to sinners? I answer, The assumptions behind such a question are wrong: it is erroneous to admit of judgment according to righteousness in the blood of Jesus, and yet look elsewhere for a positive justifying righteousness as if that were some future work. We are 'justified by his blood', Rom. 5:9. Then, at the cross, judgment according to righteousness, and righteousness to be accounted, are one and the same thing.

At the cross God's judgment of sin, according to the measure of divine righteousness, removed all distance. Nothing was left between God and the sinner. God in righteousness met the sinner, in the blood of Jesus, according to divine righteousness. If the blood of Jesus is to the account of the sinner, it is the same thing as having the cause of its being shed, the righteousness of God, to that sinner's account. The precious blood, as of a lamb without blemish and without spot, removed all the distance between the sinner and the righteousness of God. Then, God and the sinner have met together in righteousness. This is the righteousness that is 'through faith in his blood'. If so, it must follow that righteousness has been accounted to all those for whom that blood has been shed.

183

David describes the blessedness of the man unto whom God imputeth righteousness without works, Romans 4:6-8. Does he describe a 'negative' and 'positive' righteousness? He does not. Much less does he describe the grievous aberration of a 'positive' legal righteousness supposed to have been wrought on the lawless basis of works of supererogation without either the shedding of blood or the forgiveness of sins. Then how does he describe the blessing of righteousness imputed: wherein does it consist? In the forgiveness of iniquities. In the covering of sins. In the Lord not imputing sin. Who hath these things, hath righteousness imputed. And who hath righteousness imputed, hath the blessing. But the forgiveness of iniquities, the covering of sins, the not imputing of sin to the guilty, all these things stand in and depend upon the blood of Jesus Christ. Then so does the righteousness of God.

The righteousness of God judged the sinner in the Substitute, and found satisfaction in the blood. Therefore the blood of atonement quenched all wrath, acquitted from all judgment, cleared from all condemnation, and removed all offence. The blood of Christ is the answer to the distance between the wrath of God and the sin of man. In that blood the distance was fully met and removed, so that God and the sinner could meet in justice, with all guilt absolved and all righteousness fulfilled. Thus the place of the shedding of blood, and of the blood that was shed, become the ground on which God in all the perfection of his righteousness can be met by the sinner in all the iniquity of his sin. He believes and is not consumed. Why not? Because the righteousness of God does not come to him in judgment, as it did to the Substitute whose blood was shed; it comes in justification, as it must to the sinner for whom that blood was shed.

Then the same righteousness which went forth in condemnation against the sinner—identified with his Substitute—and which caused the shedding of the blood, is that righteousness which has been put to the sinner's account. Why? Because it was for that sinner that the blood was shed. Just as the right-eousness of God was fully satisfied in the blood that was shed, so of necessity the one for whom that blood was shed must have had that righteousness fully satisfied on his behalf. Then, since God's righteous judgment against both sin and the sinner, according to his own nature, have been perfectly satisfied, once and for all, in the Substitute, there can be nothing remaining in that sinner to which God in righteous judgment can ever be incensed again. All that he is, all that he has done, has already been fully exposed to and judged by the righteousness of God, and that righteousness has already been perfectly satisfied in the blood shed on his behalf.

Therefore righteousness of God fully requited, wholly at peace, in relation to the blood shed for the sinner, must answer to—or be 'unto'—that sinner. This is the sinner that shall certainly be brought to faith in his blood. Righteousness of God shall be 'upon' him. That righteousness of God is called, Righteousness imputed. And the sinner is called, The blessed man unto whom God imputeth righteousness without works. He has been justified by faith. His faith is in that blood which satisfied the righteousness of God on his behalf. This is the righteousness of God brought in by the faith of Jesus Christ at the cross. It is that of which Paul the Apostle speaks, saying, 'But now the righteousness of God without the law is manifested: even the righteousness of God which is by faith of Jesus Christ', Romans 3:21,22. It is this righteousness that is unto all and upon all them that believe.

The English 'Unto all and upon all them that believe', Romans 3:22, goes back to Tyndale, who wrote in 1525, 'Unto all and upon all that beleve'. This was followed by the Great Bible of 1539, which rendered the Greek, 'Unto all and upon all them that beleve (*on hym*).' Next came the Geneva Bible, 1560, 'Unto all, and upon all that beleve.' After this there was the Bishops' Bible of 1568, which gave, 'Unto all, and upon all them that beleeve.' The Roman Catholic Rheims publica-tion of 1582 translated as follows: 'Unto al and upon al that beleeve in him.' Finally the King James, or Authorised, Version, 1611, provided the rendering, 'Unto all and upon all them that believe.'

Thus the Greek Original of Romans 3:22 was translated into the English tongue, virtually without change, from 1525 through six versions, faithfully conveying the words of the Holy Ghost through the pen of the holy apostle by the providence of God throughout the centuries. No exponent or preacher of scripture could omit these vital words without immediately being challenged as a deceiver or a heretic, having neither care for the souls of men, nor regard for the gospel. And so it stood for ages and generations. Until 1881.

The Revised Version of 1881 made the following breach in the integrity of holy scripture: 'Unto all them that believe', with the footnote, 'Some ancient authorities add *and upon all.*' So the words 'and upon all' were rent out of the gospel by the Revisers. With sickening inevitability the Revised Standard Version, 1946, widened the breach as follows: 'For all who believe.' No footnote. In the New English Bible, 1961, it was no longer a question of a breach; the whole fabric of the Original was carried away, leaving the subsequent English fiction as a kind of law unto itself.

The authors of this novel work, the publishers, the distributors, and many others, including booksellers, may justify their capitalization of the dismissal of the *Textus Receptus*, as of the relegation of the Authorised Version, initiated by the Revisers of 1881, but their own responsibility remains both dire and heavy. The New English Bible, 1961, claims that the following is a translation: 'God's justice has been brought to light ... It is God's way of righting wrong, effective through faith in Christ for all who have such faith—all, without distinction.' No text exists for this evil mangling of the gospel.

Based upon the daring but measured onslaught commenced in and maintained since 1881, the reading of the New English Bible of 1961 represents the culmination of the contemptuous overthrow of justification by faith. This was achieved neither by argument nor by treatise, but by deceitfully altering the Bible itself, adding insult to injury with the pretence that this calculated gloss provided modern man with a more accurate and contemporary sounding scripture. After such a debacle, the remaining barriers gave way, and the succeeding volumes were subject to little more restraint than that dictated by the outlook of the sales charts.

It is perfectly clear that all this—and by 'all this' I mean the obliteration from the English Bible of words and phrases vital to justification—began in 1881 with the Revision. This was what caused the breach which led to the collapse eighty years later. Whether it was the changing of the word 'of' to 'in', with the phrase 'the faith of Jesus Christ'—or its equivalent—some five times, or whether it was the removal of the words 'and upon all', lacerating part and casting doubt on the remainder of the expression 'righteousness of God by faith of Jesus Christ unto all and upon all them that believe', the Revision of 1881 was the occasion of an attack the objective of which has been maintained to this day.

For it was an attack. Ostensibly, upon the *Textus Receptus*—Hort's 'that vile *Textus Receptus*'—together with the Authorised Version of ancient standing; but actually upon justification by faith, the bulwark which prevented the drift back to reunion with Rome. For so long as the Article of Justification stood, in the general consciousness of the English speaking people, salvation by grace through faith remained alone in the Protestant religion, and fear and foreign darkness ruled in the Roman Catholic Church. Over the centuries direct attacks upon the doctrine had the opposite effect to that desired. But in 1881 the strategy of undermining the faith of the people in their own Bible began, the first tactic of which was the Revision to which the unsuspecting populace looked forward with such eagerness. After this it was only a matter of time. With the joint publication by Anglicans and Papists of a tract—'Salvation and the Church', 1987*—that time would seem very nearly to have been fulfilled in our own day.

The Greek of the *Textus Receptus*—εἰς πάντας καὶ ἐπὶ πάντας, *eis pantas kai epi pantas*—has been correctly rendered in the Authorised Version, word for word, 'Unto all and upon all'. Westcott and Hort, together with the Revisers, did not challenge the translation of the English on this occasion. This time they challenged the Greek. The Westcott and Hort Greek text reads here, εἰς πάντας, *eis pantas*, omitting the last three words of the Greek in the *Textus Receptus*. There is a footnote in the Revised Version, though not in Westcott and Hort's text, indicating that 'Some ancient authorities add *and upon all*'. This note is a cover-up in case of a challenge to show authority for the omission of the three words from the text. But once they had got away with it, they dropped the footnote.

The questions that should be asked are as follows: On what authority did Westcott and Hort leave out these three words from their own Greek text? Who included the footnote in the English Revised Version when it was not in the new Greek text of Westcott and Hort which the Revisers, contrary to their directions, had elected to follow? What is the relative worth of the footnote over against the text? These are the queries to which our attention is now directed.

On what authority did Westcott and Hort leave out the three Greek words, *kai epi pantas*, 'and upon all'? They left out these words on the ground that they were omitted from the oldest manuscripts—Sinaiticus and Vaticanus in particular—

*See 'The Elect undeceived', John Metcalfe Publishing Trust, 1987.

on which they based their entire textual theory. But what did so respected a Greek scholar as Prebendary Scrivener have to say of their theory? Dr. Scrivener's estimation of the system upon which Drs. Westcott and Hort constructed their 'Revised Greek text of the New Testament' will be quoted shortly. But first let it be noted that the Chairman of the Revising body, Bishop Ellicott, adopted Westcott and Hort's system in its entirety, and made it the substance of his 'Defence of the Revisers'. It is little wonder that the Bishop was on the defensive when the weighty Dr. Scrivener had this to say:

'(1) There is little hope for the stability of (Westcott and Hort's) imposing structure, if its foundations have been laid on the sandy ground of ingenious conjecture. And, since barely the smallest vestige of historical evidence has ever been alleged in support of the views of these accomplished editors, their teaching must either be received as intuitively true, or dismissed from our consideration as precarious and even visionary.'

'(2) Dr. Hort's system is entirely destitute of historical foundation.'

'(3) We are compelled to repeat as emphatically as ever our strong conviction that the Hypothesis (of Hort with Westcott) to which he has devoted so many laborious years, is destitute not only of historical foundation, but of all probability...'

'(4) (We cannot) on our part, doubt, that the System (of Westcott and Hort) which entails such consequences is hopelessly self-condemned.'

Burgon, a Greek scholar of massive achievement, says the same in principle. 'The New Greek text (of Westcott and Hort) was a wholly untrustworthy performance, was full of the gravest errors from beginning to end, had been constructed throughout on an entirely mistaken theory.' A theory that

189

was 'nothing but a series of unsupported assumptions.' 'A weak effort of the imagination.' In the Preface to 'Revision Revised', addressed to Lord Cranbrook, Burgon states, 'My one object has been to defeat the mischievous attempt which was made in 1881 to thrust upon this Church and Realm a Revision of the Sacred Text which—recommended though it be by eminent names—I am thoroughly convinced, and am able to prove, is untrustworthy from beginning to end. The reason is plain. It has been constructed upon an utterly erroneous hypothesis.'

'It is, however, the systematic depravation of the underlying Greek which does so grievously offend me: for this is nothing but a poisoning of the River of life at its sacred source. Our Revisers (with the best and purest intentions no doubt) stand convicted of having deliberately rejected the words of inspiration in every page, and of having substituted for them fabricated Readings which the Church has long since refused to acknowledge, or else has rejected with abhorrence; and which only survive at this time in a little handful of documents of the most depraved type.'

The Westcott and Hort theory was based upon the assumption that the two oldest manuscripts, Vaticanus and Sinaiticus —although not dated, probably belonging to the fourth century—were those by which all questions of doubtful or disputed readings were to be settled. Dr. Scrivener, 'probably the most able textual scholar of the 19th century', contemporary with Westcott and Hort, had this to say: 'It is no less true to fact than paradoxical in sound, that the worst corruptions to which the New Testament has ever been subjected originated within a hundred years after it was composed; and that Irenaeus and the African Fathers, and the whole Western, with a portion of the Syrian Church, used manuscripts far inferior to those employed by Stunica, Erasmus, or Stephens thirteen centuries later, when moulding the *Textus Receptus*.'

In other words, the basis of the Greek text of Westcott and Hort, that used by the Revisers, was the corrupt, few, 'oldest manuscripts'. Whereas the great mass of manuscripts and vast body of testimony that supports the *Textus Receptus*, received by the godliest ages, and the godliest men, in the history of the church, used of God in incalculable ways, for inestimable blessing, is overwhelmingly weighty and authoritative. Now, the former was the 'authority' on which Westcott and Hort left out the three Greek words from Romans 3:22, *kai epi pantas*, 'and upon all'. And the latter is the unbroken testimony on the authority of which these words had been accepted as the Greek text long centuries before the existence either of Westcott or Hort, or of this latter-day infatuation with a few manuscripts rejected as depraved and faulty by past ages and generations of the saints.

Next follows the question, Who included the footnote 'Some ancient authorities add, *and upon all*', to the text of the Revised Version of 1881, when the Greek for these words was omitted in the Westcott and Hort text? Let Dean Burgon speak. 'I pointed out that the 'New Greek Text', which, in defiance of their instructions, the Revisionists had been so ill-advised as to spend ten years in elaborating, was a wholly untrustworthy performance, was full of the gravest errors from beginning to end, had been constructed throughout on an entirely mistaken theory. Availing myself of the published confession of one of the Revisionists, I explained the nature of the calamity which had befallen the Revision. I traced the mischief home to its true authors, Drs. Westcott and Hort, a copy of whose unpublished (Greek) New Testament Text (the most vicious in existence) had been confidentially and under pledges of the strictest secrecy, placed in the hands of every member of the revising Body.'

'I called attention to the fact that, unacquainted with the difficult and delicate science of textual criticism, the Revisionists had in an evil hour surrendered themselves to Dr. Hort's guidance, had preferred his counsels to those of Prebendary Scrivener, (an infinitely more trustworthy guide) and that the work before the public (the Revised Version 1881) was the piteous (but inevitable) result.'

From which it transpired that when the Revisers came to Romans 3:22—following, as they did, Westcott and Hort's text—in the absence of the Greek *kai epi pantas*, they were obliged to assist the enemy in his blatant attack on justification by faith by omitting the English words 'and upon all'. But this was more than some of the Revisers could stomach. Hence they weakly stuck out for the margin, or footnote. They agreed to omit the three vital words from the text—after all, it was not in the Greek!—but to save their faces insisted upon the note in the margin. But it was too little, too late.

It was much too late. The breach had been made. And in the next version, the Revised Standard Version, 1946, no such inhibitions frustrated the wreckers of the *Textus Receptus* and of the sound Authorised Version. The footnote was dropped. Yet it should never have been a footnote. The words were part of the verse. But then, the words, *kai epi pantas*, 'and upon all', were part of the Greek. For it was just here, in failing to resist this monstrous evil of deceitfully supplanting the sound, and infinitely more authoritative, Greek of the *Textus Receptus*, that the main body of the Revisers—in defiance of their clear brief—fulfilled in themselves the truth of the words 'The godly man ceaseth; the faithful fail from among the children of men', Psalm 12:1.

From the foregoing it is evident that the faithful need have no fear concerning the correctness of the word for word translation in the Authorised Version, 'Unto all and upon all them that believe', Romans 3:22. They may proceed to the exposition of the phrase with perfect equanimity, having not a shadow of doubt as to its veracity according to the Greek text attested by the Holy Ghost and preserved by the providence of God, that is, the *Textus Receptus*.

To the fearful and unbelieving, the stolen mantle of scholarship assumed by those who have attacked both *Textus Receptus*
and Authorised Version appears daunting. And yet neither
the usurpers nor their fabrications can stand the test of
sound scholarship. How much less will they be able to resist
the sword of the Spirit, and the spirit of faith: for the truth is
that they are no better than infidels who steal the treasures of
the sanctuary. Such as the three words in Romans 3:22.
However, to those born of the Spirit, to the believing, to
those taught of God, every word unites in the integrity of '*εἰς
πάντας καὶ ἐπὶ πάντας* '—*eis pantas kai epi pantas*—combining
together to cry with a loud voice to all that be of little faith,
'Do thyself no harm: we are all here', Acts 16:28.

Recall that the apostle is speaking of the righteousness of
God in the gospel. It is the righteousness of God by faith of
Jesus Christ that is 'Unto all and upon all them that believe'.
The righteousness of God is unto all. The righteousness of
God is upon all. The righteousness of God is both unto all and
upon all. It is not unto all without being upon all; neither is it
upon all without being unto all; nor is it upon all without
first being unto all. That is, given the premise that 'all' refers
to 'all them that believe', not 'all' indiscriminately.

Rightly to divide the word of truth at this point, in this
statement, is of the utmost importance to the understanding
of justification by faith. That is why the enemies of the doctrine sought to sow confusion by mutilating the passage in the
name of Textual Criticism. They grasped—better than others
who claimed to be the friends of justification—how vital was
the integrity of this phrase. Evidently the crucial words are
'unto' and 'upon'. Granted that the righteousness of God is
the common benefit, and that 'all them that believe' are the
common beneficiaries, the question arises, Why both words:
why both 'unto' and 'upon'? The answer is in the context of
time.

'Unto' and 'upon' are divided by time. Whilst the apostle refers to the same righteousness, that of God by faith of Jesus Christ, it is one thing for that righteousness to be 'unto', and another thing for it to be 'upon', all them that believe. The first has application at one time, and the other at another time, the two being divided by a more or less widely spaced interval. From this observation the question naturally follows, When is the righteousness of God by faith of Jesus Christ 'unto', and when is it 'upon' all them that believe, respectively?

Just as previously, Romans 1:17, the expression 'from faith to faith' answered to the faith of Jesus Christ, and the faith of his people, respectively, so now, Romans 3:22, the phrase 'unto all and upon all' answers to the bringing in of the righteousness of God by faith of Jesus Christ, and the accounting of that righteousness to the faith of his people, respectively. The righteousness of God by faith of Jesus Christ which discharged transgressors from the law and its curse, likewise took away all that stood between them and the presence of God. It is a righteousness therefore which, by the broken body and shed blood of Jesus Christ upon the cross, fully satisfied God in his own nature in respect of those for whom Christ died. That death, witnessed by the blood, brought them to God in righteousness, just as it brought God in righteousness to them in the sacrificial atonement.

There is therefore now nothing between that people—identified with and in their Substitute—and the righteousness of God perfected on their behalf in his death. Just as there is nothing between God in righteousness—identifying that people in and with the Substitute—and the people of God perfected in righteousness by the broken body and shed blood of their Sacrifice. They have become the righteousness of God in him. This was effected when he died for them, and as them, since that sacrifice which was consummated in death caused divine righteousness to be wholly at rest in respect of those for whom it was made. This means that when he died, righteousness was theirs through his death. That is, righteousness was unto them because of the shed blood and broken body of the sacrifice that had satisfied the righteousness of God on their behalf to the very uttermost. Then, righteousness of God by faith of Jesus Christ, in death, and witnessed by blood, was unto all the people of God.

At the cross righteousness of God, justifying righteousness, was brought in by Jesus Christ. Not some vague, general, universal and inapplicable righteousness, potential to 'all' but effectual to none. But a specific, intended, particular and applicable righteousness, effectual to 'all them that believe'. In a word, when justifying righteousness was wrought in death, then it was 'unto' them. It was not that they had received it: it was not 'upon' them. But it was wrought on their behalf: it was 'unto' them.

At the cross, by the faith of Jesus Christ, God wrought righteousness to the account of all his people. Then, it was 'unto' them. When in the process of time they were brought to believe the gospel, that righteousness which had been wrought for them, which was unto them, was revealed to their faith in the gospel. They believed God, and it was accounted to them for righteousness. Then, that righteousness was 'upon' them. That is, 'Unto all and upon all them that believe.'

As a result of the work on the cross, justifying righteousness is said to be unto all them that believe. As opposed to any that disbelieve. Thus it cannot be a work general to all but particular to none. Otherwise justifying righteousness could not be called justifying righteousness. If righteousness of God was brought in for all them that believe then justification was already effected on their behalf. Justification must have been accomplished when Christ died and brought in righteousness of God to their account in such a way that it is said to be 'unto' them. Their believing is never said to make particularly effectual a work that is construed as being generally potential.

195

Their believing answered to a work that was already effectual. It was already effectual when Christ died. Then righteousness was unto them. In particular. When they believed, that same righteousness was upon them. Their believing added nothing whatsoever to the righteousness: it was the response of faith to the revelation of what God had wrought for them, and put upon them, in particular.

When Christ died, righteousness was brought in, and justification was effected, for all that believe. That is why Paul calls it ἑνὸς δικαιώματος —*henos dikaiōmatos*—'one accomplished righteousness', Romans 5:18. It was this that was 'unto all' them that believe. The work must have been accomplished. Otherwise it could never have been said to be 'unto' a people. But it is said to be unto a people. Then, it must have been accomplished. As to that people, they are described as 'all them that believe'. Their believing in no way qualified, activated, or made effectual the righteousness. How could it? It was already effectual. It was already 'one accomplished righteousness'. That is what they believed. And since they are the ones for whom it was wrought, and to whom it was imputed, how should anyone else know better?

The fact of an accomplished righteousness wrought through substitutionary atonement is everywhere attested in holy scripture. In the Bible there is no question of a conditional atonement or of a righteousness that must be qualified to become effectual. When the Messiah came, according to the prophet Daniel, he would shortly 'finish the transgression, make an end of sins, make reconciliation for iniquity, and bring in everlasting righteousness', Daniel 9:24. Where his suffering for our transgressions, covering our sins, reconciling us to God in a substitutionary sacrifice, are not only synonymous with bringing in everlasting righteousness—so that all are said to happen at the same time, that is, at the cross—but everything is put in the past tense, so that all these things are seen as already having been accomplished, from the moment that the cross was declared to be a finished work.

The writer to the Hebrews teaches the same thing, declaring, 'By one offering he hath perfected for ever them that are sanctified', Heb. 10:14. Here the perfecting of a people took place in the past without their presence, by the one offering on their behalf. So the writer states in Heb. 9:12, assuring us that when Christ ascended into the heavens—'into the holy place'—he had already done the work that had conclusively redeemed his people by nothing other than the shedding of his blood, without the need of any further qualification, 'having obtained eternal redemption for us'.

Any amount of sophistry drawn from other parts of scripture can be raised in objection to this doctrine, which we are able to explain and answer, more or less with ease. But what no amount of sophists can do at any time, in any wise, is explain or answer the least one of these scriptures which we bring forth to affirm the comfortable doctrine of substitutionary atonement and its corollary, justification by faith. And the reason why none of them can answer us is that these things are not their experience, and neither have they any faith.

Saith the prophet, 'I have blotted out, as a thick cloud, thy transgressions, and, as a cloud, thy sins: return unto me; for I have redeemed thee', Isaiah 44:22. He saith not, I will blot out, but, I have blotted out. Then, it was accomplished, and, if so, together with justifying righteousness, at the cross, as an effectual verity. Nor is this to be qualified, because the prophet does not say, 'return unto me; and I will redeem thee', but he says, 'return unto me; for I have redeemed thee.' The former conditional notion may act on the arm of the flesh, which will take delight that so much depends upon its own ability, but afterwards it shall surely fall away. The latter is the truth, and the truth brings in a heart-broken, soul-melting contrition, overwhelmed with the love of God, 'I have—have, have—redeemed thee', the bowels yearn, the eyes become a fountain of tears, and the soul cries, 'I will return unto thee'. And this is a repentance not to be repented of; but it cannot come without the preaching of this truth: 'I have redeemed thee'.

Again, Rev. 5:9, 'Thou hast redeemed us to God by thy blood', then, if so, by nothing else. So saith the Apostle Paul —also in the past tense, placing the whole work at the cross— 'Christ hath redeemed us from the curse of the law', Gal. 3:13, and, I Cor. 6:20, 'Ye are bought with a price'. The prophet Jeremiah taught the same doctrine, 'In those days, and at that time, saith the LORD, the iniquity of Israel shall be sought for, and there shall be none; and the sins of Judah, and they shall not be found: for I will pardon them whom I reserve', Jer. 50:20. The iniquity and the sins of God's people, whom he had reserved, disappeared for ever in the sacrifice at the cross. After this they could not be found, though sought for. Therefore the people are pardoned. There is no other reason for pardon.

So Peter assures us, 'Christ hath suffered for sins'; What, and not taken them away for ever? Or hath he suffered for sins so ineffectually that they can only be taken away with the subsequent assistance of man? God forbid, for, saith the Apostle Paul, 'Christ died for our sins', I Cor. 15:3, and rose again, demonstrating their removal in death. Once more, Peter declares, 'He bare our sins in his own body on the tree', I Pet. 2:24; and shall they not be borne away? Then how can they ever return to us? Here is an effectual atonement, in which Jesus says, 'This is my blood of the New Testament, shed for many for the remission of sins.' He laid down his life for the sheep; he gave his life a ransom for many; he was wounded for our transgressions; he was bruised for our iniquities; the LORD hath—hath, hath—laid on him the iniquity of us all; yea, God's righteous Servant shall justify many, for he shall bear their iniquities. Then, he shall justify them by the death of the cross, because that was the time, and there was the place, when he bare the iniquities of his people, and bare them away for ever, world without end, Amen.

198

In no other way can justification be a reality, than in the way of the gospel which was once delivered to the saints by the apostles. Justification must be rooted and grounded in substitutionary atonement, which, in turn, must have brought in everlasting righteousness 'unto' the account of every one for whom that atonement was made. That is, seen from heaven, for all those chosen in Christ and given to him by the Father before the foundation of the world. Or, seen upon earth, for every one that believeth, that is, all those brought of God to faith, without distinction. This justifying righteousness, wrought at the cross, Paul calls, 'one accomplished righteousness'.

This is that which was actually effected at Golgotha for every believer, from the beginning of the world to the end of it. This is the righteousness which was accomplished when Christ, united with his people in the place of sin and judgment, as their sacrifice, received in his own body every last measure of the righteous judgment of God according to his own nature against that people. Such a sacrifice having been accomplished, in which every state of the whole people suffered full exposure to all the righteousness of God, that people must therefore be without fault before the throne of God.

The very righteousness which consumed the offering now reposes in the consummated sacrifice. That which had judged the offerers in the Substitute now absolves them in the atonement. In him who had taken away the righteousness of God against them, they had become the righteousness of God justified and accepted, the transition being measured by the hours upon the cross during which the Saviour bore the wrath and indignation of the Almighty.

Having absorbed all God's righteousness in judgment on their behalf, in death all God's righteousness rested upon him in peace and equanimity on their behalf. Even as the blood flowed, so the righteousness of God without a veil, without a shadow, without a hindrance was unto all that should ever

199

believe, who were all seen in him who had died in their place, already clothed with everlasting and divine righteousness. This is called, Being justified by grace. There remained however, the imputing of this same righteousness, pertaining, as it does, to the experience of the believer. This, in turn, is named, Being justified by faith. The one is unto, the other upon, all them that believe.

Confusion arises when the proud imagination of man dismisses the kernel of the doctrine—being enraged at the very idea of God bringing in his own election—whilst retaining the shell in order to garnish human sovereignty and free will with the husk of justification. This cannot be done, and must result in darkness and perplexity. It is God that justifieth, Rom. 8:33, not man. All man can do is to confuse the issue. But every poor heart-broken sinner, every sincere penitent, all those of a contrite spirit, are more than happy to lay aside the weapons of their rebellion and repose with thankfulness upon the mercy of God alone, believing upon the Lord Jesus Christ.

Here appears the folly of those who rob God of his justifying truth by saying, Justification is a general work for all the world. This is false, and contrary to the apostolic doctrine: justification is the work of God for every one that believeth, there being no difference between any believers, for all of them have sinned and come short of the glory of God, whether Jew or Gentile. Together with the modern evangelist, the Arminian theorist imagines, God has a justification for all the world, provided every one accepts it. If so, God actually justified none. For, to them, he potentially justifies all.

Then his work can only be completed if the good will of man concludes it by particularly accepting what he has generally offered. Equally, that work must remain ineffectual, and his love unrequited, if the ill will of man refuses to fulfil all righteousness by receiving it. All depends upon man. And some men, more religious and better than others, apparently make the divine effort somewhat more worthwhile by their relatively virtuous wills assisting the Almighty to make it all possible. If this is not salvation by works, and the righteous being called rather than sinners, what is?

Hence Christ ought to cry 'It is finished', only when the essential condition of man's acceptance is added to God's general work in order to make it complete. Thus the righteousness of God by faith of Jesus Christ is made defective, because it is not by this alone that men are justified, neither is it through his blood only. No, it is by the will of man ratifying the shedding of his blood; it is by man adding his work of acceptance to the righteousness of God in order to make it effective.

But the Lord Jesus Christ, and his holy apostles, taught us that we were bought with a price, and that he had paid it. That we were redeemed by his blood, and by nothing else. That we had been justified freely by his grace, and that this was already in the past tense when his blood was shed. That we had been justified by blood alone. That was what we believed. And now men come to confuse us with this novel doctrine, to mutilate our Bibles, to take us back to the anti-christian system of the man of sin, who, with his predecessors —we are informed by Anglican as well as papist authorities— has been preaching justification all this time after all. By what means? The Mass?

Who could have conceived of righteousness of God being manifested on a principle of faith? Or, given the departure of Christendom, of Protestantism, of evangelicalism, of denominationalism, of Brethrenism, of independency, and, alas, of the poor, discouraged and apathetic remnant of the spiritual yet alive upon the earth at this present, who could conceive of it now? But it is so, and faith, which comes by hearing, and hearing by the word of God, the principle of faith, I say, and

righteousness of God revealed by it, is of the essence in the
gospel, without which it is no gospel. This is that righteousness
of God which is by faith of Jesus Christ. Christ brought in
justifying righteousness by his death. For he died in faith,
and by faith he brought many sons to glory. Because, by his
death, righteousness was therefore to their account, and,
through his blood, they were already justified.

Christ brought in the righteousness of God in the New
Testament. And, when he had done so, by his death, it was
already 'unto' all them that ever did, or ever should believe.
It was not yet in the awareness of those for whom he had
died. But it was certainly in his awareness who had died for
them. They may not have known of what he did, indeed, the
vast majority of them had either died in faith, or were not yet
born. But God knew what he had done. And, when it was
done, God had already justified every last one of his people.
Righteousness was 'unto' them.

J.N. Darby, whose faintly whispered overtures to election
are soft and vagrant as the zephyr breeze, supposes in this
passage that the righteousness of God is unto all the world.
But the apostle holds that it is unto all them that believe, and
none other. Moreover, Paul teaches that when such persons
are in experience brought to faith then the same righteousness,
which was unto them, shall be upon them. But not to
Mr. Darby. To Mr. Darby, justification is by union with
Christ risen from the dead. This is not correct. Justification is
by faith, not union: and faith in Christ's blood, not in his
resurrection. Justification commences by union for Mr. Darby
where it has already been accomplished by faith for the
Apostle Paul. And Mr. Darby's union is potentially for all.
But the Apostle Paul's faith is the faith of God's elect.

The very idea of a prior righteousness of God 'unto' the
believer through the death of Christ—a 'quantum' righteousness, as he calls it with distaste—is anathema to Mr. Darby.

Righteousness in existence, already wrought out, brought in at the cross, righteousness to be imputed, righteousness 'unto' the believer, he cannot away with. And the reason for this, I believe, is a reluctance to come out clearly in respect of election and its consequences. And the reason for that was a preoccupation with the unity of the body—in which his views, as such, were most enlightened—to the detriment of truths wont to cause offence among the shallow, carnal, and argumentative.

The righteousness of God by faith of Jesus Christ, which is unto all, is also upon all them that believe. That is to say, by the work of God they are brought to the knowledge of what God has done for them in Christ, that they might be justified by faith. This entails those outward providences and inward states which bring men to a knowledge of their bankrupt and lost condition. How clearly this appears in the four gospels. Not the righteous, the rich, the healthy, the religious, the see-ing, the hearing, the speaking, the walking, but the sinners, the poor, the sick, the possessed, the blind, the deaf, the dumb, the paralytic, were those who came to Jesus.

Not the Pharisee, who went up to the temple full of his good works, but the publican, who stood afar off, not so much as lifting his eyes to heaven, but smiting his breast, saying, God be merciful to me a sinner, was justified. Not the elder brother, but the prodigal son, came to himself, and found the riches of his father's grace. Not Simon the Pharisee, but Simon the leper; not the rich, who were sent empty away, but the hungry were filled with good things; not the mighty, who are put down from their seats, but the mean men of low degree are those to be exalted in the gospel.

A woe is pronounced on the rich, the full, the laughing, and upon those persons of whom men speak well. But the blessing rests on the poor, the hungry, the weeping, upon those whom men hate, and separate from their company, and reproach, and whose names they cast out as evil, for the Son of man's sake. Why? Because the blessing of Abraham is upon those that are of Abraham's faith, whereas the curse of the law is on them that trust in their own righteousness. And who are the latter? We are all of the latter, until God makes us to feel our lost estate, know our penury, and discover in ourselves our own inward leprosy, so that we are brought to fall at Jesus' feet, worshipping him, saying, Lord, if thou wilt, Thou canst make me clean.

Before anyone can be brought to faith, so that the righteousness of faith may be upon him, God must open that person's eyes to see his true condition, to feel his lost estate, and to know what he has done in the sight of God. The first part of this work occurs when the alarm sounds in the sinner's soul, by which he is awakened and convicted of sin. He then starts up with a sense of eternity, of his own immortality, of his tremendous accountability, and sets to work with a great zeal for outward reformation. Soon he finds all his righteousnesses are as filthy rags, all his vows are broken promises, and all his intentions are nothing worth. He discovers that his heart is deceitful above all things, and desperately wicked. He was blind to this before he was awakened to seek after God, but now he knows it of a truth.

Soon the day of judgment appears to him as a dreadful and inescapable reality, the wrath of God is revealed from heaven to his inward vision, and the curse of the law sounds sensibly within his soul. Sin revives, as the commandment comes within, and the sinner dies to all hope of salvation. Languishing between unbelief and despair, he now knows that he can do nothing. False comforters crowd in upon him, offering him a multitude of platitudes, consolations, alleviations, and textual deliverances. Eagerly they offer him instant salvation, pointing to their wares both in Bible and church, ministry and sacrament, worship and evangelism, assuring him of 'all he needs to do'. But he is sick at heart, he has discovered the plague of his heart. God's hand is heavy upon him, the anger of the Almighty is gone forth, he feels deeply that he is helpless under the judgment of God, and, as to all these put together, 'Miserable comforters are ye all'.

The broken-hearted sinner is aware that God has awakened him, God has convicted him, God has slain him, and God must quicken him. He knows that he can do nothing, and that man can do nothing for him. God brought him into this condition, and none but God can bring him out of it: God must be his Justifier. He turns from all false comforters, all light healing of the wound, and, sobbing to his own soul, 'Cease ye from man, whose breath is in his nostrils: for wherein is he to be accounted of?' he waits daily upon God alone for his salvation.

When once the sinner is brought to this point, hoping in God's mercy, waiting continually upon him, sooner or later occurs the second part of this divine work. God, who commanded the light to shine out of darkness, shines in the poor man's heart, to give the light of the knowledge of the glory of God in the face of Jesus Christ. His eyes are opened. The Father sends to him a spirit of wisdom and revelation in the knowledge of his Son. It pleases God to reveal his Son in this vessel of mercy. His ears are unstopped. He hears the Lord whisper, 'The world seeth me no more; but ye see me.' It is from this sight that the fountains of the deep are opened, the rocky heart breaks, every barrier and hindrance is instantly removed, and faith springs up with a witness as the word of God, the word of righteousness, the word of faith, sounds sweetly in his ears.

Full of wonder, in the freshness of first love, the eyes of newly-born faith hardly discern the righteousness of God that is unto, or that which is upon, the young believer. Overwhelmed with joy, faith regards the cause, the death of Christ, not the effect, the righteousness of God. New-born, all things new, Christ fills faith's wondering gaze. Christ crucified for me! is all the cry. Faith regards the blood, Romans 3:25. And so confirms David, saying, Blessed is the man whose iniquities are forgiven, whose sins are covered, unto whom the Lord will not impute sin. The love of God, the love of Christ, these fill the heart, and the new-born soul cannot see beyond the crucified Saviour for very joy.

This is the case with every justified sinner. He sees that God has forgiven his sins by the shedding of Christ's blood, that God has righteously judged him in the sacrificial Substitute, and that God can justly forgive him because he has been punished in his Sin-bearer. The sinner is brought by faith into a consciousness of what Christ has done, and done for him. He feels that Christ died for him, that his blood was shed for him, that Christ loves him, and that his iniquities are forgiven, that his sins are covered, and that God will not impute sin unto him. His faith appreciates the cause of his pardon, it is Christ crucified.

With every passing moment, with every impulse of the Spirit, with every bending of the knee, with every turning of the page, with every lifting of the eyes to heaven, the breadth, length, depth, and height of the love of Christ, which passes knowledge, bring fresh openings into the profound, the wonderful work of God in saving him. Yes, and saving his brethren withal. And by a salvation which is in Father, Son and Holy Ghost. Rejoicing with joy unspeakable, and full of glory, he perceives by the blood of Jesus Christ that he is justified, and knows by the witness and teaching of the Spirit that the righteousness of God is upon him, that it is imputed unto him, and that his faith is counted to him for righteousness.

The Apostle Paul cites David in confirmation of this doctrine, Psalm 32:1,2. David, whose faith was conspicuous, declared his awareness of the imputing of God's righteousness by that spirit of prophecy through which he foresaw the death of Christ. In Psalm 32 he speaks of iniquities being forgiven, sins being covered, and of sin not being imputed. Here it is evident that David perceived a sacrificial and substitutionary atonement in which iniquities should be borne, blood would be shed, and a sentence of condemnation passed upon the Substitute, in order to justify God in showing mercy, and in pardoning the iniquities of the transgressors. Paul cites this as David describing 'the blessedness of the man, unto whom God imputeth righteousness without works.'

The provision of an atonement through which righteousness of God would be assured 'unto' the account of all that should believe is one thing. The imputing of that righteousness to the present faith of the believer, so that it is 'upon' him, is another. Of the latter experience, in which the sinner is first brought to a knowledge of himself, and of the wrath of God, and then by way of true humility to saving faith, so that righteousness might be 'upon' him, David now speaks, Psalm 32:3-5. 'When I kept silence, my bones waxed old through my roaring all the day long.'

Here David, resisting the conviction of sin that was upon him, refused to confess his iniquity to God. He 'kept silence'. But when he did so, the piercing reproofs of his own con-science, the accusing voice of the law, the rumblings of the judgment to come, and the inward distress of resisting the Spirit of God, caused such interior turmoil that David calls it 'roaring all the day long'. This continuous disquiet broke down the stout structure—spiritually the bones—by which hitherto he had supported himself against any such divine drawings. Now the support crumbled, the stoutness collapsed, his bones 'waxed old', and he could resist no more. This was no temporary remorse, no religious self-pity, no passing vex-ation. This was the work of God in bringing him to himself; this was the alarm of God sounding within his soul; this was that divinely wrought conviction of sin which could not be resisted. This revealed to David the perversity of his heart, and showed him his reluctance humbly to seek God for pardon, Ps. 32:3.

Next, Ps. 32:4, David feels the sensation within himself of wrath going forth against him. Not for a few days, or intermittently, this was constant. Just as his conviction was 'all the day long', so his sense of wrath was 'day and night'. The hand of the LORD was upon him with intolerable pressure, and the fountain of his life was dried up within him. He was shut up to his interior sensations. Under conviction of sin, inward torment, vexation of spirit, fear of judgment, the sounding of God's trumpet in his soul, the consciousness of the day of wrath ever before him, David had no strength left. His moisture was dried up as the drought of summer. He could hold out no more. Broken in spirit, contrite in heart, his stubborn will yielded. At once his soul melted, and, bowing humbly, with his whole heart he sought the LORD in earnest.

'I acknowledged my sin unto thee, and mine iniquity have I not hid. I said, I will confess my transgressions unto the LORD', Ps. 32:5. Brought to a true knowledge of himself, his sins, his corruptions; made aware of God, his holiness, his indignation, and his wrath against sin, David was thus prepared by the Spirit of God for the knowledge of Christ and of the atonement. At last he confessed his transgressions; and in consequence could say, 'Blessed is he whose transgression is forgiven'. He acknowledged his sin; and hence could cry, 'Blessed is he whose sin is covered'. He no longer hid his iniquity; therefore he could confess, 'Blessed is the man unto whom the LORD imputeth not iniquity'.

Thus it was that David, first describing the blessedness of the man unto whom God imputeth righteousness without works, Psalm 32:1,2, afterwards continued to show how he was brought into this experience of blessedness by the alarming, awakening, quickening, and converting operations of the

Spirit of God, bringing him to repentance and confession, Ps. 32:3-5. David therefore in the whole psalm confirms the apostolic doctrine, by showing the spiritual experiences and consequences of righteousness being 'upon' the believer.

And so Paul teaches. For he does not regard the experience of David as some rare or singular occurrence peculiar to him as a prophet. Rather he cites David's experience as common to 'all them that believe', when righteousness of God is to be brought 'upon' them. For just as it was God who wrought the righteousness by the faith of Jesus Christ at the first, so it is God himself who imputes that righteousness, and, if so, by the process which David describes as common to all who receive the blessedness of the forgiveness of sins. The account which David gives, and Paul cites, provides the perfect description of the way in which the people of God as a whole are brought to the faith of God's elect.

This is a work that is wholly of God, as the experience of Abraham testifies. He heard within himself the voice of God, as it is written, 'Abraham believed God, and it was counted to him for righteousness.' The Patriarch Abraham and the King David combine with the Apostle Paul to describe that divine work which brings home the righteousness that is unto every one that believeth. That is, the voice of God through his word calls his people to faith, by which the righteousness which was first unto them, is now upon them, and they experience within themselves the blessedness of that justification in which God imputeth righteousness without works, 'unto all and upon all them that believe'.

XI

Righteousness and the Doctrine of Christ

THE righteousness of God by faith of Jesus Christ is unto all and upon all them that believe, and none other. No distinction is made in the righteousness of God unto and upon all believers: it is the same righteousness. Neither is there any difference between believers: it is the common faith. It is a faith which owns that all have sinned, and—what is worse—come short of the glory of God. Totally depraved, wholly condemned—both as to the rule of the law of God, and as to compatibility with the glory of God—yet all for whom Christ died shall be brought to faith, all 'being justified freely by his grace'.

The basis on which those once cursed by the law, and condemned from the glory, have been justified—that is, accounted to be just, or righteous, in the sight of God—is the imputation of a righteousness not their own. Such an accounting, or imputing, of righteousness is free and unmerited; it is neither deserved nor earned. There is nothing in the vessels of mercy to warrant mercy, no quality in them to endear them to their Justifier, nothing to incline him to be favourable to them above any other. If anything, they are worse, lower, poorer, more base, the more contemptible than others. Righteousness is irrespective of their sinful and depraved condition before God. Then it is free.

More, it is of grace. It is despite what had been earned. They had earned death, gendered wrath, and deserved punishment.

They had merited the curse, kindled indignation, and warranted vengeance. The holiness of the Almighty required him, in the nature of his sovereignty, to do away with such a race from the earth. The righteousness of God, in the integrity of his character, necessitated his pouring forth his anger and fury from the heavens. The rectitude of the Judge, in the immutability of his justice, obliged him to execute the sentence due upon both the heathen and the apostate religious. But God did not do away with the race, neither did he pour forth his anger and fury from the heavens upon the earth, nor did he execute judgment upon the heathen, or upon the lost sheep of the house of Israel. He decreed condemnation, he poured out wrath, he executed judgment upon his Son. Sinners, and those short of his glory, he justified. Then righteousness of God put to their account is of grace. 'Being justified freely by his grace.'

Whence came the righteousness without which sinners could not be justified? To Abraham, for example, it lay well over two thousand years in the future. To us, that righteousness lies just under two thousand years in the past. It came by the death of Jesus Christ in the midst of time, being testified by his blood. When that blood was shed for all that had ever believed, and for all that should ever believe, then, then their iniquities were blotted out, their sins were covered, and God ceased to impute sin unto them. That blood, shed to satisfy the righteousness of God in judgment against them, having satisfied it, brought the righteousness of God to their account. All, in that instant, were 'Justified by his blood', Rom. 5:9, 'being justified freely by his grace', Rom. 3:24.

Thus it is very clear that the heart of justification by faith lies in the righteousness of God both secured and assured unto all believers by the death of Jesus Christ. This is 'the righteousness of God without the law ... even the righteousness of God by faith of Jesus Christ unto all ... them that believe.' Just as justification by faith is central to the gospel, so righteousness of God lies at the heart of justification. Thirteen times righteousness of God is mentioned in the New Testament, and of these references eight are to be found in Romans, the epistle most concerned with the revelation of justification by faith.

The righteousness of God on account of which believers are justified can never be called abstract. It is not righteousness of God abstractly, it is righteousness of God in relation to me, a sinner, for whom the blood of Christ was shed. If the blood was shed for me at all, then it was shed because the righteousness of God in judgment met and condemned me in my Substitute on the cross. Therefore the blood of Jesus speaks with a voice which testifies that all God's righteousness is satisfied and at peace for ever in respect of my deeds and my person.

It follows that the righteousness of God is assured to me, it is mine, because of him who loved me and gave himself for me. The attribute or quality of righteousness in God can never be abstract to me, nor can it be abstract to God in relation to me. How could it be? It is personal to me. It is personal to God. It is personal to Christ. Shed blood, five wounds, unendurable torment, everlasting love, vicarious atonement, requited justice, substitutionary sufferings, satisfied righteousness, and a sacrificial death make it personal in Christ both to God and to me. My iniquity was the cause, in my Substitute, of that righteousness exacting that vengeance at that time. Then, such a righteousness, by such a faith, must be unto me in particular, because of him who 'loved me, and gave himself for me'.

Justification is to be regarded as having two distinct stages. The first of these consists of the bringing in of the righteousness of God by faith of Jesus Christ at the cross on behalf of all those for whom he died. The second stage follows. This consists of the imputing of that righteousness of God—brought in at the cross by faith of Jesus Christ—to the faith of every one that ever did or ever shall believe. Of necessity there is more or less of an interval between the two parts, or stages, which together constitute the whole of justification by faith.

Given the significance of this doctrine, why do we not hear more of justification by faith in what is preached in the name of Christ today? If the immortal souls of men depend upon it—and they do depend upon it—why is it not with us as burning and constant an issue as it was in the times of the Reformation? Yes, and if the words 'justification by faith' are conspicuous by their absence from the modern evangel, from present-day evangelism, and from the contemporary church—and they are conspicuous by their absence—how much more deafening is the silence on the righteousness of God? Well might the people say, 'We have not so much as heard whether there be any righteousness of God.'

Yet righteousness of God is at the core of what Christ wrought in his death, Gal. 2:21, it is at the centre of the gospel, Rom. 1:17, it is at the heart of the knowledge of Christ, Rom. 10:4, it is the essence of justification by faith, Rom. 3:21,22, and the substance of what is believed, Rom. 10:6,8,10. Righteousness of God by faith of Jesus Christ is what the apostle preached for justification, Phil. 3:9, it is what Martin Luther declared to be the standing article of the Christian church, and it is what Christ preaches in the great congregation, Ps. 40:9. No one can be saved without believing this word of truth: it is the gospel of our salvation. Moreover, none can rightly hear of, know about, or believe upon Christ, save by preaching, and preaching according to this same apostolic doctrine, called The word of faith, Romans 10:8,14-17.

The apostle shows, Rom. 3:24, that justification is through redemption: 'being justified freely by his grace through the redemption that is in Christ Jesus.' Whereas justification is a positive word, having to do with the imputing of righteousness, in which a man is accounted to be righteous before

God, without regard to his real condition, or his actual state, redemption is otherwise. Redemption is negative in that it views the enemies, the calamities, the debts, the states and conditions which bound the sinner, but from which, by the grace of God, he has been 'unloosed'. Redemption delivers from the host of enemies and calamities which had condemned the lost, declaring a loosing away from everything to which before they were in bondage. This redemption is therefore the setting at liberty from the slavery in which before one had been held.

In the Epistle to the Romans men had been seen as laden with sins, sunk in guilt, wilful in rebellion, blind in self-righteousness, depraved in their inward parts, possessed of a foul and polluted fountain of inbred sin, given up of God, under the curse, awaiting the judgment and vengeance of that great day, without excuse, and with the wrath of God revealed from heaven against the whole fallen race. Now a redemption is proclaimed. It is the redemption in Christ Jesus. Here the guilty, condemned at the bar of God's justice, under sentence of a fearful execution of everlasting punishment, are 'loosed away from' all that in which they had been held, and by which they had been condemned.

The price of such a deliverance follows: it is blood. 'By faith in his blood.' Now, says the apostle, this righteousness, this being justified, is through the redemption that is in Christ Jesus, the anointed Saviour. Because by redemption through blood sinners are redeemed from curse of the law; redeemed from bondage to the law; redeemed from among men; redeemed from all iniquity; redeemed from death and the grave; redeemed from hell and destruction; and redeemed by an eternal redemption. What precious blood this is! Having loosed condemned sinners from all this, from all that was against them, the same precious blood preaches peace to their souls, a free righteousness, and a propitiated God, 'through faith in his blood', Rom. 3:25.

The price of this jubilee which is sounded in the ears of those sunk in debt, perishing in their sins, and without hope or inheritance in this world or the next, is clear: it is in the blood of Jesus Christ. This is that precious blood which achieves remission, secures ransom, and pays the price of redemption. It is the blood that is upon the propitiatory, the place of communion, the blood by which the people of God have been sanctified, Heb. 13:12, and it is the same blood that has brought in justification, Rom. 5:9, 'being justified by his blood'. This is the blood of sprinkling that speaketh better things than that of Abel, from which arises virtually every single branch of the saving and powerful doctrine of Christ.

Justification, the being declared, or reckoned, righteous, when one is not, is in itself a purely positive act of God. It is the conferring upon the sinner of a free and imputed righteousness. The condition, the state of that sinner, has no bearing on the matter. Neither, strictly, is it a question of the origin or nature of the righteousness to be imputed. In the act of justifying the ungodly the existence of the righteousness is taken as a matter of fact. Justification presumes an objective, distinctive, extrinsic righteousness, declared to be the gift of God to the ungodly. It is imputed so that by gift it is to the account of the ungodly. In that sense justification is wholly positive. A divine righteousness, coming down from heaven, is by so much added to the sinner. By this gift of God he is immeasurably the richer. It is also true that by this righteousness the sinner has the blessing of the forgiveness of his iniquities, the covering of his sins, and the certainty that the Lord will never again impute sin unto him.

The blood of atonement, which satisfied the righteous judgment of God in respect of the iniquities, sins, and sin of the ungodly, is that which likewise paid the price of redemption. If the blood brings righteousness to the account of the ungodly, it also secures redemption for the sinner. At the point at which the blood brings in the righteousness of God, and takes away the sins of the people, that is, remission, or forgiveness, justification and redemption meet.

The apostle speaks of the blessing of iniquities being forgiven as commensurate with God imputing righteousness without works, Rom. 4:6,7. Yet he also speaks of the same forgiveness of sins in terms of 'redemption through his blood', Eph. 1:7, Col. 1:14. Evidently therefore justification and redemption converge at the place where the blood of Christ secures the righteousness of God, the remission of sins, and the forgiveness of the sinner. Thus Paul can say, 'being justified freely by his grace through the redemption that is in Christ Jesus', Rom. 3:24. Redemption sees the sinner forgiven through the remission of sins, just as justification views the righteousness of God satisfied in sins having been judged, and consequently remitted. Hence, at the cross justification and redemption converge, but from the cross they diverge, each distinct branch of the doctrine of Christ unfolding with coherent definition.

Both justification and redemption are achieved by the shedding of blood. And both are conveyed by faith in that blood. But in the fulness of the work of Christ in death, brought home to the sinner's conscience, Paul speaks of the blood bringing in the righteousness of God on the one hand, and of its paying the price of redemption on the other. This he expresses as 'Being justified freely by his grace through the redemption that is in Christ Jesus.' The apostle is exclaiming, as it were, It is not that God, in justifying the ungodly by faith, disregards their ungodliness, dropping a kind of cloak over their unrighteousness and sin, God forbid. Rather, this justification is through the redemption, that is, through the loosing away of the sinner from all his guilt and filth, bondage and corruption, darkness and death.

The imputation of righteousness is, in the awareness of the ungodly, a positive gift, an addition to their account above all that they could either ask or think. But this gift comes through the experience of what is negative, taken away, a subtraction from the conscience of all that in which the ungodly were held, all the debt, guilt, wrath, punishment, and judgment to come. It is through the same precious blood of Christ by which the ungodly are justified and reckoned to be righteous, that they are also loosed, freed, and redeemed from all that which was against them, and which was contrary to them, 'being justified freely by his grace through the redemption which is in Christ Jesus.'

Therefore as to all that was against us, all that was negative, we can truly say, If God be for us, who can be against us? He that spared not his own Son, but delivered him up for us all, how shall he not with him also freely give us all things? Who shall lay anything to the charge of God's elect? It is God that justifieth. As to every one of our enemies, all that was for our destruction, by the redemption that is in Christ Jesus, God has set us free. It is a positive justification, through the redemption, which, looking back, discharges us completely from everything that was contrary to us. By the redemption we are forgiven, our sins are remitted, our souls ransomed, and our persons are delivered. The flesh has been condemned, the body of sin has been destroyed, the curse of the law silenced, we are no longer under the law, out of reach of law, we shall not come into judgment, we are washed, cleansed, sanctified, at liberty, loosed entirely.

Withal by the imputing of righteousness, even the righteousness of God by faith of Jesus Christ, we are made to soar above into the realm of the heavenlies. We are accounted to be righteous with a righteousness that is divine, which came down from God out of heaven, by which we rise over everything unhindered, translated into the kingdom of the Majesty on high. By the imputation of righteousness we transcend all that from which we were delivered by redemption, being elevated to that with which we are invested in justification.

We are translated from one kingdom to another, we are found in Another, we belong to another world, are citizens of another country. We are heirs of God, joint-heirs with Christ, partakers of the divine nature, indwelt by the Holy Ghost, are the sons of God, have the earnest of the Spirit, and, united in one body, wait for the coming of the Lord from heaven. All this the righteousness of God by faith of Jesus Christ has achieved for us, and secured to us, 'being justified freely by his grace through the redemption which is in Christ Jesus.'

Continuing to preach Christ Jesus, the anointed Saviour, who redeemed his people when he brought in everlasting righteousness through the shedding of his blood, on the one hand setting them free from all below, and on the other justifying them with a righteousness suited to all that is above, the apostle proceeds to what is further unfolded by the work of justification. The blood of Jesus Christ having both met and brought in the righteousness of God for all his people, the way into the holiest is therefore made manifest by that same blood. The grace of God having reckoned divine righteousness unto his people, a place commensurate with that righteousness, in the heavenlies in Christ Jesus, is accorded to them. Thus they are seen as elevated in position with the Saviour in the ascension. This brings in the heavenly propitiatory, Rom. 3:25.

The apostle therefore now declares the work of God in the Person of Christ in terms of his 'being set forth a propitiation through faith in his blood', Rom. 3:25. Christ Jesus, raised up to heavenly glory in consequence of his work on earth, is himself that propitiation—'*whom* God hath set forth'—or place of appeasement, being set down on the throne of his Father. Or ever the Saviour ascended on high, he had already redeemed, already justified, his people. Then he is seated in the heavenly glory for them, just as they are seated in him.

The propitiatory was the cover of beaten gold, of one piece with the cherubim of glory, that covered the ark of the covenant—overlaid round about with gold—in the tabernacle in the wilderness, Heb. 9:1-5. This propitiatory cover is commonly—but not accurately—called the mercy seat. The propitiation as such was effected by the blood of the sacrificed goat, in the figures of the true under the Old Covenant, but once a year, on the day of atonement. On this day the high priest entered into the Holiest of all beyond the veil to sprinkle the blood of propitiation seven times with his finger, amidst clouds of incense, upon the propitiatory of pure gold, of beaten work, covering the ark of the covenant.

Romans 3:25 shows the fulfilment of this type. Christ set forth as a propitiation becomes the reality of which the sprinkling on the day of atonement was the figure. The true propitiatory, or mercy seat, is not that seen on earth, but that prefigured by what was seen on earth. The propitiatory in the heavens is not that inanimate form of pure gold, beaten and fashioned by the hand of man, but it is the once-crucified, ever-glorified Saviour, the Son of God, Jesus Christ the Lord. Not an object on earth, as was the form, but a Man in heaven, as is the reality. Not sprinkled by the blood of beasts, as was the shadow, but sprinkled with his own blood, as is the substance. Not for time, but for eternity. Not annually, but everlastingly. Not for the land of promise, but for the world to come. Not in an earthly sanctuary, but made higher than the heavens.

This propitiatory, which is Christ Jesus raised from the dead, ascended into glory, set down at the right hand of the Majesty on high, now sits and reigns in glory on behalf of that people whom he had redeemed and justified by his work on earth. This propitiatory, I say, now raised to sublime heights, exalted before the face of God in the heavenlies, bears before that holy presence the scars which marked his sufferings and death, and the sprinkled blood the shedding of which occurred in death after he had wrought righteousness and secured deliverance for every last one of his people upon the cross at Golgotha.

This exalted place of appeasement, set forth by the propitiatory in the glory, high over all the earth, shows the rectitude of God in the forgiveness of the Old Testament saints. Here was an evident declaration that God was righteous in forgiving his ancient people who had put their trust in him, and who had died in faith. Yet at the time of their death God seemed not to have had justification for the pardon which he had bestowed upon them during their lifetime. What of his own avowed righteousness? What of natural justice? What of the judgment? Where was the impartial administration of the rule of law, in the apparently indiscriminate disposal of absolution? If God forgave them, why not the heathen? If the heathen, why not devils? What was the difference, that was not arbitrary?

Now the propitiation showed the difference. Not one of those who had received the promise of pardon, and who had died in the faith of that promise, was forgotten in the substitutionary sufferings, in the broken body and shed blood, of the Saviour upon the tree. The blood of sprinkling in the glory declared the pardon of each one of that great company of just men made perfect, sounding the names of all who had trusted in the coming Seed, the promised Messiah, the Christ who should save his people from their sins.

They had looked to him from ages and generations, whether it were Adam with his coats of skins, Abel with the firstlings of his flock and of the fat thereof, Noah with his burnt offerings of a sweet savour, offered up on the altar which he had made, or Abraham, who believed God and it was counted to him for righteousness: all trusted in God, all set forth in type, figure or promise their faith in him that was to come. Now, at last, after ages and generations, in the midst of time, at

Golgotha, Christ believed God, and received all their sins, transgressions and iniquities, who had trusted in him and had died in faith, received them, I say, in his own body on the tree, God justifying them freely by his grace through the redemption which is in Christ Jesus.

Raised from the dead, ascended into glory, his visage so marred more than any man, and his form more than the sons of men: carrying with him his justified and redeemed people in his own Person, and by his own blood, God hath set him forth a propitiation, to declare his righteousness for the remission of the sins of a past and bygone age. Both the sprinkled blood and the blood sprinkled propitiatory in the heavenly glory declare through righteousness the perfect satisfaction of an atonement made on earth in which mysteriously there appeared in the one great Substitute the names and the persons of every one of the Old Testament saints that had believed upon him from the foundation of the world. Thus it appeared that their faith was justified in the issue, just as their persons were justified by the event.

By his death Christ glorified God with a witness. In twelve ways he magnified God in his Being, justified God in his sayings, and cleared God in his judgments. By that death the justice of God was abundantly manifest, the justification of God was manifestly just, and God appeared as both just and a Justifier. In the death of Christ mercy and truth met together, and righteousness and peace kissed each other, with mercy rejoicing against judgment.

Christ believed that his death would justify God, he believed that his death would justify the elect, and he believed that his death would bring in justifying righteousness. By his death Christ fulfilled the promise, the oath, and the covenant of God. At the cross he glorified God in his character, attributes, and nature. By the shedding of his blood Christ consummated the works, ways and word of God. When he cried, It is finished, and gave up the ghost, Christ effected the purpose, the will and the counsel of God. Nothing was lacking for God that Christ did not accomplish in death. It was finished. He had glorified God on the earth.

This vital passage, Rom. 3:22-26, shows that justification is not isolated from the Person of Christ. Earlier in the epistle we had observed the titles, Jesus Christ, his Son Jesus Christ our Lord, seed of David, Son of God, the Lord Jesus Christ, and Christ. Here, within this short compass of five verses, we read of the names, Jesus Christ, Christ Jesus, and Jesus. Then justification by faith is not isolated from the Person of Christ. It is in Christ. Hence it cannot be separated from his living Person as though it could be reduced to data for some detached study. To deduce intellectual subject matter from 'historical theology', as they call it, to lard this matter with texts foraged from the Bible, to call the result 'justification', to incorporate this into the syllabus of some philosophical system of religious speculation, some kind of abstract, academic study, is singularly obnoxious to the Lord of glory, offensive to the Holy Ghost, contrary to the truth, and destructive of sound doctrine. Justification by faith is the blessing of Abraham in the heavenly gift of the Father of mercies, to be dispensed in life and power from the glory through mystery and revelation by the Lord Jesus Christ.

Neither is justification ever to be isolated from the doctrine of Christ, properly so-called. The apostle had taught, earlier in the epistle, the truth concerning the gospel of God, the gospel of Christ, and the faith, just as later he would fully deliver that form of doctrine which was to be obeyed from the heart on the part of his people. He had spoken of Jesus Christ being made of the seed of David according to the flesh, of the Son of God with power—mark that, power: Not word only, but power also—according to the spirit of holiness by the resurrection from the dead. The apostle had declared the righteousness of God revealed from faith to faith, the wrath of God revealed from heaven, and the day of wrath and revelation of the righteous judgment of God.

Paul had spoken of God judging the secrets of men by Christ Jesus, according to the apostolic doctrine, and had shown how the law had judged the whole world to be guilty before God, silencing every tongue, convincing all the earth of the knowledge of sin, altogether excluding justification from its realm and competence. Now, Rom. 3:22-26, he speaks of the grace of God, of being freely justified by grace, and of the manifestation of the righteousness of God by faith of Jesus Christ. He directs the faith of believers to the blood of Christ, and declares justification, redemption, propitiation and remission, all in the limited number of five verses. Then justification cannot be dissociated from the doctrine of Christ.

Not only does justification find its own place in the doctrine of Christ, that is, the doctrine which reveals his Person and work, and which he himself teaches from heaven, but it has an importance in that doctrine which may be used to include and sum up many other truths. It is clear from Rom. 3:24,25,26, that the apostle uses the word justification in a way that comprehends and contains the truth of redemption, remission, propitiation, and, indeed, of righteousness itself. That justification is employed doctrinally to convey every truth necessary to its realisation—as well as to describe the act of justification in and of itself—is apparent from I Cor. 1:30, where the apostle, speaking of Christ Jesus being the wisdom of God, informs the faithful that it is of God, not of themselves, that they are in Christ. As to that wisdom which Christ Jesus has been made of God to all saints, it stands in three parts: righteousness, sanctification and redemption. This is not to imply that, say, remission is not part of the wisdom of God to the church, it is to affirm that everything is considered as being comprehended and summarised under the three brief heads of righteousness, sanctification and redemption in the doctrine of Christ. As to 'theology', so-called, the apostles knew nothing of it, and neither they nor the Lord Jesus ever used the term. To them, the word had no meaning.

The word justification therefore may be used to imply the inclusion of related truths necessary to its being effected. This is clear from Rom. 3:24,25. But why is this, and when is it so? It is because justification entails the pre-eminent and ultimate consequence of the death of Christ on behalf of his people. That their sins are remitted, that redemption has been secured through his blood, is all true; but what is consummately true is that the same blood which paid the price of remission and secured redemption is also that which has brought the righteousness of God to the account of every one that believeth.

It is this that has opened heaven, thrown wide the gates of the house of God, brought in the adoption, and achieved union and communion with Father, Son and Holy Ghost. Every stage must be involved, but none surmounts such heights as this culminating glory of justification itself. When, therefore, the apostle would summarise the work accomplished by the death of Christ nothing could be more apt than that he should use the word which of necessity includes everything else, yet in itself is indicative of the ultimate triumph of the cross.

Implied in justification is the truth that Jesus Christ is come in the flesh. The incarnation of the Son of God—made of the seed of David according to the flesh—the life and ministry of the Son of man, the fact of the divinity of Christ, the nature of his divinity, his becoming incarnate, his assuming human nature into union with his divine nature in one Person, the revelation of the deity through his manhood, all must be inferred from a doctrine which teaches the crucifixion of Jesus Christ the Son of man and Son of God.

The revelation of the four evangelists is necessarily assumed in the truth of the death of Christ. That Messiah had come, that the kingdom of heaven had been preached, and would be preached, that its mysterious, divine, heavenly and spiritual nature had been manifested, that both Messiah and the Kingdom had been rejected by the Jews: all these things are necessarily implied by the death of Christ. That it was the Jews who had crucified him, that God had raised him from the dead, and that the Kingdom had turned under the apostolic ministry to the Gentiles, likewise followed from the crucifixion.

The cry from the cross, Eloi, Eloi, lama sabachthani, showed that the Servant of God had appeared, that he was the Son of God, without father, without mother, without descent, having neither beginning of days nor end of life, able both to discern and to fulfil the good pleasure of God in the divine Service. Accordingly it followed that this Service of God must be first to the Jews, next to the Gentiles, principally to the heart, and always for the world to come. Similarly it followed that both the Servant and the Service of God were rejected by the carnal outward Jews in favour of a worldly, legal and exterior religion, that the Servant whom they despised God had magnified, and that from the ascended glory the Son of God continues in a spiritual and evangelical ministration to the Gentiles unto this day.

Implicit in justification is the coming of the promised Saviour. Conceived in the womb of the virgin, the Holy Ghost had come upon Mary, and the power of the Highest had overshadowed her, therefore also that holy thing which should be born of her should be called the Son of God. Heralded and baptised by the forerunner, the heavens opened, the Father proclaimed, and the Spirit descended to reveal the Saviour who should declare and make manifest the Grace of God. Relating not to the Jews only but to the Gentiles also, answering to the whole of mankind, peace was pronounced on earth, good will toward men. Such grace was displayed to the poor, the needy, the mourning, the sick, the lost sheep of the house of Israel, and the stranger within their gates. The Saviour's birth, baptism, transfiguration, visitation, crucifixion, resurrection and ascension conspired together to set forth the gospel of the Grace of God.

Also inferred from the death of Christ is the truth that the Word which was in the beginning, which was with God, and was God, which was in the beginning with God, by whom all things were made, and without whom was not anything made that was made, in whom was life—which was the light of men—that he, even he, should come into the world. That he who made the world, was in the world. He was made flesh, and dwelt among us, full of grace and truth. To him testimony was borne by six signs and seven, by the voice of one crying in the wilderness, by Moses' writings, by the Father's speech, by the works which he did, and by the scriptures which spoke of his coming.

But he received not honour from men. He received neither witness from the Jews, nor testimony from the rulers. They received him not. For all their law, their heritage, their scriptures, their sacrifices, their feasts, their temple, and their glory, they cast him out and crucified him. Yet this was he— unlike the servant, Moses—who was Son over his own house, the Son of the Father, who, by the Spirit whom he should send, would bring the children of God into union with the Father and the Son, that they might be one, and dwell in holy communion in the house of the LORD for ever.

All this, all the content and doctrine in the four evangelists, is implied in justification. For justification is founded upon substitutionary atonement, and substitutionary atonement is what was accomplished by this same Jesus upon the tree at Golgotha. The crucifixion was the culmination of his life upon earth. But that death—and his blood shed in death—has become the foundation upon which he proclaims and dispenses justification from the glory. For justification is from the glory. Justification was accomplished on earth but it is proclaimed from the glory.

Justification cannot be conveyed by human authority or priesthood, it cannot be ministered through the sacraments or rites of the—or any—church, and it cannot be claimed by the will of man out of the dead letter of scripture. Justification is administered by the Lord Jesus Christ from the glory, defined by the apostolic doctrine of the gospel, preached by the ministry sent of God and subject to the apostolic rule, witnessed by the Holy Ghost from heaven, and ratified by the sprinkling of the blood of Jesus Christ. Justification is not for this world, it is for the world to come. It does not pertain to an earthly inheritance, but to the everlasting glory. Justification can never be trapped in an ecclesiastical system, or in a form of words, it is for free-born sons, for the heavenly bride, for that Jerusalem which is above, for that which is at liberty, that which is the mother of us all.

Justification is secure to all the seed. Nothing in this world or the next, no power in heaven or on earth, no being above or beneath, no event within or without, nothing shall undo that work of Christ on the cross by which he effectually justified every last one of his people. Nothing shall prevent the almighty power of the Spirit of God, nor shall anything obstruct the all-prevailing providence of the grace of God from bringing every one of these Christ's brethren, from the least to the greatest, from the most wayward to the most unfaltering, to dwell in the house of the LORD for ever. How can anyone doubt it? It is God that justifieth.

Justification embraces everything that Christ accomplished in his death. Justification, though administered from the glory of heaven, does not in itself speak of what Christ is doing, or what he will do. Justification declares what Christ has done, and done in death, and it declares everything that he has done in death. However, it is a declaration that is made by

227

the ascended Son above, through the descended Spirit below, to the heart of every poor and contrite sinner, mourning over his lost condition, shut up under the law, and groaning from the fear of the wrath to come. To every one of these, the Lord's prisoners, there is sent a declaration of pardon, peace, and liberty, a sounding of the heavenly jubilee carried by the Holy Ghost from Christ above to the interior heart of the convicted sinner below, and to none other.

Such lost sheep know the blessing of Abraham. These are in the secret. They know the doctrine of Christ, because he has proclaimed it to them himself, who died for them. Now they know in their day what he suffered for them in his. They know the truth not from the clergy, not from books, not from studying, not from the schools, not by the intellect, not by understanding, but by the revelation of the mystery, by the spiritual opening of the word of God, by the voice of the Shepherd, by the work of the Holy Ghost from heaven. Hence it is that all these are brought to feel their sinful condition, the burden of their sins, their lost estate under the wrath of God; but all, I say, all shall hear his voice within, saying, 'Son, be of good cheer, thy sins be forgiven thee.'

Remission of sins, forgiveness for sinners, ransom from bondage, pardon to the guilty, and deliverance from the wrath to come resound with a personal witness in the heart by the Spirit sent down from on high, as the word of faith is preached by the mouth of ministers of the New Testament sent by Jesus Christ to proclaim the glorious gospel. He to whom the burdened soul had lately cried, 'O LORD, rebuke me not in thine anger, neither chasten me in thy hot displeasure', now appears through faith in the blood of Jesus Christ as propitiated, appeased, one whose anger is abated, and whose good pleasure beams forth in the smiling countenance of the Son of his love. Now, iniquities are forgiven, sins are covered, sin is no longer imputed, God is rendered propitious, every debt has been paid, and the Father welcomes and embraces the weeping child bewildered by such overwhelming love. This is justification.

Justification proclaims the reconciliation. Indeed, everything that was accomplished in the death of Christ, by his broken body and shed blood, everything is gathered up and encompassed with sublime certainty to enhance the divine heights of justification. The reconciliation, the thorough exchange of places, fulfils every sacrifice figured under the Old Covenant. Christ is at once the passover, the substitute, the oblation, the sacrifice, the wave offering, the heave offering, the meat offering, the peace offering, the burnt offering, the sin offering, and the trespass offering. He is Melchizedek's bread and wine and David's sacrifice at the threshingfloor of Ornan. His death answers to the slain beast from which came Adam's coats of skins, and the slaughtered lamb of Abel offered with the fat thereof; he is Abraham's ram, the slain goat and the scapegoat, the bird slain and the bird set free. He is the Lamb slain from the foundation of the world, the great atonement, and the one substitutionary sacrifice. He is the reconciliation.

So interwoven is reconciliation with justification, so united with righteousness in the body, the blood, the death of the crucified Son of man, that the Apostle Paul, when teaching the nature of the reconciliation, Rom. 5:12-21, six times over refers to justification or righteousness in the process, in no more than ten verses. The change of places may express the fulfilment of every ancient sacrifice, it may answer to the unique revelation of each distinct offering, it may be the substance of every shadowy oblation, it may be grounded in the age-old atonement, it may be based on substitutionary sacrifice, it may issue forth in reconciliation through the thorough exchange, but in the doctrine of Christ as a whole it is expressed as one of a series of cumulative steps towards the ultimate place gained by Jesus Christ for his people through his sufferings and death. Hence reconciliation is expressed in the doctrine as an essential part of justification and of the righteousness of God. That is the place to which the exchange of places brings the reconciled people of God in Christ Jesus.

The people of God, being justified freely by his grace through the redemption that is in Christ Jesus, hear those preachers that are sent—for how can one preach except he be sent? Rom. 10:15—and they cry aloud, How beautiful are the feet of them that preach the gospel of peace, and bring glad tidings of good things! For the ministers of Christ were not sent without a purpose, but to preach the gospel, to teach the doctrine of Christ, to divide the earth, to be a savour of life unto life, and death unto death to all mankind. Whilst they give forth the word of faith by the Holy Ghost from heaven, there sounds from above the glorious trumpet, as from on high there follows the heavenly administration of the apostolic succession, the ministry of the New Testament, the ministry of righteousness, the ministry of the Spirit, the ministry of glory, and the ministry of liberty.

Whilst many may hear outward preaching, this inward sound none can catch but those who, having inward ears to hear, do hear. They hear his voice, they feel his power, they receive his witness, and they find and rejoice in the testimony of God within themselves. They experience, they cry with joy, It is God that justifieth! as justification, their own justification, is sealed to them by the Holy Ghost from heaven. This is accomplished through the shedding and sprinkling of the blood of Christ, who, by one sacrifice, hath finished the transgression, made an end of sins, made reconciliation for iniquity, and brought in everlasting righteousness, sealing the vision and confirming the prophecy unto the coming of the everlasting kingdom and glory, world without end, Amen.

PART THREE
THE CONSEQUENCE

THE CONSEQUENCE

XII

The Righteousness of Faith

WHEN God judged and wrought in righteousness through the faith of Jesus Christ at the cross, it followed that justification was effected and secured for all his people in that substitutionary death. Nothing was to be added to make justification effectual or secure: it was effectual and secure. What God had wrought through the death of Jesus Christ was exterior to the persons for whom he wrought, it was outside of their lifetimes, beyond the realm of all that was earthly or of man. This was a work wrought between the Father and the Son, and wholly between the Father and the Son, and the result was that the entire election was actually justified by the time that the blood of Christ was shed.

In consequence, the Person of the Holy Ghost was sent to commence his age-long work. This work brings home to the conscious awareness of every one for whom Christ died, that he did die, and that he died for them. This is achieved through each one being brought to faith in turn, throughout the age, until Christ comes again in glory. The Holy Ghost inwardly

233

reveals what was wrought by the Father and the Son at the cross when everlasting righteousness was brought in for all that shall believe. When faith comes in, the righteousness of God, already put to account in the knowledge of God, is reckoned to those for whom Christ died in their own exper-ience and to their knowledge. This is called, being justified by faith. It is the imputing of righteousness.

This is the imputing of righteousness of God, wrought at Golgotha for persons foreknown—mostly of generations yet to come—to the faith of those persons themselves, so that they know what God did for them by Jesus Christ so long ago. This is not what passed between the Father and the Son con-cerning the bringing in of the righteousness of God at the cross. It is what passes between the Spirit and the believer concerning the accounting of that same righteousness to faith. That which had been wrought, of which the believer knew nothing, is now counted to him so that he himself believes and knows what God had known from the beginning. The sinner having been brought to faith by the Holy Ghost, the know-ledge exclusive to the deity is now shared by the sinner: righteousness had been wrought for him, he believes that, and his faith is counted to him for righteousness.

Whereas justification had been effectually accomplished by the faith of Jesus Christ at the cross, so that there everlasting righteousness was accounted to the entire election, neverthe-less the work of bringing the elect, one by one, to the knowledge of what God had wrought remained to be fulfilled. Whilst they were justified in the sight of God by what he had done, they knew nothing of it, they were not justified in their own exper-ience: God knew of it, but the knowledge was hidden from them. In fact, sooner or later, they would come to the place where they would be convinced by their spiritual experience that justification was an impossibility for such unworthy and sinful persons as themselves.

But then the Spirit of God would bring them from this place of condemnation, spiritually called Sinai, to another place, called spiritual Zion, where their justification would become a reality. It had been a reality all the time: but not to them. The bringing of those for whom Christ had died, and whom God had justified, to the place where that justification became real to them, so that they themselves knew of it and felt it, was and is the work of the Holy Ghost from heaven.

This in itself demonstrates the truth that there are two parts to justification, the one in which God by Jesus Christ brought in righteousness for all his people through the cross, and the other in which God by the Holy Ghost accounts that righteousness to the faith of such a people by the word of God. Whence it appears that the knowledge of God concerning the justification of his people is one thing; but the knowledge of their justification by that people is another. Both may be referred to indiscriminately by the term justification; but only the latter may be called justification by faith, because the words 'by faith' entail the experimental work of the Person of the Holy Ghost within themselves.

The justification of a sinner is therefore that act of God by which the sinner is accounted to be righteous when in fact he is not. This act of God's accounting a sinner to be righteous may have a cause, and may be on a certain ground, but it, itself is not that cause, neither is it that ground. It is the effect of that cause: it rests upon that ground. It is a sentence from the mouth of God in heaven by which a man sinful in himself is pronounced righteous before God. It is this that justifies the sinner by faith.

The cause of the act of justification lies in the everlasting love of God for his people, in sending and giving up his Son to die for them, that they might be saved. The Father loved a people in Christ before the foundation of the world, predestinating them to everlasting glory, Eph. 1:4,5. This was according to his own purpose and grace, given to them in Christ Jesus before the world began, II Tim. 1:9. Such are the called according to his purpose, the election whom he fore-knew, predestinated to be conformed to the image of his Son.

Moreover whom he did predestinate, them he also called: and whom he called, them he also justified, Rom. 8:30. Of his own will begat he them with the word of truth, that they should be a kind of firstfruits of his creatures, Jas. 1:18. This was not of him that willeth, nor of him that runneth, but of God that showeth mercy, Rom. 9:16. And of his mercy, he chose a seed in Christ before the world began. This is the seed that shall serve him; it shall be accounted to the Lord for a generation. This is the generation of them that seek him, that seek thy face, O Jacob. Selah.

The Father gave that people to Christ whom he had chosen in him, that by righteousness the Son should give eternal life to as many as the Father had given him. This election was of the Father; but they were given to the Son, that through the Son righteousness might be imputed unto them, who had no righteousness of their own. For them Christ prayed; he prayed not for the world, but for those which were given to him by the Father. And the world hated them, because they were not of the world, even as he was not of the world. The Father had given to the Son all those whom he had chosen out of the world. By the Son's giving himself for them, the world would know that the Father had sent the Son, and that the Father had loved them, even as he had loved his own Son. And this was the cause of their being justified.

The ground of that act by which God would justify sinners appeared in the righteousness of God manifested without the law, even the righteousness of God by faith of Jesus Christ. This justifying righteousness wrought of God through the death of his Son is unto all those that should be brought to faith thereafter. It was wrought in substitutionary atonement.

As their sacrifice, Christ really took the place of the whole election, so that it was not as himself that he was upon the cross in the counsel of God, but as them, in all their state, and with all their deeds. This was what was judged in righteousness, and judged in righteousness till that righteousness found nothing to judge. Thus the substitutionary Saviour brought in righteousness of God for all his people, and thus God justified that people in him by the shedding of his blood. On that ground, God passes the sentence of justification upon them that believe thereafter. This is the only ground of justification for a just God and a Saviour.

No reason can be found in sinners, before or after believing, with or without repentance, which could possibly incline God to justify them, or bring him under any obligation to effect their justification. Their faith is no reason for him to justify them. Or their unbelief for his not doing so. In fact, God had already concluded the whole work of justification before the existence of multitudes that should afterwards repent and believe. That the sinner believes adds to and takes nothing from his justification. The reason for the sinner's justification lies wholly in righteousness of God through the death of Jesus Christ, not on the sinner's believing it; his belief brings him into the knowledge of what God had done for him, but God had already done it: that is what is believed by the justified.

Faith is not a reason for, but a consequence of justification. When the sinner knows that Christ has died for him, that God has freely justified him, this works a vast change. Enmity is turned to amity, hostility to peace, hatred to love. Unbelief gives way to faith, darkness to light, distance to communion. Trust takes the place of suspicion, hope of despair, and submission of rebellion.

The knowledge that God has already forgiven, pardoned, cleansed, washed, purged, and delivered the sinner brings down every barrier, removes all hardness, and overcomes every constraint. Indeed nothing but the knowledge that the sinner has not to change in order to be justified, but that God in everlasting love to the self-condemned had already justified him by grace, could work such a transformation as now becomes evident. The sinner is radiant. He is filled with joy unspeakable and full of glory. This brings in faith of course. If so, far from being a reason for justification, faith appears and is seen to be a consequence of justification.

Faith is wrought by the Holy Ghost in the heart when God opens the sinner's eyes to behold Jesus Christ and him cruci-fied. No man can do this work. Much less can the sinner do it for himself. Under the preaching of men of God sent as a savour of life unto life God opens the interior eyes by his own quickening operation, so that the sinner knows for himself that Christ loved him, and gave himself for him.

This revelation to the inward man, in which the Father reveals the Son, and the Son makes known the Father, is not without prior spiritual experience. The first part of this preparatory work—in which the word of God comes with power—brings a divinely inwrought conviction of sin, together with the sounding of an alarm in the sinner's soul. This makes him set to work with a fiery zeal, as he labours to please God and earn favour by fabricating an outward reformation in the letter of scripture. Soon he finds all his vaunted righteousness as filthy rags, and discovers his heart to be deceitful above all things, and desperately wicked. Filth boils up within him, rebellion stirs his heart, desperation takes hold of him as an armed man, and, as he stands trembling under the frown of God, the sentence of death sounds forth without a hope of remission in this world or the next.

A sense of wrath now descends on the sinner groaning under the burden of his sins, whilst the curse sounds its legal terrors in his soul, and a horror of great darkness falls upon him. As he casts about for relief, thunder and lightning seem to reverberate and flash from Sinai, conspiring with the voice of words that cannot be borne to sink the desperate man into a morass of despair. Now the waters are come into his soul; there is no standing; confusion is with him by day, and perplexity by night, so that it is a vexation but to hear the report. All his lovers and kinsmen stand afar off, the sinner feels that none has been where he finds himself, and in consequence he dies to any and all expectation from man or from within himself. Turning with abhorrence from worldly company and all false comfort, at last he submits and resigns himself to the just judgment of Almighty God.

Next, to his astonishment, a voice of kindness and of compassion sounds out of the darkness round about him: 'Wilt thou be made whole?' Hardly able to believe his ears, he finds in himself a thousand causes as to why he is beyond mercy, unfit for the Lord's pity, a worthless reprobate on whom compassion would be utterly wasted, and, in any event, one long past hope and quite beyond all help. His language is like that of the man at the pool of Bethesda, 'Sir, I have no man, when the water is troubled, to put me into the pool'. But now the Lord himself has come for his salvation, and what has he to do with man or pools? 'Rise, take up thy bed, and walk!' And immediately the man was made whole. And so it is with the sinner.

Righteousness is imputed, life is bestowed, healing follows, sight is restored, the ears are opened, the tongue unloosed, the lame leaps as an hart, and the dead is raised to life again. It pleases God to reveal his Son in him, a spirit of wisdom and revelation in the knowledge of Christ is bestowed upon him, according to the riches of the Father's glory he is strengthened with might by his Spirit in the inner man, and Christ dwells in his heart by faith. Rooted and grounded in love, he comprehends with all saints what is the breadth, and length, and depth, and height, and knows the love of Christ, which passes knowledge, being filled with all the fulness of

239

God. And shall not such a revelation from the Father in heaven, such an enlightenment from the Holy Ghost below, such a vision of Christ, bring in faith?

When the sinner believes, as he does, that Christ died for him, that his blood was shed for him, and that he himself was judged in the sacrificial offering of his Substitute, I say, when he believes, it is said of him that 'his faith is counted for righteousness', Rom. 4:5. It is not simply that God is righteous in forgiving him, or that God imputes righteousness unto him —though both these things are true—what is also said is that when the sinner 'believeth on him that justifieth the ungodly', then 'his faith'—mark that, his faith—'is counted to him for righteousness.' How can this be?

It is both irresponsible and mischievous to suppose from this statement that the apostle meant that faith is a substitute for righteousness. And yet some have supposed that it is, and have taught others so. As if to imply, well, some passages show that righteousness is imputed, but others say that faith is imputed for righteousness, and so it must follow, faith is reckoned to be equivalent to righteousness, it is a substitute for righteousness. God forbid! However, such destructive nonsense has been advocated by certain academic clergymen in their wisdom as the only explanation for what they think of as a contradiction. But it is not a contradiction: it is a revelation. Had these learned men bowed in humility before what has been revealed, they would have owned that none but the Spirit who gave the revelation to the apostle, could lead others into the spiritual meaning of that heavenly doctrine which came forth from God. But no, reason and intellect, philosophy and speculation, constitute their stock in trade, and about their trading they must go.

The expression 'faith being counted for righteousness', does not and cannot mean that faith is righteousness, or a form of righteousness, or that it is considered in the sight of God to be acceptable instead of righteousness. Oh, into what a miry ditch do these blind guides and their sightless followers get themselves, doting upon what is highly esteemed among men, quite cutting off themselves—and multitudes besides—from the revelation of the Holy Ghost, sent to lead the humble into all truth.

As if God were unrighteous, and winked, making out that since we cannot attain to righteousness, poor things, no matter: faith will do nicely. That is, faith is a perfectly acceptable substitute. Is it? Then since no one questions that justification is by faith, it would follow from the use of the word 'by' that justification must be conditional upon the faithful merit of the sinner in bringing forth this equivalent 'righteousness'. Then faith becomes a saving labour, the truth that none is justified by works is overturned, and the sinner who can produce sufficiently meritorious 'faith' by dint of his hard labour, is thereby justified to the chagrin of his less virtuous brethren. If this be not confusion worse confounded, what is?

The appearance may seem specious when those who are so foolish as to make faith equivalent to righteousness put their error in their own terms, but the terms they use, like the legs of the lame, are not equal. They say, faith is an acceptable equivalent or substitute for righteousness. Oh? Whose righteousness? In their statements, it is just righteousness, period. And since this is in connection with faith, it would appear to juxtapose two qualities in man. But with justification we are not considering what is of man. With them, however, everything is of man, for craftily omitting the words 'of God' from 'righteousness', they propose faith as a kind of alternative to righteousness in man, and thus sound all very plausible. But to propose the faith of man as an equivalent, or alternative, to the righteousness of God sounds what it is: blasphemy.

Again, if the accounting of a believer's faith for righteousness meant that God accepted faith as if it were an equivalent

241

or substitute for righteousness, then, since we are justified by faith, it would follow that faith becomes the reason, ground or cause of justification. But we have shown that faith is not the reason for but the consequence of justification; that far from faith being the ground of justification, justification rests on the ground of a substitutionary atonement; and that the cause of justification is not faith but the free and everlasting love of the Father.

In the death of his own dear Son, God wrought out and Christ brought in a righteousness for the sinner which was complete and everlasting. Thus God effected a justification for the ungodly, the ground or basis of which was in the death of Christ. Yet if faith be a substitute for righteousness, and we are justified by faith, then the basis of justification must be faith. What? faith in the sinner a substitute for the righteousness of God in the blood of his Son? Faith the ground then on which both the efficacy and application of the atonement must be dependent? God forbid.

Faith may be a witness to the possession of the righteous sentence of justification, but the ground or basis of that righteous sentence lies in the atonement itself. The righteousness in justification is divine, and was wrought once and for all at the cross by the Father and the Son. But the faith in justification is wrought within the sinner, generation by generation, by the Holy Ghost through the word of God. This effectual inworking of the Holy Ghost is sure and certain to all those for whom Christ died, on whose behalf God wrought righteousness, to whose account that righteousness was placed, and who were justified by his blood.

When a sinner's eyes are opened, and he believes that Christ died for him, and that Christ's blood was shed for his sins, his belief is on the ground or basis upon which God brought in everlasting righteousness. He is believing that God in righteousness judged him in his Substitute. He is crediting that

God wrought a righteousness for him and put it to his account. His faith freely owns that God, having fully discharged his righteousness in judgment, through the blood of Jesus Christ, thereupon placed that righteousness to the account of him for whom Christ died. Hence righteousness is reckoned to him, not by his believing it, but by God's effecting it, God's righteous judgment being satisfied and at rest regarding his person through the death of Christ. He is 'justified by his blood.' When the sinner is brought to faith, that is what he believes.

Whence it follows that all the ungodly who are brought to faith by the interior calling and work of the Holy Ghost, believe that Christ died as their Substitute, and that all that Christ endured as their Substitute is effectually theirs. Otherwise substitution is no more substitution. The ungodly feel and know by the Holy Ghost within themselves that Christ shed his blood for them, and that in turn God wrought out a righteousness on their behalf in the death of Christ. They believe that this righteousness was unto them, and, indeed, that it is now upon them. How do they know that it is upon them? Because they believe. 'Unto all and upon all them that believe.'

They believe that they, the ungodly, now brought to faith, are the ones for whom God wrought out and brought in a righteousness by faith of Jesus Christ, which was thereupon accounted to them. But not then to their knowledge, who had not attained to the knowledge of God, much less to that of countless multitudes for whom Christ died in far-off places and distant times yet to come. However, each in his generation brought to faith, they know, they believe, they credit by the death of the Son of God on their behalf, by his blood shed for them, that the righteousness before unto them, is now upon them. And when they do so believe, their faith becomes the evidence of what they believe. They believe with their heart, yes, but they confess with their mouth also. From this confession the mystery hidden in the heart is made evident. Faith becomes the evidence of things not seen. Righteousness of God by faith of Jesus Christ unto and upon them is not seen, but their faith is seen, and in consequence their faith makes unseen, divine things apparent.

Evidently therefore their faith witnesses to divine righteousness being upon them, and so does the Holy Ghost. This is to be seen, men may see it, the world stands convicted by it, the Spirit himself bearing record as they testify with a joy in believing that is at once divine and palpable. Thus the coming of the Spirit to dwell in all them that believe convinces an unbelieving world 'of righteousness, because I go to my Father, and ye see me no more.' Nevertheless all those that are of faith see the Son by the Spirit, and bear witness, and show that his departure in death brought in righteousness and life to every one that believeth. This is 'justification unto life' with a witness.

The righteousness of God which was unto and is now upon every one that believeth is evident by their faith. Righteousness is no longer hidden in the deity, it is manifest in the faithful. It is no more a secret in heaven, it is revealed on earth. It does not remain a mystery in the sacrifice, it is evident in the faith of all those for whom that sacrifice was made. Thus the faith of the sinner, the believing of the ungodly, makes known of a certainty before God, to men, and to angels, that righteousness is upon them. What they believe is so evident by their believing it, that it may be said, their faith is counted for righteousness. One may count on it, that where such faith is, of necessity, there is righteousness.

It is evident from the faith of believers that righteousness is accounted to them, the Spirit himself bearing record, with the word as testimony. Faith is not the righteousness, God forbid, faith lays no claim to righteousness, faith renounces all righteousness of her own, faith believes in the righteousness of God wrought by Jesus Christ at the cross. Faith looks not at the things which are seen, but at the things which are not seen: for the things which are seen are temporal; but the things which are not seen are eternal. Faith looks to and believes in a righteousness that is eternal, that cannot be seen now, and could not be seen when it was mysteriously wrought by the Father and the Son two thousand years ago. Of this mysterious, divine, spiritual, invisible transaction of everlasting righteousness at the cross, recorded in the word of God, faith is the indisputable, visible, and tangible evidence.

So certain is it that every one whom the Father gave to the Son from eternity, for whom Christ died in time, to whom justifying righteousness is secure for ever, so certain is it, I say, that the Holy Ghost shall bring every one of these elect to saving faith, that it is said of them, their faith counted to them for righteousness. He who witnesses saving faith in the believer is as if he witnessed righteousness wrought for that believer at the cross. So sure is the righteousness of faith, and the faith that pertains to righteousness, that the evidence of the one is the witness of the other.

When such faith as this is in evidence, there righteousness of God is certain to have been imputed. Faith is an infallible witness of that righteousness. For every one that is of faith, Christ died, for them his blood was shed, and to their account righteousness of God is as certain as the fact that they believe. Then faith is an infallible testimony to the bringing in and imputing of righteousness. That is why it is said of him that worketh not, but believeth on him that justifieth the ungodly, his faith is counted for righteousness. The visible possession of the one is the seal of the invisible accounting of the other. So much so that the one is pledge for the other, as it is written, Abraham believed God, and it was counted to him for righteousness.

XIII

Faith Counted for Righteousness

GROUNDED in the atonement, righteousness of God was brought in by the blood of Jesus Christ, to be established through grace to the account of all the people of God. Because of righteousness, generation by generation, God pronounces the sentence of justification upon that people in their ungodliness. This sentence is believed, and hence sinners are justified by faith, righteousness having been imputed to them. It is not the atonement, but the righteousness of God brought in by the atonement, that is imputed. Thus faith is reckoned for righteousness, and righteousness is reckoned to faith.

The ground of justification is therefore the substitutionary atonement in which the Son of God was made a sacrifice for the redemption of his people. Whatever may be the bearing of the death of Christ upon the world, the atonement itself is specific, it is peculiar to the elect, it is an effectual redemption for all the chosen people. The atonement did not make their redemption possible, it made it a reality, it effected their redemption: 'thou hast redeemed us to God by thy blood.'

Justification rests on this. Take away the effectual redemption of all the chosen people of God by the blood of Christ, and the ground of the justification of the elect is destroyed. It is utterly destroyed, it becomes meaningless. The avoidance of election, hence of both effectual redemption and accomplished righteousness, makes the Bible an interminable maze, it turns the doctrine into an inextricable labyrinth. Because of fear of unpopularity, and the lust for worldly fame and honour, modern theologians, so-called doctors, clergymen and evan-gelists take the bottom out of justification by explaining away election, effectual redemption and accomplished righteousness in the death of Christ. Then everything falls through. Nothing remains but justification by relative merit on the part of those who 'accept', or, alternatively, universalism.

Take away election, and a general atonement for nobody in particular ensues. Bring in a general atonement, and a uni-versal justification for every one who chooses must follow. Then no one is justified. Not by the death of Christ. That death was for all. Then is universalism true? Are all justified thereby? No, it depends upon the choice of each. Then not one is justified by the death of Christ. If any are justified, it is by their ratifying the death of Christ, making it workable, on account of their meritorious choice. As to others, they are not so meritorious. Then the merit of one, as against the demerit of another, becomes the moving cause which permits God to have any effect whatsoever in the salvation of men. What a system.

Bastard Calvinists, who get their notions from the libraries of Ashdod, and call themselves Reformed for dropping the names of a few pass-word Puritans—but who, themselves, cannot say Shibboleth—hover with one eye on the public, and the other on the party line. 'How long halt ye between two opinions? If the LORD be God, serve him.' But they love the praise of men more than the praise of God, and hence set the word of God at nought by their traditions.

They have a head full of notions, and a judgment blocked by prejudice, whilst their heart remains void of experience. They prate about the biblical doctrine of justification, but what they mean is the human tradition of 'active and passive obedience'. They pay—whispered—lip-service to election, but their practice extols free will, intellectual pride, and human invention. They set about their tortured and tortuous wanderings through a series of quotations from the dead in order to explain the truth of the God of the living which they have already destroyed by their traditions, and confounded by their contradictions. Why seek ye the living among the dead? They themselves were never taught one gospel truth by the quickening Spirit, much less were they sent in the power of the Holy Ghost by the Lord of glory to teach others also. Let them alone: if the blind lead the blind, both shall fall into the ditch.

The Greek word λογίζομαι, *logizomai*, variously translated Impute, reckon, count, account, is derived from the verb λέγω, *legō*, To arrange, to gather, to say. The noun form of this word is λόγος, *logos*, A word, the word, speech, a thing uttered. There are eleven passages in which the word *logizomai* has been used in connection with the imputing of righteousness, or of faith for righteousness, although, in all, the word occurs in a variety of contexts some forty times in the New Testament.

Of the eleven occasions on which *logizomai* has been employed in connection with righteousness, twice the word has been translated Count or counted, twice Reckon or reckoned; twice Account or accounted; and five times Impute, imputed, or imputeth. No less than nine out of the eleven references occur in the Epistle to the Romans, and, of these nine, every one is in the fourth chapter. Out of the eleven occurrences of *logizomai* denoting the accounting, reckoning or imputing of righteousness to faith or faith for righteousness, the preponderance is heavily in favour of accounting faith for righteousness. In fact, only twice in the New Testament is it said that God imputes righteousness or that righteousness is imputed; nine times over, however, it is said that faith is imputed—counted, reckoned, accounted— for righteousness. It is to these nine passages that attention is now drawn.

In the third chapter of the Epistle to the Romans Paul the Apostle declares the righteousness of God manifested in the gospel by the faith of Jesus Christ, and goes on to show the nature of justification and the manner of God's justifying his people. In the fourth chapter the revelation proceeds to the imputing of righteousness, or of faith for righteousness. Here righteousness is assumed, and so is justification. Now the question is, How is the righteousness by which God justifies his people, imputed in their experience? To answer this question the apostle points to Abraham, in whose life and experience justification by faith had been fulfilled prophetically so as to provide a pattern for all who should follow after, and particularly for those upon whom the ends of the world are come, in the times of the gospel.

'Abraham believed God, and it was counted unto him for righteousness.' Three times over Genesis 15:6 is quoted in the New Testament, twice by Paul, Rom. 4:3 and Gal. 3:6, and once by James, Jas. 2:23. The revelation given prophetically in Abraham provides a well of salvation from which with joy the apostle draws the water of the Holy Ghost to set forth justification by faith. Abraham is seen as the exemplar, his believing as exemplary, and in him justification is set forth as an example the radiance of which shines to the ends of the earth and to the closing days of time.

More than any other person, and more than any other place —save, perhaps, 'The just shall live by his faith', Habakkuk 2:4— Abraham in Genesis 15:6 is cited to show the substance of the gospel and the essence of the faith. It is true to say that to the Apostle Paul the gospel of Christ could not properly be preached, nor could faith in him rightly be declared, without opening, enlarging, and applying the truth that 'Abraham believed God, and it was counted to him for righteousness.'

Here was the father of the faithful, the heir of the promises, the friend of God, the one in whose hearing was sworn the oath of the Almighty, who heard his immutable counsel, saw the vision of the righteousness of faith, of Christ, of Christ crucified, of the resurrection from the dead, of the heavenly country, and of the holy city. Here was the one in whom the gospel was preached before to the heathen, the one in whom all nations should be blessed. Here was the father of all the children of promise, the one in whom the gospel was ministered four hundred and thirty years before the law was given: in a word, here was the one of whom it was written, 'Abraham believed God, and it was counted to him for righteousness.'

From his quotation of Genesis 15:6 Paul proceeds, Rom. 4:3, to expound the truth that God accounts righteousness without works, bringing in David himself—'Even as' David, Rom. 4:6— as witness to the truth established in Abraham. Abraham was the source, and from that source Paul draws the doctrine which excludes boasting, includes the Gentiles, and establishes the law, developing each branch of the teaching with telling conviction. But in the last analysis everything stems from the moment that 'Abraham believed God, and it was counted to him for righteousness'. Then since this belief, and that occasion, was so vital, it behoves us to enquire, What did Abraham believe? He believed God, yes; but about what?

Genesis 15:6 states precisely, 'And he believed in the LORD, and he counted it to him for righteousness.' That is, he, the LORD, counted it, Abraham's belief, to him, Abraham, for righteousness. But it was not righteousness, it was faith. Yes, but that faith was counted to him for righteousness, and counted to him for righteousness by the LORD. Why? There can be but one answer: Because of the nature of that which Abraham believed. It is certain that faith in general is not, and Abraham's faith in particular was not, righteousness itself. Then righteousness, reckoned to Abraham, was objective to his faith. The righteousness was not in his belief, but in that which he believed. Yet that in which he believed was of such a nature that his belief could be counted—reckoned as if it

were, when it was not—for righteousness. What was it that
Abraham believed, that this should be so?

The immediate and obvious occasion of Abraham's belief,
Gen. 15:6, appears in the previous verse, in which the word
of the LORD came to Abraham, saying, He that shall come
forth out of thine own bowels shall be thine heir. And he
brought him forth beneath the stars of heaven that night,
and showed him, and said unto him, So shall thy seed be.
And he believed in the LORD, and he counted it to him for
righteousness, Gen. 15:4,5,6. But what has that statement—So
shall thy seed be—to do with righteousness? A great deal, and
Abraham knew that it had a great deal to do with righteousness, indeed, he believed that it had everything to do with
righteousness, and thus it was that he believed God and it
was counted to him for righteousness. However, in order to
understand how this was so, it is necessary first to enquire
more deeply into the events preceding and surrounding this
great promise to Abraham.

Faith being counted to Abraham for righteousness in
Genesis 15:6 was that root the sap of which the Holy Ghost
drew into Romans chapter four to bring to fruition the New
Testament teaching of the righteousness of faith. Abraham's
faith was the prototype of that faith by which the just should
live, and yet the extraordinary thing is that what Abraham
believed, Gen. 15:6, appeared to concern neither justification,
nor righteousness, nor atonement, but rather Abraham's heir:
'So shall thy seed be', Gen. 15:5. In fact, less is said about
what Abraham believed than that he believed. Certainly he
believed the promise, but more precisely, 'He believed in the
LORD', Gen. 15:6, or, Rom. 4:3, 'Abraham believed God'.

Here then, it is not what the LORD said, but the LORD himself
that is believed. The question follows, In what respect did he
believe the LORD? This is best answered by enquiring, In what
respect could he have believed the LORD? At the very least, in

respect of all that which had been revealed by the LORD to his saints in times past. At the most, in relation to all that had been revealed to Abraham personally, and was being revealed even at that moment.

Concerning the faith of Abraham, the father of the faithful, there existed a vast heritage of the work, ways and word of God which had been revealed to the patriarchs before his day. Without doubt, believing the LORD, Abraham believed all that had been wrought, revealed, and declared by the LORD from the very beginning. For example, he believed 'that the worlds were framed by the word of God, so that things which are seen were not made of things which do appear', Heb. 11:3.

Faith coming by hearing, and hearing by the word of God, it being given that Abraham believed in the LORD, it follows that he believed that 'In the beginning was the Word, and the Word was with God, and the Word was God. The same was in the beginning with God. All things were made by him; and without him was not anything made that was made. In him was life, and the life was the light of men.' Abraham believed that, he believed that the worlds were framed by the Word of God, that the Word was God, that the Word was with God, that the same was in the beginning with God, and that in him was life. He knew that only righteousness could bring in life. This was Abraham's light, and he rejoiced to see the day.

Abraham believed that by faith Abel offered unto God a more excellent sacrifice than Cain, by which he obtained witness that he was righteous, Heb. 11:4. Abraham knew that Abel's offering was of the firstlings of the flock and of the fat thereof: and if of the fat, then of the blood with the fat; and if of the blood with the fat, then of the sacrificial lamb. He knew that Abel offered the sacrifice by faith, by which he obtained witness that he was righteous, God testifying of his gifts. It follows of course, that Abel's righteousness was the righteousness of faith. Abraham believed that. How do we know that he even knew of it? By a twofold testimony. First, because God testified of Abel's gifts, Heb. 11:4, and second, in that Abel himself 'being dead yet speaketh'. If we at the ends of the world receive God's ancient testimony to Abel's gifts, and likewise hear the speech that still sounds forth, how much more Abraham at the dawn of time? Then if we believe the twofold witness, who are children of Abraham by faith, how much more the father of the faithful himself?

Likewise Abraham believed the testimony which God bare to believing Enoch, that he pleased God; for of all men Abraham knew that without faith it is impossible to please him. Just as he knew that he that cometh to God must believe that he is, and that he is a rewarder of them that diligently seek him, Heb. 11:5,6. For Abraham himself, called the friend of God, believed God, and pleased him by faith, and looked to him who translated the believing out of this present world, into the world to come, counting it a sure pledge to all the heirs of promise, set forth in the faithful testimony of believing Enoch.

Abraham believed God, despite the darkness, despite the serpent, despite the fall, despite sin, despite the curse, despite death, despite the judgment to come, he believed God. He believed God to overcome the darkness, the serpent, the fall, sin, the curse, death, and the judgment to come which he feared. Like Noah, he was moved with fear, knowing that God would judge the world in righteousness not by water for a generation, but by fire for evermore, of which the fire which fell upon Sodom and Gomorrah—Abraham having seen the country burning as a furnace with his own eyes—was but a token. Observing Noah's belief, Abraham looked for a spiritual ark by faith, an ark that would carry him and his seed through the coming deluge of eternal fire. Like Noah, Abraham builded an altar, Gen. 8:20; 12:7,8, and 13:18, becoming heir with him of the righteousness which is by faith, Heb. 11:7. And how should Abraham know so much of Noah, that he should follow the faith of him who found grace in the eyes of the LORD? Because for well over half a century Abraham and Noah were contemporaries.

By faith Abraham, when he was called to go out into a place which he should after receive for an inheritance, obeyed; and he went out, not knowing whither he went. By faith he sojourned in the land of promise, as in a strange country, dwelling in tents with Isaac and Jacob, the heirs with him of the same promise. Yes, by faith he went out into a place, the land of promise, but he never received it as an inheritance, he dwelt in it as in a strange country. What did he think of this, did his faith fail him? No, for he looked through the earthly sign to the heavenly reality. He gazed beyond time into eternity. He saw past death to the resurrection and the life. Hence Abraham endured as seeing him who is invisible, receiving the promise of earthly Canaan as a heavenly pledge that he should be heir of the world to come, Rom. 4:13.

In this world, Abraham received not so much as a foot's breadth of land. For all the promise, he must needs purchase a burying place, a graveyard, from the sons of Heth, to lay to rest his wife. Nothing. Abraham had nothing. No land. Despite the promise, he was a stranger in the land, a sojourner, he wandered as a nomad, dwelling in tents to the third generation. No land to build a house. No permanent building. No city for his posterity. Did he still believe, this ancient patriarch Abraham, yet dwelling in tents with Isaac and Jacob, still believe, after all that? Yes, by faith he 'looked for a city which hath foundations, whose builder and maker is God', Heb. 11:10.

Abraham's faith, the faith of God's elect, true faith, saving faith, the faith that is of God, did not, and could not fail. Nor shall that of his spiritual seed. 'These all died in faith, not having received the promises, but having seen them afar off, and were persuaded of them, and embraced them, and confessed that they were strangers and pilgrims on the earth.' Abraham, and his seed, looked for fulfilment after death, by a better resurrection, in the world to come, and regarded all earthly promises and inheritances as but figures of the true. 'For they that say such things declare plainly that they seek a country.' 'They desire a better country, that is, an heavenly: wherefore God is not ashamed to be called their God: for he hath prepared for them a city', Heb. 11:14,16. Now, this is of the essence of the faith of Abraham, who 'believed in the LORD, and he counted it to him for righteousness.'

Abraham, who rejoiced to see Christ's day, believed in the LORD when he met Melchizedek, Gen. 14:18,19,20, and gave him tithes of all. What did Abraham see in this Melchizedek, that he should give him a tenth part of all? And who was this that blessed even Abraham, for 'without all contradiction the less is blessed of the better'? Indeed, who was this, said to be Abraham's better, and what did the friend of God, the father of the faithful, see in him? Abraham saw one 'without father, without mother, without descent, having neither beginning of days, nor end of life; one made like unto the Son of God, abiding a priest continually', Heb. 7:3. And Abraham believed in the LORD, and it was counted to him for righteousness.

In the person of Melchizedek, by faith Abraham beheld the King in his beauty. The name Melchizedek is a compound which unites the Hebrew word for King, *melek*, with that for Righteousness, *tsedeq*. It is, by interpretation, King of righteousness. Then he was one who reigned over righteousness, over every form of righteousness, over it as such; his dominion was over the quality, whether human or divine in degree. Of necessity therefore, righteousness was his to dispense: it was in his royal gift. He reigned over human righteousness, legal righteousness, divine righteousness: otherwise, where were the dominion? He was King of righteousness, had dominion over it in all its forms, had the disposition of it, there could be no area of righteousness as such in which he had not prevailed. Righteousness, absolutely, was his dominion: it was his administration.

His was a dominion of peace. Melchizedek was first by interpretation, King of Salem, which is, King of peace. Then, righteousness and peace have kissed each other. The basis of peace is righteousness established: being justified by faith we have peace with God through our Lord Jesus Christ. This Prince of peace who reigned through righteousness upon mount Zion, brought forth bread and wine, symbols of a broken body and shed blood to come, which should bring in everlasting righteousness. Melchizedek blessed Abraham. 'Peace be unto thee.' The ground of peace, the only ground of it, lay in the satisfied righteousness of the most high God. This brought in the blessing. Nothing but a vicarious sacrifice, nothing but substitutionary atonement, could ever satisfy divine righteousness. Till there was found a broken body, and shed blood, there could be no established righteousness, no justification, no peace, and no blessing. But in a figure the King of righteousness brought forth bread and wine, and blessed the believer in peace, and with peace. And Abraham believed in the LORD, and he counted it to him for righteousness.

All this, and much else, was embraced and experienced by the faith of Abraham: indeed, it constituted the background of the occasion on which the word of the LORD came to Abraham, saying, 'he that shall come forth out of thine own bowels shall be thine heir. And he brought him forth abroad, and said, Look now toward heaven, and tell the stars, if thou be able to number them: and he said unto him, So shall thy seed be.' Gen. 15:4,5. This was the first promise, the promise of an heir. The second promise was like unto it. 'In the same day the LORD made a covenant with Abram, saying, Unto thy seed have I given this land, from the river of Egypt unto the great river, the river Euphrates', Gen. 15:18. This was the second promise, the promise of an inheritance.

The promises were alike in that both had an immediate earthly object, the figure of an ultimate spiritual reality. Isaac was the immediate earthly object of the first promise, but, Paul assures us, Christ, the true seed of Abraham, was the ultimate spiritual fulfilment: 'Now to Abraham and his seed were the promises made. He saith not, And to seeds, as of many; but as of one, And to thy seed, which is Christ', Gal. 3:16. Likewise the promised inheritance was Christ's, and passed beyond the immediate earthly land of Canaan to the ultimate spiritual fulfilment of the world to come, as saith the Apostle Paul, 'that he should be the heir of the world', Rom. 4:13.

The promises to Abraham, of an heir and of an inheritance, took occasion from the earthly circumstances of Abraham's lifetime. But the spiritual reality in the mind of God—and in the faith of Abraham—soared beyond those circumstances into the realm of what was eternal, spiritual, divine, and supernatural. For all this, the ultimate fulfilment of the promises, that of Christ as opposed to Isaac, and that of the world to come in contrast with Canaan, still retained a connection with the immediate circumstances of Abraham, and with their earthly signification, so that the heavenly reality really did answer in every way to the thing promised. Christ was of the seed of Abraham as pertaining to the flesh, just as much as Isaac, and the world to come will be constituted from the purged elements of the world that now is, and therefore from the land that was immediately promised.

There can be no doubt but that Abraham perceived by faith the ultimate, the divine, the spiritual meaning behind and beyond the immediate, the earthly, and the ostensible realisation of the promises. Nor can there be any doubt but that he clearly grasped what stood in the way of that ultimate fulfilment. Two impassable barriers, insuperable obstacles, stood in the way of divine accomplishment. Abraham perceived this. The first was death. And the second was judgment. Death stood between Abraham and a natural heir: how much more a spiritual? And judgment, the righteous judgment of the world, stood in the way of Abraham gaining the inheritance of what was promised in the present world: how much more of the world to come? And Abraham understood perfectly that his own sin, his own death, and his own condemnation stood in the way of his enjoyment of either.

Resurrection was the divine answer to the first. The world to come was the counsel of God in response to the second. And substitutionary atonement, bringing in everlasting righteousness for all the heirs of promise, was the provision of the Almighty which should meet every need of Abraham both in this world and in that which is to come. Hence it followed that inherent in the promise of an heir lay the assurance of the power of God in the resurrection from the dead. Immanent in the promise of an inheritance appeared the creation of a new heavens and a new earth. And implied in the promise to Abraham that he should receive the blessing were the dawning rays of the coming manifestation of the righteousness of God by faith of Jesus Christ unto all and upon all them that believe. 'And he believed in the LORD; and he counted it to him for righteousness', Gen. 15:6.

The LORD brought Abraham forth abroad that night, bidding him 'look now toward heaven, and tell the stars, if thou be able to number them.' And Abraham went forth abroad, and stood, the sand beneath his feet, and he looked up, and saw the stars innumerable shining against the dark of the night sky. 'So shall thy seed be.' And he felt the myriad grains of sand under his soles, between his toes, yet stretching out along the strand incalculable in number. 'So shall thy seed be.' And the LORD said to Abram, 'I am the LORD that brought thee out of Ur of the Chaldees, to give thee this land to inherit it.' An heir and an inheritance. But between him and the realisation, between promise and fulfilment, stood his own body, now dead, when he was about an hundred years old, and the deadness of Sarah's womb, she being some ninety years of age. Death. Death lay between.

Although he himself was alive, his body was as good as dead, past bearing seed, past living for an inheritance: 'now dead'. And likewise Sarah, his wife, of whom it was said, 'The deadness of Sarah's womb'. Dried up, past conception, past bearing children. Death stood in the way, the vitality of their bodies necessary to the fulfilment of the promise 'now dead', their faint, flickering hold upon the mortal frame almost gone. Death stood in the way, and if so, sin. Unforgiven sin, unatoned sins: sin brought in death. And after death the judgment. A judgment, as the flood had shown, certain to all the world, and the whole earth. Sin, death, and the judgment to come. If the promises were sure, what was the answer? Abraham believed God, yes, but precisely because he believed God about the heir, and therefore the resurrection, and about the inheritance, and hence the world to come, he also believed God about sin, death, and the judgment to come.

Because of this, Abraham asked 'Lord GOD, whereby shall I know that I shall inherit it?' Gen. 15:8. That is, How can this be, in view of unforgiven sin, imminent death, and certain judgment, standing unresolved between the promise and its fulfilment? 'And he said unto him, Take me an heifer of three years old, and a she goat of three years old, and a ram of three years old, and a turtle dove, and a young pigeon.'

And Abraham took unto him all these, and divided them in the midst, and laid the pieces one against another, but the birds divided he not. Thus Abraham stood between the great reeking sides of the heifer which he had divided, the bloody flanks of the goat, and of the ram, the slain pieces high about and around him, the dead birds at his feet, blood on his hands and body, blood a widening circle darkening the sand beneath his feet: he stood upon the blood, the blood soaked pieces of the slain sacrifice surrounding him, in a manner enclosed in the death of the substitute. By this means he would know in his experience how the promises should be fulfilled.

Standing upon and sprinkled by the blood of the atonement, enclosed in the substitutionary death on his behalf, here was a death that he himself had caused by his own deeds, here was blood which he himself had shed with his own hands. Abraham knew, Abraham knew by the three beasts of sacrifice, by the hint of resurrection three times over, by the heavenly witness of that which was undivided in death, by the lamb slain from the foundation of the world, he knew that divine righteousness would be answered by substitutionary atonement. 'And he believed in the LORD, and he counted it to him for righteousness.'

Abraham knew how and he knew that the righteousness of God would be met in vicarious judgment upon the substitutionary sacrifice. He knew it experimentally, he knew it as taught of God; he knew it inwardly, and he knew it by faith from afar off: 'Every man therefore that hath heard, and hath learned of the Father, cometh unto me.' And Abraham had heard, and had learned, and had come to Christ in a figure, and had been found in him, and found in him at the place of atonement, and had rejoiced to see his day.

Also at this time the father of the faithful was taught of God concerning the giving of the law to his seed some four hundred years in the future; of the darkness and obscurity of the legal dispensation; of the ages that lay between his receiving the promises and their fulfilment in the coming of Christ; and finally of the justification of all the children of promise by substitutionary atonement. And Abraham believed in the LORD, and it was accounted to him for righteousness. Sin would be covered, death would be abolished, judgment would be met and everlasting righteousness would be brought in world without end.

Abraham would be justified by faith. How should he know of the righteousness of faith? 'And it came to pass, that when the sun went down, and it was dark, behold a smoking furnace, and a burning lamp that passed between those pieces', Gen. 15:17. This answered to the angel of the LORD kindling the fire, and ascending in the flame, of Manoah's sacrifice, Judges 13:19,20. It answered to the fire of God falling on the burnt offering of Elijah at mount Carmel. And it is interpreted by the word of the LORD to Isaiah the prophet, 'For Zion's sake will I not hold my peace, and for Jerusalem's sake I will not rest, until the righteousness thereof go forth as brightness, and the salvation thereof as a lamp that burneth', Isa. 62:1. This was fulfilled when the legal dispensation had run its course, and when the righteousness of spiritual Zion, and of Jerusalem above, Abraham's seed, went forth. This righteousness is called the righteousness of God by faith of Jesus Christ, which went forth against all those divinely hidden in him for whom he was substitute at the cross, and when the lamp of the law burned against the transgressors concealed in his side who was made a curse for them at Golgotha. Of this Abraham was a prophetic witness, a promised partaker, and a distant believer: 'And it was counted to him for righteousness.'

What was counted to him for righteousness? Faith. 'But to him that worketh not, but believeth on him that justifieth the ungodly, his faith is counted for righteousness', Rom. 4:5. Abraham's belief about himself, was that he was ungodly. Abraham's belief about God, was that he would justify the ungodly. Abraham's belief about righteousness was that God would bring in righteousness to the account of the ungodly through substitutionary atonement.

These were the things about which he believed the LORD: it was his faith. He believed that the seed of promise, by whom righteousness would be accomplished, was very far distant in the future. He believed that the great atonement, of which

261

animal sacrifices were the figure, was ages and generations ahead in time. He believed that whilst justifying righteousness lay in the remote future, present faith was counted for the distant object in which it reposed, that is, it was counted to him for righteousness.

The atonement for sin lay vastly distant in the ages to come, but Abraham believed in that atonement, he believed that God would account righteousness to him, he believed that he would be justified by faith, vast distance or not. Such belief is called, The faith of God's elect. It is the faith that is of God, a faith no less certainly wrought of God than the atoning work in which it believes, whether that atonement be in the future, as it was with Abraham, or in the past, as it is with us. The faith and the justification, the work of the Spirit and the work of the Father and the Son, the work in the believer and the work in Christ, alike are wholly of God.

The apostle calls justifying righteousness the righteousr.ess of faith. Hence the patriarch Abraham's faith—for all that when his belief was present, the righteousness in which he believed was distant—Abraham's faith was the divine—mark that, the divine—pledge of Abraham's justification. His faith was therefore counted to him for the thing in which it reposed: it was counted to him for righteousness.

Of the nine passages in which faith is said to be imputed, counted, or accounted for righteousness, seven are in the fourth chapter of Romans. In Rom. 4:3 the apostle commences his teaching by quoting Genesis 15:6. The remaining six references to faith being counted for righteousness in this chapter follow in sequence as the apostle expounds this quotation. Twice more reference is made to faith being counted for righteousness, and in both cases, Gal. 3:6 and James 2:23, the passage concerning Abraham—Gen. 15:6—is quoted directly. All the references, whether the developed argument of Romans four, or the quotations in Galatians and James respectively, apply the words spoken of the faith of Abraham, to that of all his spiritual seed. What was true of the father is true of all the children of promise, that is, of every one that is of the faith of Abraham, the father of the faithful.

The justification of both Abraham and David, described in Romans chapter four, clearly rests upon the basis of the atonement. If so, the imputation of righteousness must be grounded upon the effectual remission of sins, the actual forgiveness of the sinner, and the accomplished redemption of all the heirs of promise through the blood of Jesus Christ. However, it is not the atonement itself but the righteousness brought in by the atonement that is imputed. Therefore, since righteousness stands to the sinner's account for no other cause than that of the shed blood of Jesus Christ, it follows that the imputing of that righteousness to faith in the experience of the sinner neither adds to nor subtracts from the righteousness itself. Such faith, wrought by the Holy Ghost, testifies to a righteousness accomplished outside of the sinner's experience on the one hand, and unaltered by it on the other.

Faith is counted for righteousness precisely because it is the evidence that righteousness has been accounted to the believer by the blood of Jesus Christ. When faith is counted for righteousness, what is not seen—not in evidence—is the substitutionary atonement wrought for that sinner. What is not seen—not in evidence—is the righteousness of God put to the account of that sinner when atonement was made on his behalf. When the Holy Ghost brings that sinner to faith, what is seen—what is in evidence—is the faith of God's elect: this bears witness to the unseen and divinely wrought atonement; it is the evidence of the invisible righteousness of God put to his account in heaven before God.

Then that visible, evident, confessed faith, the faith of God's elect, to which the Holy Ghost bears witness, is an infallible and certain testimony that to this believer both atonement and righteousness pertain. This faith cannot fail:

it can never fall away. Such faith may safely and surely be credited as certain witness of effectual atonement, just as it may be counted as irrefutable evidence of imputed righteousness. In a word, faith may be, and faith is, counted for righteousness.

The covenant cannot be seen. The atonement cannot be seen. The righteousness cannot be seen. None of these things was visible aforetime to Abraham, none was visible during the crucifixion, and none is visible to us in retrospect. These are things that pertain to the unseen work of the invisible God, declared in that sealed doctrine which, without the teaching and revelation of the Holy Ghost, appears but a maze of confusion even to the wisest and most prudent of men. But the Holy Ghost brings in faith, teaching the spiritually exercised soul by the powerful and inward application of the word of truth. Thus faith comes by hearing, and hearing by the word of God.

Now, faith is in a manner visible. Faith can be seen, must be heard, confesses the work of God, answers to the truth, beholds the Saviour, comes from God, subsists by the Holy Ghost, and is attended by a divine testimony from heaven above. The Spirit of God must and shall bring to faith all those given to the Son by the Father before the world was, for whom the Son came into the world to die at Golgotha, and to whose account righteousness of God was reckoned when the blood of atonement was shed. How could the Spirit fail in such a work? The work of God in Christ is certain to the man with faith, just as his faith is certain because of the work of God in Christ. Righteousness by the blood of Christ witnesses to the man that is to be brought to faith, and faith by the Holy Ghost witnesses to righteousness by the blood of Christ. Then faith can be as sure of righteousness as righteousness can be of faith. If so, faith may be counted for righteousness. It is the visible proof, the incontestable witness of righteousness. Then, being in evidence, faith may certainly be counted for righteousness.

The manifestation of true saving faith wrought by the Holy Ghost from heaven, formed by the word of truth, to which witness is borne by the presence of the living God, plainly testifies of eternal election, particular redemption, substitutionary atonement, imputed righteousness, effectual calling, assured endurance and everlasting glory. It shows the faith that stands not in the will of man, neither in the arm of the flesh, nor in the letter of scripture, but in the mighty power of God. This is faith not in word only, but in power also. It must be so, just as the Holy Ghost must bring to faith all the heirs of promise. Otherwise, the promise could never be certain any more than the inheritance could be secure.

The heirs of promise were chosen before the world was created or Adam was formed. They were secure in Christ before the serpent came in or the fall took place. They were given the promise of life before sin and death existed. They were delivered from this present evil world by the death of the second Man, the last Adam, the Lord from heaven. On their behalf everlasting righteousness was brought in by the Father and the Son. For them the Holy Ghost was both received and sent from heaven by the Lord of glory ascended to the right hand of the Majesty on high. That same Holy Spirit has come to fulfil in them the work of faith with power according to the will of the Father and the word of the Son. Hence of them it can and must be said, Their faith is counted to them for righteousness.

This can be said of none other. Neither can it be said of any faith other than their faith. There is none other. It is fatuous, nothing other than perversity, to talk of 'other faiths'. There are no other faiths. According to Christ's apostle, there is one faith, Eph. 4:5, just as there is one Lord. I am the way, the truth, and the life: no man cometh unto the Father but by me, said Jesus, Jn. 14:6. To speak of heathendom as possessing 'faiths' betrays an ignorance of divinity that is as black as the night. There may be various religions; numerous systems of works; many spirits and demons; multitudes of idols; varieties of superstitions; countless perversions of the faith: 'For though there be that are called gods, whether in heaven or in earth—as there be gods many, and lords many—to us there is but one God, the Father, of whom are all things, and we in him; and one Lord Jesus Christ, by whom are all things, and we by him', I Cor. 8:5,6. Therefore, 'One Lord, one faith, one baptism', Eph. 4:5. One faith, that is, the faith of God's elect, Titus 1:1. Everything else is heathendom and fallen Christendom, being under the darkness of the god of this world. Any faith other than the one faith is presumption, the blinding delusion sent of God to those who despise the truth in the last days, II Thess. 2:10,11,12.

Nevertheless even to the end of the age, to the last day, the foundation of God stands sure, and its seal remains unbroken. As certainly as in the beginning so to the end the rod of Christ's strength shall go forth out of Zion, and he must rule in the midst of his enemies. The Holy Ghost remains more than able to bring to faith every one whom the Father gave to Christ, for whom Christ died, to whose account the Father and the Son brought in everlasting righteousness. Of these it can, it must, and it shall be said to the very end, Their faith is counted to them for righteousness.

Such faith issues from the quickening and regeneration of the Holy Ghost, it is wrought through belief of the truth, it comes by hearing, and hearing by the word of God, and it is preceded by that conviction of sin and wrath which brings the sinner self-condemned and without strength to Jesus Christ, and him crucified. Therefore it is written, Blessed is the man whom thou chastenest, O Lord, and teachest out of thy law. Presumptuous false faith, however, blown about by every wind that stirs up the religious world, and the worldly religious, rests on nothing more solid than the will of man, having no deeper foundation than the fall, and no stronger anchor than the arm of the flesh.

Presumptuous false faith, as opposed to that precious faith which stands in the power of God, appeals to the flesh, it does not convert from the flesh; it entices into the world, it does not call out from the world; it draws down to earth, it does not soar up to heaven. Presumption beholds man: it cannot see God. False faith views the outward creeds, churches, ministries, and evangelisms of Christendom: it has no heavenly vision of Christ, neither spiritual power from his ministry, nor has it been taught by divine revelation of his evangel. Presumptuous false faith rests upon popular applause and acceptance, the consensus of the majority, the traditions of man, and the outward letter of scripture. It has no idea of the living God, of the power of the Holy Ghost, or of the word of God. It knows nothing of what is spiritual, heavenly, divine, or supernatural. Presumption will not stand when the rains of heaven fall, when the floods of judgment come, or when the winds of eternity blow. 'For this shall every one that is godly pray unto thee in a time when thou mayest be found: surely in the floods of great waters they shall not come nigh unto him', Psalm 32:6.

To suit the flesh, presumptuous false faith patches together a gossamer light garment of biblical inconsistency, which will never cover the poor soul in the day of wrath. Woe be to them that cover, but not by my Spirit, saith the Lord. To accommodate worldly ease, intellectual freedom, liberty of choice, and the pride of life, the presumptuous unite their opinions with what they consider to be the more agreeable parts of scripture, fashioning a maze of contradictions in which the wanderer can never rest, nor be stable for two moments together in his conscience. Of such it can never be said, no, not even by themselves, Their faith is counted to them for righteousness. To them, these words present an unintelligible dilemma which can never be resolved.

Nevertheless, of all those to whom presumption is the abominable thing which their soul hateth, that is, of all the children of promise, of all the heirs of glory, it can properly, intelligibly, and consistently be said—it must be said—Their faith is counted to them for righteousness. Blessed of the Father before all worlds, redeemed by the Son in the end of the world, called by the Spirit till the world is no more, this is that people which shall hear the words at the threshold of the world to come, 'Come, ye blessed of my Father, inherit the kingdom prepared for you from the foundation of the world.' Happy is that people, that is in such a case: yea, happy is that people, whose God is the LORD.

This is that people which shall not escape chastisement: humiliation and afflictions abide them; they may be sure of straitness and tribulation; persecution and the worst kind of vilification shall be their portion. They are poor in spirit, they mourn, weep, lament, are contrite in heart, melted in soul, meek in disposition. They are pilgrims and strangers, in a strange country, sojourners in the earth. Yes, but to them atonement is certain, redemption secure, righteousness assured, and the resurrection of the just settled. Already 'justified by his blood', of each one of this people it can be said of a truth, by the witness of the Holy Ghost, by the word of the Son of God, and by the oath of the Almighty, 'His faith is counted unto him for righteousness.'

XIV

Righteousness Imputed

W HILST the phrase 'faith counted for righteousness' and the word 'justify' each occur several times over in the New Testament, the expression 'righteousness imputed' and the word 'justification' appear but two or three times respectively. The first reference to 'righteousness imputed' occurs in Rom. 4:6, 'the blessedness of the man unto whom God imputeth righteousness without works', and the second and last in Rom. 4:11, 'that righteousness might be imputed unto them also.'

The blessedness of the man unto whom God imputeth righteousness without works is described by David in the thirty-second psalm, quoted by Paul in Romans 4:6-8. The blessing stands in the forgiveness of iniquities, the covering of sins, and in sin not being imputed. The Apostle Paul interprets the words used by David in a way that emphasises the lawlessness of what has been forgiven, the wilfulness of what has been covered, and the inwardness of what is no longer imputed: what a blessing, then, comes to the man unto whom God imputeth righteousness without works!

The blessedness which David describes, and which Paul calls imputing righteousness without works, is neither an explanation of the righteousness imputed, nor a description of the atonement, it is an account of the experience of forgiveness. David does not describe and neither does Paul reiterate the cause of forgiveness but the effect of it. The effect upon a man of being forgiven—whatever may be the cause of that forgiveness—is that he is 'blessed'. 'Blessed' is he whose transgression is forgiven; 'blessed' is the man unto whom the LORD imputeth not iniquity, Ps. 32:1,2. David is not describing the basis of the man's experience, but the experience itself: 'Even as David also describeth the blessedness of the man.' It is the blessing, and the consequent sensation of blessedness, that is stated by Paul to be the effect of 'God imputing righteousness without works', that is, the experience of righteousness being imputed.

Then that which David describes and Paul quotes is not the work of God in bringing in righteousness for his people, but the work of God in imputing righteousness to that people. This is a work commensurate with the forgiveness of iniquities, the blotting out of sins, and of the Lord not imputing sin. This is not the work that accomplished salvation, it is the work that applies salvation. It is not the work on which a just pardon is based, but the work of granting a just pardon on that basis. It is not what was done for sinners at the cross, it is what conveys to sinners what was done at the cross. It is not how forgiveness was wrought, but how it is received. It is not the work of atonement, but the application of the atonement. Then, David neither describes nor does Paul quote the work of God in Christ, but the work of God by the Holy Ghost.

Nevertheless both Psalm 32:1,2 and Romans 4:6-8 assume an effectual atonement; they imply the accomplishment of redemption by the death of Christ. Both passages take for granted the bringing in of justifying righteousness by his blood, and the completion of salvation by the offering up of the body of Jesus once and for all. Vicarious atonement, substitutionary sacrifice, bear mute witness to the truth that only upon such a basis could forgiveness justly rest. The burnt offering, the meat offering, the peace offering, the sin offering, and the trespass offering alike point to the foundation of David's experience and Paul's confirmation: 'Once in the end of the world hath he appeared to put away sin by the sacrifice of himself.' A broken body and shed blood provide the only basis for the forgiveness of iniquities, the covering of sins, and the not imputing sin, that is, for the imputing of righteousness without works: 'that God might be just, and the justifier of him which believeth in Jesus.'

Assuming such a basis of blessedness, David describes and Paul declares the actual granting of remission, the effectual inworking of salvation, the vital application of redemption, in a word, the experimental imputing of righteousness. Thus as one the holy men combine; the voices of Old and New Testament agree; the psalm and the epistle unite; the king and the apostle declare in unison: 'Salvation belongeth unto the LORD: thy blessing is upon thy people. Selah.'

It is God that applies the word of righteousness. It is the Holy Ghost by whom the blessing is brought. It is the Spirit who bears the inward witness that righteousness is imputed. Salvation is brought home to the interior man, the hidden man of the heart, by the Spirit of God. This is the blessing, but modern evangelism has utterly destroyed that blessing.

How is this? Because modern evangelism stands in the technique of man, finding its response in nothing but the decision of men. How can this deliver from the flesh or from worldliness? It is itself of the flesh, it is of the essence of worldliness. It is a system that is for man, that bends divinity to please man, that accommodates both methods and 'message' to the world. This sets aside the election of God: 'According as he hath chosen us before the foundation of the world.' It dispenses with the will of God: 'It is not of him that willeth, nor of him that runneth, but of God that showeth mercy.' It makes nothing of the decision of God: 'Ye have not chosen me, but I have chosen you.' It makes the salvation of God at the cross dependent on human agreement: 'Who hath saved us, and called us with an holy calling, not according to our

271

works, but according to his own purpose and grace, which was given us in Christ Jesus before the world began.' And it degrades justifying righteousness into a generality for the whole world, in which man has the say, and God is a helpless bystander: 'Whom he did predestinate, them he also called: and whom he called, them he also justified: and whom he justified, them he also glorified.'

Again, modern evangelism has utterly destroyed the blessing because it dispenses with—nay, it denigrates—feelings, sensations, and vital experience. Was it not a matter of feelings to David, when he cried out in an agony of conviction, 'O Lord, rebuke me not in thine anger, neither chasten me in thy hot displeasure'? Was he void of sensation when he groaned under conviction of sin, 'My sin is ever before me', and, 'I have roared by reason of the disquietness of my heart'? Was Paul empty of inward experience when a light shone from heaven, the voice of words thundered in his soul, and God revealed his Son in him? The truth is, substituting human art and persuasion for the interior sensations of the Holy Ghost, and putting the will of man in place of the mighty power of God, the modern evangelist and the modern evangelical must deny feelings, sensations, and saving experience, because their whole system is one which denies the powerful operations and spiritual inworking of the living God in bringing vital regeneration to every one of his purchased people.

But all who have felt the word of God come with power, all who have been under the conviction and operation of the Holy Ghost, all in whom the Father has revealed the Son, are brought to know the blessing in their experience, and hence can say from the heart 'It is God that justifieth'. To such as these, the forgiveness of transgression, the covering of sin, the not imputing of iniquity is nothing to do with the intellect, or dead letter of scripture; neither does it stand in the form of godliness, or in human sentiment, but in the mighty inworking of the Holy Ghost, and in the power thereof. Hence David describeth the blessedness of the man unto whom God imputeth righteousness without works: the blessing is, that God does it, not man, not the church, not oneself, God does the work, and God applies the work: O, what a blessing! Unspeakable; divine. Here is the blessedness: God has done this, even God Almighty. How certain to the soul, how joyful. Precisely because it is of God: God by the Holy Ghost does the work.

It is God that writes forgiveness upon the heart, the Holy Ghost who testifies within that sin is covered, it is the LORD that imputeth not iniquity: what sweet, what heavenly, what unutterable comforts are these: God himself descends and condescends to reveal Christ, fill with the Spirit, seal the pardon, settle the forgiveness, and impute righteousness to the helpless and convicted sinner. And of this blessedness, and these divine consolations, the fallen church, the apostasy, bastard Calvinists, superficial Arminians, letter-learners, dead-letter salvationists, and modern evangelicals know nothing, absolutely nothing. How could they know? It is what they despise. And yet what they despise is the doctrine by which, the experience through which, and the way in which God imputeth righteousness without works. Yet not satisfied with the writing of 'Ichabod' over their own doors, latter-day evangelical opportunists have set about deceiving the generation that is to come also, which is removing the old landmarks with a witness.

But what does David mean by 'transgression', Ps. 32:1, and why does Paul call this 'iniquities'—plural—Rom. 4:7? The word David uses is *pesha*, generally translated 'transgression', an English compound word derived from the Latin *trans*, 'across', and *gradi*, 'walk, step'. To transgress, therefore, as David uses the word, means To trample underfoot, to walk over the holy commandment of God. Out of a total of ninety-three references, *pesha* has been translated transgression eighty-four times. It is a word that has God's holy law in view. It is a matter of law.

Hence the word Paul uses—and multiplies, using the plural, as if to indicate the increase of the transgression—is *anomia*, a Greek compound comprising the preposition *a* and the noun *nomos*, 'law'. The use of the prefix *a* before the word for law however, radically qualifies the meaning, it dismisses and makes void the whole idea of law. It is not merely anti, or against law, it is nullification of law, it is to be utterly contemptuous of the law. The meaning, and correct translation, of *anomia*, therefore, is 'lawlessness'. Then the apostle speaks here of lawlessness, showing that the transgression of the transgressor is not simply a question of trampling the law underfoot, defying the Lawgiver, but one which shows complete contempt for the existence of law, thereby dismissing the Lawgiver as unworthy of notice. And if in the plural, the implication is that the transgressor continues in this course as a habit of life, a bent of existence. So Paul properly interprets and enhances David's meaning.

Whether it be the Hebrew *pesha* or the Greek *anomia*, it is a question of relationship to law. The law predicates man's obligation firstly towards God. It asserts God's rights over man. The assertion of rights, and the corresponding existence of obligation in those held accountable, is the basis of law. This may be expressed as an all-embracing concept, 'Thou shalt love the LORD thy God with all thy heart, and with all thy soul, and with all thy might.' Or as that concept applied to various—say, ten—areas of accountability, so that its essential light is caught by distinct facets of obligation, as, The right of God constantly to receive, and the duty of man wholeheartedly to give, the worship of total devotion as the object of human being. Again, that God should be fully recognised, known, and hallowed, according to his revealed nature and real character. That man should not debase, misconstrue or misrepresent that nature or character; nor should he add to, subtract from, multiply or divide the sum of the revelation of God and his worship, much less invent contrary religions or notions which rob God of his glory, giving it to another.

Moreover the law requires that God should be the cause of man's rest, confidence, trust, and true repose, as set forth in the Sabbath. That man ought not to work, either with mind, heart, will, intention, conversation, hand, or foot, so as to disturb that rest, presuming to bring God in as debtor to his works of supposed merit. The law speaks of God's right to holy reverence, awe, and constant fear from man, and of man's obligation to live so that God is ever the reality of his existence. Once more, that man should utterly and wholeheartedly submit to God's absolute and Almighty authority, and every expression of that authority, without doubt, question, or rebellion, inwardly or outwardly. Likewise to bow and yield willingly to all superiors and powers raised up by God above one's own station. These facets of the law pertain to God and his worship. There are those that pertain to man and his rights.

The law, which has respect to the Being of God, and that of man, and of the obligation of accountable man in respect of that Being, and of human being, requires the safeguard and support of the life of mankind. That is, by deeds and words, by rebukes and encouragements, life, especially that which is lived to Godward, is to be preserved. Likewise man's right to his own property, both physical and moral, such as reputation and honour. This applies also in relation to the right of women, which is to be respected, and not violated, particularly as it pertains to the wife of another. The law forbids the wickedness of slander, talebearing, false report, and evil speaking, besides deceiving, lying, and misrepresentation. This is so of all coveting whatsoever things may be in the world that have not fallen to us as our lot in the providence of God, as all discontent with our station, ambition to change our estate by the acquisition of money, status, power, position, or property. In all these things, and wheresoever the law looks,

275

and at whatever facet of life or affairs, the legal rule draws a straight line, an immutable line, and legislates according to the one concept of the right of divine and human being to the constant fulfilment of every proper obligation from every creature under heaven.

That is the line that has been drawn, but transgressors step right over it, the lawless constantly trample it underfoot, going across it as if it did not exist. They put their feet on it, walk away from it, depart from it, as if no law had ever been given. This is called, Transgression. Transgressors actually transgress for the entirety of their lives, with their being as such, in relation to the concept of law, flaunting its very existence, despising Almighty God, as though he had not spoken, and as if there was no day of reckoning. It is the concept of law that is transgressed, not just one or another facet of it: 'Whosoever shall keep the whole law, and yet offend in one point, he is guilty of all.' The lawless therefore transgress not sometimes, with some commandments, but always, with the commandment; they transgress not with a member or action, but from their heart, with their being; they transgress not simply a rule, but the rule, not only a law, but the Lawgiver: hence they are called, Transgressors. And the wonder is, that any of these should ever be pardoned.

Secondly, David, Psalm 32:1, and Paul, Romans 4:7, refer to sin and sins respectively. But what does David mean by sin, that Paul calls sins? David employs the Hebrew word *chataah*, which means 'to err', or 'fall short'. This is in the singular. Paul however uses the plural Greek *hamartiai*, 'errors, missing the mark again and again'.

This does not so much view the law, as the heart. Firstly, with David, it views the heart in the sense of the interior motion of the will, the thing that one has purposed, it is sin. Secondly, in the plural, as Paul interprets, it is the heart viewed in its various intentions, in those motions of the will which result in outward action, such actions first err in the heart, they are sins. So many intentions that miss the mark of what ought to have been, multiplied beyond number, all proceeding, however, from a deeper heart resolution, an interior purpose, that in itself in the most inward sense misses the mark in the entire purpose of life and end of being.

This that David indicates is what the Lord Jesus teaches, 'That which cometh out of the man, that defileth the man. For from within, out of the heart of men, proceed evil thoughts, adulteries, fornications, murders, thefts, covetousness, wickedness, deceit, lasciviousness, an evil eye, blasphemy, pride, foolishness: all these evil things come from within, and defile the man', Mk. 7:20-23. And again, 'The light of the body is the eye: if therefore thine eye be single, thy whole body shall be full of light. But if thine eye be evil, thy whole body shall be full of darkness. If therefore the light that is in thee be darkness, how great is that darkness!' Mt. 6:22,23. Now that is what David meant by sin. Not the acts in themselves, nor even the intentions by which the acts are conceived, but the end, the purpose for which one lives: that gives rise to every resolution. It is the heart.

Nevertheless, Paul uses the plural: sins. But he does not mean outward, bodily actions; rather the intentions of the heart—pointing out how diverse and seething these are—from which all the exterior deeds spring. And this is Christ's teaching, in respect of righteousness: 'Except your righteousness shall exceed the righteousness of the scribes and Pharisees, ye shall in no case enter into the kingdom of heaven', Mt. 5:20. And murder: 'Ye have heard that it was said by them of old time, Thou shalt not kill; and whosoever shall kill shall be in danger of the judgment: But I say unto you, That whosoever is angry with his brother without a cause shall be in danger of the judgment: and whosoever shall say to his brother, Raca, shall be in danger of the council: but whosoever shall say, Thou fool, shall be in danger of hell fire', Mt. 5:21,22. It is the intention, not the act. Indeed, it is the intention, whether the act occurs or not. And of such intentions, the heart of the sinner is full.

Likewise with adultery: 'Ye have heard that it was said by them of old time, Thou shalt not commit adultery: But I say unto you, That whosoever looketh on a woman to lust after her hath committed adultery with her already in his heart.' All the guilt and culpability of the adulterer stands in his inward intention. This is true whether the outward act takes place or not, Mt. 5:27,28. So with oaths. 'Ye have heard that it hath been said by them of old time, Thou shalt not forswear thyself, but shall perform unto the Lord thine oaths: but I say unto you, Swear not at all.' No, no outward oaths, but the inward intention of honesty: 'But let your communication be, Yea, yea; Nay, nay: for whatsoever is more than these cometh of evil', Mt. 5:33,37.

Thus it is with retaliation: 'Ye have heard that it hath been said, An eye for an eye, and a tooth for a tooth: But I say unto you, That ye resist not evil: but whosoever shall smite thee on thy right cheek, turn to him the other also', Mt. 5:38,39. How meek, how gentle, the followers of the Lamb. They do not practice sin. And love: 'Ye have heard that it hath been said, Thou shalt love thy neighbour, and hate thine enemy. But I say unto you, Love your enemies, bless them that curse you, do good to them that hate you, and pray for them which despitefully use you, and persecute you', Mt. 5:43,44. But who has this intention? Not the sinner.

The same applies to almsgiving, 'Take heed that ye do not your alms before men.' It is a question of the motive of the heart, the real intention, not the outward action. Virtue is not in the outward action: it is in that which brings it forth. The intention of the heart may be all vile, and yet the outward action shining and illustrious: 'Therefore when thou doest thine alms, do not sound a trumpet before thee, as the hypocrites do in the synagogues and in the streets, that they may have glory of men. Verily I say unto you, They have their reward. But when thou doest alms, let not thy left hand know what thy right had doeth: that thine alms may be in secret: and thy Father which seeth in secret himself shall reward thee openly', Mt. 6:1-4. This is equally applicable to prayer, Mt. 6:5-8; and fasting, Mt. 6:16-18; and, indeed, it is applicable to everything in religion, and all that is in this world, and the entire period that constitutes this earthly life, Mt. 6:24-34.

This doctrine of Christ places virtue not in the outward deed, where men place it, but in the inward resolution, in the hidden man of the heart, which God alone can see. So many outwardly virtuous actions, wonderfully approved of men, appear as nothing but abominations in the sight of God. It is these that Paul calls 'sins', Rom. 4:7. Such outwardly approved actions are therefore so many hypocritical sins, because the intention is rotten and corrupt, a cynical abuse and manipulation of God and of true religion for no other purpose than self-glory. These may cleanse the outside of the cup and platter, with alms, prayers, reformed conversation and orthodox appearance, but within they are full of extortion and excess. Assuming biblical creeds, forms of worship, scriptural ordinances the hypocrite outwardly appears righteous unto men, but within he is full of hypocrisy and iniquity. Such dead-letter persons trust in the text, and form their outward appearance and meetings by what they consider conformity to the Bible, but they are as whited sepulchres, which indeed appear beautiful outward, but are within full of dead men's bones, and all uncleanness.

So Christ teaches, and so Paul reiterates. How then shall God cover these inward sins, or blot out this interior sin? That he should ever do so, might well seem beyond comprehension or understanding. But who can find out the love of God to perfection?

279

Then, finally, what does David mean by iniquity, Ps. 32:2, that Paul calls sin, Rom. 4:8? By the use of the Hebrew *avon*, here called iniquity, David draws attention to the depravity that is in man. Man is discovered to be so corrupt, fallen, and crooked, his will so biased, and his mind so blinded, his heart so full of perversity, that he is utterly offensive to a holy God. He is iniquitous: that is the character of his sin. 'The iniquity of my sin', says David, Ps. 32:5. It is perverse. Now Paul calls this sin, *hamartian*, singular, not, as David, viewing sin morally in terms of its wilfulness, but constitutionally, in terms of man's state of corruption in the fall. This is the condition of the race, the fallen nature of man in Adam, man's depravity by generation.

Although David first emphasised the moral character of sin, here he shows its constitutional depravity passing from fallen Adam by natural generation. 'Behold, I was shapen in iniquity; and in sin did my mother conceive me', Ps. 51:5. This David confirms in another psalm, saying, 'The wicked are estranged from the womb', Ps. 58:3. The same is Paul's doctrine, 'Wherefore, as by one man sin entered into the world', Rom. 5:12, and again, 'As by one man's disobedience many were made sinners', Rom. 5:19. Hence he speaks in another place of 'the body of sin', and, once more, of 'sinful flesh'. This is the nature of man in the flesh, of which John says, 'That which is born of the flesh is flesh'. And what is born of the flesh is a state of inbred sin from the fall, and hence it is written, 'Now this I say, brethren, that flesh and blood cannot inherit the kingdom of God; neither doth corruption inherit incorruption', I Cor. 15:50.

How is it that God can ever cease from reckoning this to a man, since it is proper to him, his by birth, ardently embraced by him in his will, and is the embodiment of all his own volition? How can he not reckon sin to man, when he made man upright, but man made himself perverse, and when sinful flesh is a state totally obnoxious to the wrath of God? And yet—be astonished, O heavens, at this!—it is evident that there are those to whom sin is not imputed, because it is said, 'Blessed is the man to whom the Lord will not impute sin', Rom. 4:8.

It follows therefore that, despite the awful state described by David, and interpreted by Paul, God does forgive, he does pardon, there really are those to whom the Lord does not impute sin, and they really do know it experimentally. Observe then, firstly, the LORD does forgive transgression and pardon iniquities. David says, 'Blessed is he whose transgression is forgiven', Ps. 32:1. How can these things be? Because, saith the prophet, speaking of Christ, 'He was numbered with the transgressors', Isa. 53:12, and again, Isa. 53:12, 'He made intercession for the transgressors.' And the basis of his intercession appears thus: 'He was wounded for our transgressions', Isa. 53:5, and, once more, 'For the transgression of my people was he stricken', Isa. 53:8. This striking, in which God struck the Substitute of his people, was, Heb. 9:15, 'For the redemption of the transgressions that were under the first testament'; that is, transgressions against the law. And because he was struck instead of us, we may boldly say, He has blotted out our transgressions for his name's sake, Isa. 43:25, 44:22.

Paul, however, uses the word 'lawlessnesses', that is, in the text, iniquities. Hath he found forgiveness for these also? Yes, for, Isa. 53:5, 'He was bruised for our iniquities', that is, Christ, the Saviour, was bruised for them, and, if so, paid the penalty for them, so that the prisoner must and shall go free, as it is written, 'He shall justify many; for he shall bear their iniquities', Isa. 53:11. Indeed God forgives iniquities also, as it is said, 'Who forgiveth all thine iniquities', Ps. 103:3. But, if God be wroth, can they not be recalled again? What if one should commit future iniquities? Saith David, 'All thine iniquities', not some; then at the end of thy life, not the midst of it. So God testifies, because of the sacrifice of Christ for thee, and for all his elect, saying, 'Their iniquities will I remember no more', Heb. 8:12. Then, their iniquities, and all their iniquities, are forgiven them, and forgiven them for ever. Here is a forgiveness commensurate with the everlasting love of God in Christ. And who could have dreamed of so great a forgiveness as that?

Secondly, the LORD does cover sin, and it is a truth that he really blots out sins. Jesus is, John 1:29, the Lamb of God which taketh away the sin of the world. Then, Isa. 53:10, 'When thou shalt make his soul an offering for sin', surely, that sin is covered. For as David cried out, 'I have sinned', thereupon Nathan replied, 'Thy sin also is forgiven'. And how could that be, without the Lamb slain from the foundation of the world? Hence the psalmist confesses, 'Thou hast covered all their sin', Ps. 85:2, which is what the prophet confirms, saying, 'I will remember their sin no more', Jer. 31:34.

But Paul calls these sins: are these blotted out? Yes, for the Apostle Peter assures us 'He bare our sins in his own body on the tree', I Pet. 2:24. No wonder, then, that 'he hath not dealt with us after our sins', Ps. 103:10. Indeed not, for, saith he, 'Though your sins be as scarlet, they shall be as white as snow; though they be red like crimson, they shall be as wool', Isa. 1:18. How is this? Because 'He bare the sin of many', Isa. 53:12, and therefore they are called, 'Sins that are past', Rom. 3:25. For, Gal. 1:4, 'He gave himself for our sins', so that the gospel is 'for the remission of sins', Acts 2:38, and, Acts 13:38, 'Through this man is preached unto you the forgiveness of sins', which are blotted out by the blood of Jesus Christ, for his name's sake.

Lastly, it is perfectly true that there is a people, marked out by mutual experience and like common faith, unto whom the Lord imputeth not iniquity, neither reckoneth sin. This is because 'Thou hast forgiven the iniquity of thy people', Ps. 85:2;

and so the prophet is to 'cry to her that her iniquity is pardoned', Isa. 40:2. Wherefore? Because 'The LORD hath laid on him the iniquity of us all', Isa. 53:6. Then it cannot be reckoned to us, since it was reckoned to him, for he is a just God, and a Saviour.

As to the Lord not reckoning sin, I Jn. 1:7, 'the blood of Jesus Christ, God's Son, cleanseth us from all sin.' He has borne away sin, so that, Heb. 9:28, 'He shall appear the second time without sin unto salvation.' This is because God 'hath made him to be sin for us, who knew no sin; that we might be made the righteousness of God in him', II Cor. 5:21. The body of sin is therefore destroyed, Rom. 6:6, because, Rom. 8:3, God, who sent his own Son in the likeness of sinful flesh, and for sin, condemned sin in the flesh. Then what condemnation remains for those whom he thus justified? Who is he that condemneth? 'It is God that justifieth', Rom. 8:33. And, if so, by his ceasing to impute to his people that sin which was taken away by condemnation in the body of his own dear Son. What was taken upon him, that he really bore away, cannot be reckoned to them again, for, Rom. 6:10, 'in that he died, he died unto sin once.' Wherefore we may boldly say, in the full assurance of saving faith, spiritual understanding, and experimental blessing 'Blessed is the man whose transgression is forgiven, whose sin is covered. Blessed is the man unto whom the LORD imputeth not iniquity, and in whose spirit there is no guile.' This, based upon the atonement, is interpreted by Paul as being the same thing as 'the blessedness of the man unto whom God imputeth righteousness without works', Rom. 4:6-8.

Following Rom. 4:6, that is, David's description of the blessedness of the man unto whom God imputeth righteousness without works, the Apostle Paul gives the second and last specific reference to righteousness being imputed. Speaking of faith being reckoned to Abraham for righteousness, and observing that these words were spoken of him when he was in uncircumcision, the apostle concludes that this was a providence to Abraham 'that he might be the father of all them that believe, though they be not circumcised.' Immediately afterwards, the apostle makes this direct reference to righteousness imputed, Rom. 4:11, 'That righteousness might be imputed unto them also.'

But if Abraham was already counted righteous before God, and was already the father of the believing uncircumcised, what was the purpose of his being circumcised afterwards? Much every way, but chiefly as a sign on the one hand, and a seal on the other. 'Abraham received the sign of circumcision, a seal of the righteousness of the faith which he had yet being uncircumcised.' Circumcision, following after the being accounted righteous, signifies the removal of the flesh in those who are justified.

They are not born of the flesh, they are born of the Spirit. They are not in the flesh, they are in the Spirit. This is the seal of those for whom God has wrought righteousness in the promised Seed, to whom righteousness has been imputed, and whom God has justified: this is how they are to be recognised. They mind the things of the Spirit, they are spiritually minded. They dwell in the Spirit, and the Spirit of God dwells in them. By the Spirit they mortify the deeds of the flesh, they live in the Spirit. They do not walk in the flesh, they are led by the Spirit, they walk after the Spirit. This is the seal of their justification.

The expression 'a seal of the righteousness of the faith which he had yet being uncircumcised' shows that a righteousness belonged to the faith and a faith to the righteousness. It was 'the righteousness of faith', just as it was 'the righteousness of the faith'. Faith was as certain of the righteousness as was the righteousness of the faith. Just as it was certain that God would bring in righteousness according to Abraham's faith, so it is certain that all those for whom God brought in righteousness would be brought to faith.

Abraham believed God to bring to light the promised Seed and to bring in the promised inheritance, despite sin, death, and the judgment. He believed that this would be through substitutionary atonement according to the righteousness of God. 'And he believed in the LORD; and he counted it to him for righteousness.' Observe carefully that what was accounted to Abraham was righteousness. It is not said simply that Abraham was accounted to be righteous, though he was: righteousness itself was accounted; 'It was accounted to him for righteousness.' Abraham's faith anticipated the righteousness of God being wrought in the sacrifice of the promised Seed. If not, why the sacrifice which followed, by which Abraham knew of the righteousness which was to be imputed, and of the promise which was to be inherited, Gen. 15:6-17? Again, if not, why did Abraham offer up Isaac upon mount Moriah, and why his unquestioning acceptance of the substitutionary ram, by which Abraham knew that the Seed was not Isaac himself, and that the sacrifice, when it came in the fulness of time, would be wholly of God, and altogether without the work of man, Gen. 22?

Then, afar off, believing Abraham regarded the righteousness of God by faith of Jesus Christ, described in promise and prophecy, and set forth in type and figure, from the foundation of the world. This was the righteousness of faith, in which faith was as certain of the righteousness, as it was certain that all those for whom righteousness was wrought would be brought to faith. Thus Abraham believed God, and it was counted to him for righteousness. Faith was counted for righteousness, righteousness was imputed to faith, and all was established upon the sacrificial death, and substitutionary atonement, of the Seed of promise.

Faith was counted to Abraham for righteousness when he was in uncircumcision. Thus he became the father of all them that believe, though they be not circumcised, 'that righteousness might be imputed unto them also', Rom. 4:11. Then faith being counted for righteousness, and righteousness being imputed, are reckoned to be the same. In both cases, it is not the bare accounting of a man to be righteous, but the accounting of righteousness to that man, that the apostle describes: it is how a man is accounted to be righteous. Hence righteousness of God, outwrought in death, sealed by blood, credited in the issue, stands to the account of all the elect seed, that is, of every one that is of faith.

But not to Mr. J.N. Darby, neither in Brethrenism. The Brethren system repudiates the very idea that there is a righteousness to be imputed. Mr. Darby: 'When scripture says Abraham's faith was imputed to him for righteousness, it means Abraham was accounted righteous on account of his faith. Hence imputing God's righteousness could not be employed or thought of by me, because I deny all such previous sum of righteousness made out and then imputed', Collected Writings, Vol. 10. Again, 'The meaning of imputed righteousness is, not a quantity of righteousness apart from the person and afterwards reckoned to him', Collected Writings, Vol. 7. 'There is no question at all of a quantum of righteousness subsisting, and then put to their account', Collected Writings, Vol. 10.

Mr. Darby denies 'all such previous sum of righteousness made out'. Brethrenism repudiates 'a quantity of righteousness apart from a person'. The Brethren system refuses 'a quantum of righteousness subsisting', which sum, quantity, or quantum is afterwards to be imputed to the believer. Now, ignoring the contrivance of putting an opponent's argument in clumsy language distasteful to the reader—'sum, quantity, quantum'—Mr. Darby, and Brethrenism, here reject the truth that God wrought righteousness by Jesus Christ at the cross in order to justify his people thereby. Calling it a 'quantum' cannot disguise the fact that what he disparages is the very idea that God brought in righteousness to the account of his people by the blood of Jesus Christ, afterwards to be imputed to them. It is Mr. Darby himself who invents the idea of quantity or quantum. It was righteousness of God as such, which, having fully met the sinner vicariously in his Substitute, was 'made out', or 'subsisted', and which 'afterwards' was 'to be imputed' to the believer. Take that away, and justification is destroyed. Mr. Darby's system, Brethrenism, does take it away.

Next, J.N. Darby falls back on the argument that an attribute cannot be imputed. Having made that clear, it is necessary that he should show righteousness to be an attribute. 'As to righteousness as an attribute, this is equally true. But an attribute being imputed to us is simple nonsense, being a contradiction in terms.' And yet, in a not untypical reversal, hidden in the midst of the usual convoluted language, astonishingly we read, 'But that which was an attribute, or was in God, may be imputed, taken abstractly.' And what does that mean, taken abstractly? Especially followed by 'Nobody has said that the righteousness of God is imputed', Collected Writings, Vol. 10.

Darby, intent on destroying the righteousness that is imputed, teaches that righteousness is an attribute. But an attribute, he says, cannot be imputed. Therefore, J.N.D. concludes, righteousness cannot be imputed. His argument proposes that it is impossible for righteousness to be wrought out so that in consequence it might be imputed. But why not? All this depends upon our accepting the definitions of someone who has the predetermined intention of destroying the very idea of the righteousness of God brought in by the blood of Christ, thereafter to be accounted to those for whom Christ died. Scripture says nothing of 'attribute', and indeed such a description is irrelevant. Neither does scripture call righteousness an abstract quality. Righteousness requires persons or circumstances to call it forth from him whose righteousness it is: righteousness is exercised in relation to someone or something. And if the righteousness of God in relation to the sinner, seen in his Substitute, met that sinner at the cross in judgment, so as to be perfectly satisfied and cleared in the resultant death, why cannot that, as such—and not in quantum—be reckoned to the sinner's account?

Why not? Is it because that would be founded on particular redemption, offensive to Arminians? Is it because that would be effectual righteousness through Christ's work in death for all the elect, as opposed to potential righteousness through Christ's Person in glory for all the world? Is it because that would be an hard saying few could bear, in contrast with the easy believism all love to hear? Is it because such plainness of speech would expose the sacrifice of sound doctrine on the altar of broad unity inherent in the Brethren system? Is that too much to say?

Too much? One well-known Brethren writer summarises Mr. Darby, and sums up Brethrenism, on the passage 'unto all and upon all them that believe', Romans 3:22, thus: 'It—righteousness—is offered unto all the world, but only those who believe it are accounted righteous before God', W.F.K., Letters. Mr. Darby comments 'It was the righteousness of God unto all: it was in fact universal in its aspect and applicability. A righteousness of God for man, because no man had any for God, it was applied to all those who believe in Jesus. Wherever there was faith there it was applied. The believer possessed it. It was towards all, and upon all those who believed in Jesus', Synopsis, Romans 3.

Mr. Darby is saying exactly the same thing as W.F.K., only he is more careful, he makes his language more obscure, his wording is seldom obvious. 'The one righteousness, as God's gift, is unto all, but it is only upon all them that believe', Collected Writings, Vol. 21. Observe, justification is a universal work for all the world, this is what he means by righteousness being 'unto all'. However it is applied to those that believe, that is, free will secures it, it is all in the will of man to accept this general justification, or reject it. Then the blood of Christ justified none. The righteousness of God justified no one. God did not impute righteousness. No, man chose it. That was what made it work. Otherwise, justification would have been universal. But no: in Brethrenism, the easy believer is sovereign, and God must be thankful to the will of man that justification is not in ruins.

Then whatever does such a system teach about righteousness? How does Mr. Darby suppose that the ungodly are justified? What has Brethrenism to say about justifying righteousness? 'I will say one word here on the righteousness of God, as many find great difficulty in understanding what it is. The question is, How can a righteous God justify sinners? Well, the proof and testimony of God's righteousness is, that he has set Christ at his own right hand. When Christ had perfectly glorified God, and that as made sin at the cross, God places him at his own right hand in heaven; and there only do I see righteousness', Collected Writings, Vol. 32.

Let not the reader be deceived by the wily digression 'and that as made sin at the cross'. That is a typical feint, in which 'dust is thrown in the eyes'. The sentence to mark is this: 'There only do I see righteousness'. Only? Where 'only'? 'At his own right hand in heaven.' But it is not there that the righteousness in question is to be seen. It is at the cross, in the blood, having been accomplished, thereupon to be imputed to the faith of those for whom it was wrought. At the cross, in the blood, there 'only' do we see justifying righteousness.

In the same place, J.N.D. says, 'But this work, though perfectly to God's glory, was done for us, so that it is God's righteousness to give us a place with him. In Christ we are thus made God's righteousness. So that it is said, He is righteous and just to forgive. But Christ is gone there as man, and I am united to him, and I get, with this righteousness, Christ my life.' Here, hidden by misleading and ambiguous language, the errors of this system begin to be made manifest. First righteousness is for all the world by union in the glory, not by substitution for all the children of the promise at the cross. Next, the bringing in of righteousness by the death of Christ is supplanted by the life of Christ before a righteous God in glory. Hence 'righteousness' is God's response to Christ's worth in glory, not God's judgment upon sinners in their Substitute on earth. Righteousness is personal to him, not to them in him. It is not righteousness in respect of them, Therefore it cannot be imputed. Indeed, there is no imputation, because there is not a righteousness to impute. It is a case of one being accounted to be righteous because of Christ in glory, the sole ground being provided by one's own faith. So 'I get, with this righteousness, Christ my life.' No wonder, then, with this righteousness, that Brethren were soon rent asunder over the question of 'Life', under the ministry of F.E. Raven.

Further, scriptures exclusive to the substitutionary work of Christ for his people—*vide* 'In Christ we are thus made God's righteousness'—are made to apply to the whole world: for, remember, Rom. 3:22, righteousness is 'unto' the whole world, but only 'upon' those who elect to believe. 'I am united to him': then righteousness of God—seen here as a divine estimate of Christ's worth, as opposed to what was wrought out in death for the believer—appears to be by union with the Person of Christ in heaven.

What is this? Righteousness by union? In glory? This is an erroneous invention, nothing to do with justifying righteousness having been effected through substitution in the death of the cross specifically for each believer: 'Unto all and upon all them that believe.' A general, impersonal righteousness, by union, in glory, a righteousness by association with him of whom it is a divine estimate, is certainly not justifying righteousness. Neither is it scriptural. It is a jumbled confusion of ideas. It is diametrically opposed to personal, imputed righteousness, by substitution, in death, a righteousness by vicarious atonement through him who bore the divine judgment. This is called justifying righteousness. But it is neither Brethrenism nor is it the teaching of Mr. J.N . Darby.

Continuing in the next paragraph, Mr. Darby writes, 'I get righteousness manifested—how? By putting Christ, who bore my sins, at the right hand of God.' Apart from the offensive language—'I get'; 'by putting Christ'—we are not to be put off by the words 'who bore my sins'. Let the man come out into the open about justification, the foundation doctrine, the standing article of the church. Darby 'gets' it, how? By putting Christ 'at the right hand of God'. That is how he 'gets' it 'manifested'. This is in the teeth of the manifestation revealed by the apostle in the gospel. 'But now the righteousness of God without the law is manifested ... even the righteousness of God by faith of Jesus Christ.' Manifested 'by faith of Jesus Christ' observe, not by Mr. Darby 'putting Christ' at the right hand of God. Manifested 'by faith of Jesus Christ' when God judged his people in their Substitute at the cross, according to his own righteousness, through which they have been 'justified by his blood'.

Mr. Darby states, 'I affirm that scripture never speaks of imputed righteousness as a sum of righteousness, first existing in itself, and then imputed. The truth is, it never speaks of imputed righteousness at all, but of imputing righteousness', Collected Writings, Vol. 10. But scripture does speak of righteousness 'first existing in itself', in Romans chapter three, 'and then' of that 'existent righteousness' being 'imputed', Romans chapter four. The fact that Mr. Darby has noticed that the scripture does not use the form 'imputed righteousness', as such, cannot alter the reality that righteousness to be imputed is manifested by faith of Jesus Christ in Romans chapter three, and that the imputing of that same righteousness follows as a matter of fact in Romans chapter four.

Such a flimsy pretext does not warrant the erroneous conclusions, and, ultimately, the dangerous theories, deduced by

Mr. Darby from his not particularly significant observation. Just because the language and conclusions of those who hold to the active and passive obedience theory are faulty does not make Mr. Darby's language and conclusions right. The absence of the precise wording 'imputed righteousness' may seemingly provide a springboard but it most certainly cannot justify this dive into the obscure depths of speculative reasoning on the part of Mr. Darby.

The fact that the Spirit in scripture—righteousness being given—emphasises faith in imputing righteousness, hardly justified Mr. Darby in denying righteousness of God wrought at the cross thereafter to be imputed to all those for whom Christ died. This may not be called 'imputed righteousness' in precise grammatical form, but it is most certainly called 'righteousness imputed'. With equal definition, the apostle says that 'God imputeth righteousness', by which he means the righteousness of Romans chapter three. Of the same righteousness he states in chapter four, 'that righteousness might be imputed unto them also'. All the hair-splitting in the world cannot alter the fact that such language—Rom. 4:6,11 —plainly necessitates, just as the previous chapter clearly postulates, righteousness already wrought out in order that the imputing spoken of in the fourth chapter could take place.

Mr. Darby has to admit the existence of righteousness, as he does of imputing. But with his tongue in his cheek he twists it round till its plain meaning is lost in a maze of complicated contradiction. To Mr. Darby, righteousness is not imputed: what he makes this mean is that a man is accounted to be righteous: no more, no less. 'I affirm that scripture never speaks of imputed righteousness, as a sum of righteousness, first existing of itself, and then imputed.' The fact is that there is no justifying righteousness in Mr. Darby's scheme. It does not exist to be imputed. Then justification by faith does not exist in Mr. Darby's Brethrenism. What then does exist?

Speaking of the believer, Mr. Darby says, 'He has his place and portion through redemption in Christ risen.' 'He is in Christ, and in Christ accepted according to Christ's own acceptance. The value which Christ has in the sight of God, which is real and meritorious, is the value in which he stands, but as dead and risen. The death of Christ has put away his sin, and all the glorifying of God, in virtue of which Christ as man is at God's right hand in righteousness (he stands in the value of Christ) is his righteousness', Collected Writings, Vol. 10.

Now, hidden behind this perplexing jumble of words there is not only an authorship of confusion but there is also a downright attack on justification by faith. This is not immediately obvious, because it is concealed behind expressions that seem to speak well of Christ's Person and of his work. But there is only one who can do that, and it is not Mr. Darby. It is the Holy Ghost—'He shall glorify me'—and his words must be submitted to absolutely, in their 'great plainness of speech', not altered and clouded over by pseudo-spiritual theorising, hidden and obscured behind a tangle of bewildering phraseology. Mr. Darby's later questionable teaching on The Sufferings of Christ, the cause of serious division in Brethrenism, was couched in just such high-sounding and yet perplexing language.

What Mr. Darby is actually saying is that Christ as man at God's right hand, dwelling in the righteousness of God, thence becomes the righteousness of the believer. This means that righteousness to the account of the believer was not wrought at the cross. It also means that righteousness to the account of the believer was not wrought in the glory. Righteousness—to be imputed—was not wrought at all. Righteousness is entirely personal to Christ—not wrought by him for believers—it is the divine response to his worth, and is only shared by believers—being impersonal to them—by union. There is no righteousness wrought by substitution.

There is no righteousness wrought as a distinct entity. Then there is no righteousness peculiar to the believer. Therefore there is none to put to his account.

Mr. Darby's teaching on justification—mark that: on justification—is that Christ, raised to God's right hand, subsists in the righteousness of God, and that the believer is counted to be in this place by faith. Then why righteousness more than any other attribute? Why not holiness? Why not account the believer to be holy? After all, J.N. Darby teaches that Christ, for the believer, subsists in all God's attributes in glory, one not more than another. If Christ dwells, or subsists, in the righteousness, justice, holiness and mercy of God, then by faith, through union, so does the believer. It is not that the attribute of righteousness, any more than that of holiness, could possibly be imputed as an attribute. Christ is there, in all the divine attributes, as such, and that is the position in which the believer is reckoned to be by union. Overstressing righteousness—he must, to give some kind of an explanation for the justification he rejects—Mr. Darby says, 'All the glorifying of God in virtue of which Christ as man is at God's right hand ... is his—the believer's—righteousness.' But this is not righteousness imputed. Neither is it justification by faith.

Mr. Darby's teaching is not the apostle's doctrine. On the contrary J.N.D.'s system necessarily dismisses the reality of justifying righteousness by the blood of Christ, putting in its place the speculative theory of a man being accounted righteous because righteousness of God is one of the attributes—but no more than any other—in which Christ as man subsists at the right hand of God. It is not simply that this theorising is nothing to do with justification, it destroys justification, directing the mind to something as novel as it is specious. But, that man might be just with God, we are directed to the preaching of the cross, not of the glory. For, says the apostle, We preach Christ crucified, I Cor. 1:18,23.

It may be said that this is hardly fair to Mr. Darby's view of the cross. On the contrary, the question is justification, and Mr. Darby does not and will not take account of righteousness being accomplished for all the people of God at the cross. Knowingly, he denies that everlasting righteousness was then and there brought in. Hence he cannot have righteousness imputed or put to account, though there it was brought in and put to account. Thus he makes 'imputing' nothing more than accounting a man to be righteous, absolutely denying that righteousness itself is imputed to him. Arminians and papists will have no difficulty in agreeing with Darby, since they refer to righteousness imputed as 'imputed nonsense', as do all who, in principle, deny the ground and basis of particular redemption and accomplished righteousness for all the chosen seed. All these, sooner or later, must stumble on this stone of election.

The question is not about J.N.D.'s views on the sacrificial death of Christ, general as they are, the question is about the cardinal doctrine of justification by faith. As to the atonement in and of itself, High Churchmen and not a few Roman Catholics would quite agree with Mr. Darby's views. However, it is justification by faith, that is, how God justifies the ungodly, how righteousness is imputed, how the work of God in Christ is applied, that brings error to light. And it is justification by faith that the High Churchman and the Romanist abhor. But then so does Mr. Darby. That is why one must focus upon what he says about justification, and keep justification by faith in view, flatly refusing to be waylaid by high sounding words and apparently spiritual comments thrown in to take the attention from what is actually being said about justification itself.

And will some complain still? Then let them observe the measure of severity which Mr. Darby meted out to his opponents: 'What scripture does not speak of is a certain quantum of legal righteousness attributed to us, because being under law we have failed in it; because we are not under law. It is an unholy doctrine', Collected Writings, Vol. 7. In another place he accuses his antagonists of 'throwing dust in the eyes'. Darby's adversaries held views quite similar to his own on the cross itself. But the 'unholy doctrine'—which Mr. Darby, of all people, complained was being obscured by irrelevant scriptures and obtuse religious phraseology—was that which taught substitutionary legal obedience before the cross. Yes, but how can a man who holds to being 'accounted righteous' because of nothing other than the glory after the cross, object to that? Justification is at the cross. Whatever places it before, or after, is indeed 'unholy doctrine': and whoever obscures what they are teaching behind convoluted sentences, irrelevant scriptures, and spiritual sounding diversions most certainly 'throws dust in the eyes'.

Declares Mr. Darby, 'God has shown his righteousness in setting Christ as man at his right hand.' 'Righteousness is in heaven, it is a divine title to glory and in man.' Darby holds that Christ glorified God in death; as, indeed, he did. It is quite true that, in the place of sinners, Christ was made sin, so as to glorify God in all his attributes. The attributes of justice, truth, righteousness, and holiness were satisfied in his death for sinners, whilst those of mercy, pity, compassion and kindness were released by way of that death towards sinners. Veracity, longsuffering, indeed every attribute, quality and characteristic of God was glorified at the cross. Wherefore God glorified Christ by raising him to the throne of his glory.

As man in the presence of God, Christ has been raised to the right hand of God, whose every attribute he had glorified upon the earth. Including righteousness. But no more than, say, longsuffering. Christ is at rest in glory, and God in glory is at rest in him. Now, says Mr. Darby, that is the position of the believer. When he believes in Christ, that position, offered to all, becomes his. It is accounted to him—the position is reckoned as his—because he believes. Everything

Christ is as man becomes his. And because Christ is at rest in God's righteousness—just as in everything else pertaining to God's presence—therefore, says Mr. Darby, so is the believer. That position is accounted to him, and he is reckoned to be in it. Singling out righteousness—which he must, for, having dismissed imputed righteousness, he is obliged to account for righteousness imputed—and conveniently ignoring every other attribute, Mr. Darby assures the man united by faith with Christ in glory that thereby he is accounted to be righteous. This is not justification by faith. Neither is it righteousness. It is trying to account for the scriptures on justification, whilst avoiding those that speak of righteousness being imputed.

One might as well say, on such a theoretic and unscriptural hypothesis, that holiness is accounted to the believer. He is accounted holy. Mercy is imputed to the believer. He is imputed to be merciful. These are just as much attributes as righteousness. They were just as much glorified in the death of Christ on earth. God is just as much in possession of them as of righteousness in glory. Christ is just as much at rest in these attributes, as he is in the attribute of righteousness, in heaven. Why single out righteousness? In this scheme there is no more authority for accounting the believer to be righteous, than to be merciful. Nothing is substantially to his account, no, he is accounted to be what Christ is in God's presence. Then why is he not accounted to be compassionate? Why not longsuffering? These attributes of God were glorified by Christ on earth as much as righteousness. Certainly Christ is said to be at rest in the presence of God. Surely this shows the acceptance of the saints. But with equal certainty this is nothing to do with accounting the believer to be anything in particular. Much less with accounting him to be righteous. Then why single out righteousness? To attempt to explain away scriptures on evangelical righteousness whilst ignoring justification by the blood of Christ.

The heart of Mr. Darby's notion of justification is that
Christ, having glorified God on earth in all his attributes,
including righteousness, has been raised to his own right
hand on high. That is, he has been glorified in heaven, who
glorified God on earth. This, says Mr. Darby, is the position
of the believer. That may be so. But it is not justification. It is
a misapplication of acceptance, manipulated to prepare the
way for the false conclusions which follow. Hence J.N. Darby
goes on to say that because of this position in Christ, which
the believer shares by union, we are accounted to be righteous.
This conclusion is false. It is because righteousness of God
was brought in by the death of Jesus Christ that we are
accounted to be righteous. Mr. Darby beguiles us with the
truth of acceptance, with which we are bound to agree, and,
having gained our agreement, draws a succession of conclusions destructive of justification and assertive of his own
alternative speculation. This may be ingenious but it is not
justification by faith. Nor is it the righteousness of God by
faith of Jesus Christ.

To avoid the consequences of his system J.N. Darby employs
the Johannine vision to contradict the Pauline doctrine, and,
reducing justification by faith to theorising about glory,
confounds everything. Indeed, in one place, on a single page,
to explain justifying righteousness, Darby manages twenty-
one references to 'glory' in no more than forty-two lines of
tortured, confused and contradictory rationalising. But it
cannot be done. Righteousness was wrought at the cross for
all the chosen seed, to be imputed to faith generation by generation, and a woe is unto him who sets himself against this
apostolic doctrine, whosoever he may be, and however lofty
his vision of the nature and unity of the church.

Mr. Darby's position—and the position of consistent
Brethrenism—is that imputing righteousness actually means
reckoning a man to be righteous, not reckoning righteousness
to him. As Christ, being glorified, dwells in all the glorified

attributes of God, including righteousness, then, believing upon him, in virtue of that faith, by union, the believer is accounted to be in the same position as Christ. And this spiritual-sounding mixture, really calculated to destroy justification by faith, is to be called justification by faith? It is a leaky vessel empty of any real righteousness at all, void of any substantial cargo to account, launched by free will upon the uncharted ocean of general atonement, loosed to the light winds of easy-believism, adrift with sublime confidence in the tides of novel speculation. And what will be the end of such a vessel, on a voyage the like of this?

In the Darby system, the very idea of imputing must be repudiated, for the simple reason that there is nothing to impute. One may be counted, or reckoned, to be righteous when one is not, 'on the ground of faith'. But what is meant is that Christ is at rest in the righteousness of God in glory, and his place, available to all, is accounted to those that believe, because they chose to believe. But this is not imputing righteousness. There is no righteousness as such to impute. It is simply the fact that God is righteous, and Christ is in glory. It is both abstract and impersonal. Righteousness to be imputed, wrought of God in Christ for his people at the cross, is fiction to Mr. Darby, and to the free will easy-believing Brethren system. But it is sound doctrine to the apostles of Jesus Christ.

The idea of righteousness, as such, being 'accounted' or 'imputed' is anathema to Mr. Darby. The idea of righteousness, as such, being 'imputed' to the individual for whom it was wrought is 'unholy doctrine' to Mr. Darby. The idea of righteousness having been wrought through the death of Christ, thereafter to be imputed to the children of the promise, is heresy to Mr. Darby. To Mr. Darby, justification is in the glory, not at the cross. It is in the Person of Christ, not in the work of Christ. Man believes it, God did not work it. Then, to him, justifying righteousness wrought for all the chosen seed through the blood of Jesus Christ, to be imputed, does not exist.

Righteousness of God, to Mr. Darby, cannot be imputed—'one cannot impute an attribute'—one is accounted to be righteous. Therefore imputing is not a word which Mr. Darby rightly can use: there is nothing to impute. Having dismissed righteousness to be imputed, he has no further use for the word 'imputed'. But, like justification, like righteousness, it is in the Bible, and hence an explanation must be given: it will serve to 'account'—he would rather not say 'impute'—a person to be righteous. But that is not justification by faith. Let no one think that it is.

This teaching is set for the destruction of justification by faith, and avowedly so. 'Imputing righteousness is a person being accounted righteous, and nothing else', Collected Writings Vol. 7. 'The act of justification conceived of as proceeding on an underlying righteousness', Mr. Darby calls 'nonsense'. Imputed nonsense, Mr. Darby? But what saith the scripture? Does the scripture say, 'Abraham believed God, and it was counted unto him to be accounted righteous'; or does it say, 'Abraham believed God, and it was counted unto him for righteousness', Rom. 4:3? What is the apostolic doctrine? Is it, 'God accounts to be righteous without works'; or is it, 'God imputeth righteousness without works', Rom. 4:6? Which is it? For, remember, J.N. Darby says, 'Imputing righteousness is a person being accounted righteous, and nothing —nothing—else.' But what saith the Holy Ghost? Does he say, 'That they might be counted to be righteous also'; or is it, 'That righteousness might be imputed unto them also', Rom. 4:11? Let the reader mark the old paths, and observe the old landmarks.

THE
CONCLUSION

THE CONCLUSION

XV

Justification by Faith

THAT God should justify the ungodly by faith presumes, firstly, that he is righteous; secondly, that he has wrought righteousness; and thirdly, that he imputes righteousness. Without this threefold basis no flesh could be justified in his sight. On just this basis the justification of the ungodly can proceed and become a reality. The means by which, respectively, God righteously justifies, works righteousness so that sinners might be justified, and imputes righteousness to the faith of the ungodly, is the death of Jesus Christ. It is through the sacrifice of his body, and the shedding of his blood, in the death of the cross. This declares that God is righteous, that he has wrought righteousness, and that he imputes righteousness. All this is necessarily presupposed in justification by faith.

Righteousness is the groundwork of justification. Firstly in the declaration that God is righteous in justifying sinners. Why was this necessary? Because it was not possible in the nature of God's righteousness for him to overlook sin as if it had not occurred. He could not give vent to pity at the expense of judgment. Sin must be judged. The question was, how could sin be judged and yet sinners go out free? It was impossible for the Judge to dismiss law or to sweep aside the rule of rectitude as if there were no rights, no accountability, and no judgment.

Shall not the Judge of all the earth do right? If so, he must uphold the rule of law, bring transgressors to account, and pass sentence agreeable to the gravity of the offence of every soul of man without respect of persons. How then justify the ungodly? This great dilemma was overcome by the love of God in sending his own Son into the world to die in the place of sinners. God commended his love toward us, in that, while we were yet sinners, Christ died for us. Upon the dying Saviour, in the place of sinful man, the just sentence was passed, the penalty of the law fell, the curse went forth, and the full rigour of offended justice was exacted to the uttermost. This upheld God's righteousness, satisfied the law, vindicated justice, and exonerated the Judge. Exonerated the Judge? Yes, in pardoning transgressors, and justifying the ungodly.

Because the righteous punishment of the law had been paid vicariously by Jesus Christ on behalf of sinners, God could righteously justify, and justly pardon. At once, he was a just God, and a Saviour. The cross declared his righteousness not only for the remission of sins that were past, but for the remission of sins as such: that he might be just, and the justifier of him which believeth in Jesus. The cross was the declaration of God's righteousness in forgiving sinners, of his justice in granting pardon to the guilty, and of his judgment in bestowing mercy upon the transgressors. Thus the vindication of God's righteous character in justifying the ungodly was achieved when the judgment due to them fell upon the vicarious Substitute. Precisely because justice and judgment were there upheld, the cross declared God to be righteous in justifying sinners.

Righteousness is the groundwork of justification. Not only is God righteous in justifying sinners, but he wrought righteousness in order that sinners might be justified. That the death of Christ shows that God is righteous in justification is one thing; that the death of Christ shows that God wrought righteousness in order to effect justification is another. The righteousness which God brought in through the substitutionary death of Christ, put to the account of those whom he would justify thereafter, is both essential and fundamental to justification by faith. Righteousness must be wrought for those who are to be justified, in order that their justification might take place. This is the righteousness that was wrought in the death of Jesus Christ on behalf of all the people of God.

This is called 'the righteousness of God by faith of Jesus Christ.' It is 'unto all them that believe', Rom. 3:22. This is the righteousness of God, revealed in the gospel, which is 'from' the faith of Jesus Christ, Rom. 1:17, that is, God wrought it out by the faith of Jesus Christ at the cross, when he became the Substitute of all believers. 'By the faith of Jesus Christ', insists Paul, Gal. 2:16, reiterating 'that we might be justified by the faith of Christ', because by his faith, at the cross, God brought in everlasting righteousness as such for all his people. This is 'the faith of the Son of God', Gal. 2:20, and, since by it righteousness was wrought, therefore we live, 'that grace might reign through righteousness unto eternal life by Jesus Christ our Lord', Rom. 5:21.

For this cause we have obtained 'like precious faith', namely, because God wrought righteousness through the faith of Jesus Christ who took our place in death. Furthermore, we were certain to be brought to faith, for whom Christ died, and for whom God brought in righteousness. And we have been brought to faith, 'through the righteousness of God and our Saviour Jesus Christ', II Pet. 1:1. To this the early saints clave, it is the righteousness 'which is through the faith of Christ, the righteousness which is of God by faith', Phil. 3:9.

Through this same righteousness of God the ungodly, unknown to themselves, were already 'justified by his blood', Rom. 5:9. That is, they were justified when his blood was shed. If not, what do the words mean? They do not mean, any might be justified if only they believed in that shed blood, otherwise the text would read, 'by faith in his blood'. But it reads, 'by his blood'. This is because the blood by itself alone brought in the righteousness of God to the account of every one for whom it was shed, when it was shed. It is clear that righteousness is 'unto' them because of the work of the Father and the Son two thousand years ago at the cross. Then, 'justified by his blood.'

Righteousness is the groundwork of justification. Not only in that justification presupposes that God is righteous, or in that God wrought righteousness at the cross, but also because that righteousness, once wrought, is to be imputed to the justified. Righteousness of God, 'from' the faith of Jesus Christ, is 'to' the faith of all those who shall be brought to believe, Rom. 1:17. The righteousness of God by faith of Jesus Christ which was 'unto' them, is, when actually imputed, 'upon' all that believe, Rom. 3:22. It was unto them at the cross when righteousness was wrought for the elect two thousand years ago by the Father and the Son. And it is upon them when, generation by generation, they are brought to faith by the work of the Holy Ghost from heaven. When they thus believe, God imputes righteousness to them in their conscious experience. This is the blessedness of which David speaks prophetically, and Paul writes experimentally, even the blessedness of the man 'unto whom God imputeth righteousness without works', Rom. 4:6.

Of this righteousness, which, thousands of years afterwards, was to be brought in through the blood of Jesus Christ, Abraham became heir. He believed God, and it was counted to him for righteousness, Rom. 4:3. And righteousness shall be imputed likewise to those Gentiles for whom it was wrought at the cross, who shall also most surely be brought to the faith of God's elect, Rom. 4:11. Because of the certainty that the Spirit will bring to justifying faith all those for whom the Father and the Son wrought evangelical righteousness, 'Faith is counted for righteousness', Rom. 4:5,9. 'Now, it was not written for his—Abraham's—sake alone, that it was imputed to him', Rom. 4:23. Then for whose sake was it written? 'But for us also, to whom it shall be imputed, if we believe on him that raised up Jesus our Lord from the dead; who was delivered for our offences, and was raised again for our justification', Rom. 4:24,25. Where, evidently, those for whom righteousness of God was wrought in the death of Jesus Christ, being brought to faith in due time, find, like Abraham, that faith is imputed to them for righteousness, just as they discover that righteousness is imputed to them in their experience as believers.

Upon such a basis of righteousness as that which demonstrates that God is righteous, that he has wrought righteousness, and that he imputes righteousness, justification proceeds, and proceeds on the principle of faith. Everything is of God: nothing is of man. All is of grace: not a thing is of law. Faith is the principle: there is no place for works. It is justification by faith. Hence it is said that justification is of God, 'It is God that justifieth', Rom. 8:33. All those whom God justifies are called 'God's elect', just as that faith to which they shall assuredly be brought is called 'the faith of God's elect', Titus 1:1.

God justified his elect by blood, Rom. 5:9, God called them by his Spirit, Rom. 8:30, and, so certain is the work, that those whom he justified and called, are said already to be glorified, Rom. 8:30. This is being justified by his grace with a witness, Titus 3:7, as Paul says in another place, 'being justified freely by his grace', Rom. 3:24. The law has nothing to do with this work of God, it is not on a legal principle, neither is it of works. We know that a man is not justified by the works of the law, Gal. 2:16, either his own works or those done on his behalf, 'for by the deeds of the law there shall no flesh be justified in his sight', Rom. 3:20.

To the contrary, 'By him all that believe are justified from all things, from which ye could not be justified by the law of Moses', Acts 13:39. Observe, ye could not, could not be justified by the law of Moses; it could not be, justification could not be, on a legal basis or on a principle of law. Justification is by grace through faith, as opposed to its being by law through works. Therefore we conclude that a man is justified by faith without the deeds of the law, Rom. 3:28. The law was nothing but a schoolmaster to lead us to Christ, Gal. 3:24. Therefore it must follow that no man is justified by the law in the sight of God, Gal. 3:11. Indeed, whosoever of you are justified by the law—or on a legal basis, or forensic principle, whether your own, or that of a presumed legal proxy— whosoever of you are justified by the law, ye are fallen from grace, Gal. 5:4.

If the law be present, there must be works. Bring in works, and men will boast. If Abraham were justified by works, he had whereof to boast, Rom. 4:2. But what saith the scripture? Abraham believed God, and he counted it to him for righteousness. Then works are excluded. And so is boasting, Rom. 3:27. Nevertheless, we boast in God through our Lord Jesus Christ, by whom we have now received the reconciliation, Rom. 5:11. Believing on him which justifieth the ungodly, Rom. 4:5, we are on a divine foundation, we know that we have been justified, for the righteous God has brought in righteousness and imputed it to the faith which he has wrought: what blessedness! Rom. 4:6. Resting in this blessedness, being justified by faith, we have peace with God through our Lord Jesus Christ, Rom. 5:1, and by this are kept on our pilgrimage through this dark and evil world, knowing that 'whom he justified, them he also glorified'. And what could be more peaceable and certain than that?

Justification is so certain. It has a greater verification than anything else, whether of things in heaven, or things on earth, or things under the earth; whether of things in this world, or things of the world to come; whether among the quick or the dead, whether among men or angels: the greatest verification accorded to anything, is that accorded to justification. What is it? It is the resurrection from the dead. 'He is not here: for he is risen', Mt. 28:6. 'They saw him', Mt. 28:17. 'He appeared first to Mary', Mk. 16:9. 'He appeared unto two of them', Mk. 16:12. 'He appeared unto the eleven', Mk. 16:14. 'Why seek ye the living among the dead?' Lk. 14:5. 'Which said he was alive', Lk. 24:23. 'And they knew him', Lk. 24:31. 'Jesus himself stood in the midst', Lk. 24:36. 'Behold my hands and my feet, that it is I myself: handle me, and see', Lk. 24:39. 'As he blessed them, he was parted from them, and carried up into heaven', Lk. 24:51. 'Then said Jesus, Thomas, because thou hast seen me, thou hast believed: blessed are they that have not seen, and yet have believed', Jn. 20:29. 'It is the Lord', Jn. 21:7. 'He rose again the third day', I Cor. 15:4. 'He was seen of Cephas, then of the twelve: after that he was seen of above five hundred brethren at once; of whom the greater part remain unto this present, but some are fallen asleep. After that, he was seen of James; then of all the apostles. And last of all he was seen of me also', I Cor. 15:5-8.

The resurrection verifies justification. Jesus Christ is declared to be the Son of God with power, according to the spirit of holiness, by the resurrection from the dead. The resurrection from the dead declares that he is the Son of God with power. Power to do what? Power to bring in all God's elect, whom God had justified by his blood. Then, the resurrection testifies to the certainty of their justification. It verifies justification. Which is what Paul teaches, 'Now it was not written for his sake alone that it was imputed to him; but for us also, to whom it shall be imputed, if we believe on him that raised up Jesus our Lord from the dead; who was delivered for our offences, and was raised again for our justification', Rom. 4:23-25.

In what sense was Jesus our Lord 'raised again for our justification'? The interpretation of this verse, Rom. 4:25, depends upon the meaning of the twice-used preposition διά, *dia*, translated 'for' in the Authorised Version, 'delivered *for* our offences, raised again *for* our justification.' This translation presses, if not forces, upon the reader the idea that the resurrection was in order that believers might be justified. This is incorrect. The resurrection was because believers had been justified. Whilst the preposition *dia* will bear the meaning 'for', this is but one of many possible variants, and is certainly one of the worst choices for this text from the wide band of permissible meanings. It is one which, in effect, misleads the reader as to the sense of the verse.

The preposition *dia* occurs some five hundred and forty-nine times in the New Testament, using no less than twenty-two English words to convey its varied and admittedly difficult meaning. The meaning varies firstly according to whether the word is with an accusative or a genitive. If an accusative—and on one hundred and eighty-one occasions *dia* is with an accusative—twelve English words have been employed carrying the range through Because of, By, For, Through, With; and so on. If with a genitive—and *dia* occurs with a genitive some three hundred and sixty-eight times—the translators saw the need of some sixteen English words in order to render the varied meanings. These words range through After, Among, At, By, From, In, For, Through, Throughout, With; among others. The meaning of the word *dia* varies secondly according to the context, and here the translators' skill, not to mention spiritual sensitivity, comes into play, to find exactly the nuance required in each case.

In the case of Rom. 4:25 they found exactly the wrong nuance, giving the impression that justification is because of resurrection, 'raised again *for* our justification', whereas resurrection is *because of* or *through* our justification: 'raised again *because of* our justification'. The verse is in the form of a kind of couplet:

> ὃς παρεδόθη διὰ τὰ παραπτώματα ἡμῶν
> καὶ ἠγέρθη διὰ τὴν δικαίωσιν ἡμῶν

Literally this reads:

> 'Who was delivered because of the offences of us
> and was raised because of the justification of us.'

The preposition *dia*, with the accusative, undoubtedly ought to have been rendered 'because of', a meaning the translators themselves have given in twenty-nine cases. It was a matter of choice—governed by context—from the translators' own range of words. They chose 'for', as opposed to 'because of', and suggested a meaning the opposite to that intended by the apostle.

Paul showed that the resurrection verified justification. It was 'because of' justification having been accomplished in death that God raised him from the dead in triumphant victory. The translators use of 'for' implies that justification is on account of the resurrection, which makes nonsense of all that had been taught as to justification. The justification of all God's people stands in the death of Christ, 'Justified by his blood', and this is gloriously verified by the resurrection of Jesus Christ from the dead 'raised again because of our justification.'

Another passage which some have advocated as if justification were accomplished by resurrection, as opposed to resurrection testifying of accomplished justification, is that found in Rom. 5:18. Here, in a context of reconciliation, in a chapter of contrasts, Paul speaks of 'justification of life'. But the apostle means no more than that even as one offence brought judgment upon all in Adam unto condemnation, that is, the sentence of death, so likewise one accomplished

311

righteousness brought the gift of grace to all in Christ unto justification, that is, justification of life. Where the contrast lies between the sentence of death and justification of life: respectively the consequence of the transgression of Adam causing the fall, and the faith of Jesus Christ bringing in justifying righteousness. The one offence caused the sentence of death, the one righteousness brought justification of life.

It is a matter of comparisons. To wrench one expression, from one part of the comparison, out of text, context, and chapter, is little short of wresting scripture. Righteousness accomplished must issue in life, as it is said, 'Grace reigns through righteousness unto eternal life by Jesus Christ our Lord.' Whence we observe that 'justification of life' teaches us that, upon the basis of one accomplished righteousness—by which all the elect have already been justified in the sight of God through the death of their Substitute—justification is conveyed by the Spirit of life to all the chosen seed. So that 'justification of life' does not speak of justifying righteousness—or one accomplished righteousness—being effected, but of its being applied by the Holy Ghost. What term—especially in contrast with the condemnatory sentence of death—could be more apposite?

The other passage brought forward by those who suppose that justification stands in the resurrection, or rather glorifying, of Christ, is to be found in II Cor. 5:21, 'For he hath made him to be sin for us, who knew no sin; that we might be made the righteousness of God in him.' This is in the context of II Cor. 5:12-21, a passage dealing exclusively with reconciliation. Here there is a certain congruity with the verse previously considered, Rom. 5:18, in the contextual setting of Rom. 5:12-21, which likewise expounds the reconciliation.

Although mentioning righteousness—that we might 'become' the righteousness of God in him—II Cor. 5:21 is wholly concerned with reconciliation, it is not to do with justification as such. It is a sheer travesty to found a novel view of justification on two verses nothing to do with expounding that doctrine, whilst ignoring the great body of truth which does expound it. Furthermore there is no evidence that II Cor. 5:21 has anything to do with the resurrection, much less the glory. It does not speak of either. Finally, if such purveyors of novel doctrines under supposedly new light wish to overturn accomplished righteousness, the imputing of that righteousness, and justification being exclusive to faith in the blood of Christ, they may as well follow Westcott and Hort, and discover the Greek to suit their revelations, making the text read, say, 'that we might be counted to be righteous in him', *margin*, 'some authorities read, '*from the glory*'.

However the text reads literally, 'For him who knew not sin for us sin he made, that we might become righteousness of God in him.' This is in the context of reconciliation, that is, of substitution, which the apostle expounds, II Cor. 5:12-21. In the last verse he sums up his teaching, using the word 'for'. There is no reason—only the old, invalid, Westcott and Hort excuse to undermine Holy Writ—for the omission of the word 'For' in the modern versions. Any more than there is for tampering with the translation 'sin', changing the word which the Holy Ghost gave to 'sin-offering' or 'sinfulness', because the liberal authors of certain versions could not swallow the truth of total depravity by universal inbred corruption in Adam.

Notwithstanding, the words 'sin' and 'for' are correct, as such, and by the word 'for' at the commencement of the verse the apostle sums up his teaching. This introduces the essence of the substitutionary doctrine. The word 'for' ushers in the sum of the teaching, at its most conclusive, the marrow of reconciliation, or substitution, gathering up everything that had preceded in context, and setting forth the last word by definition.

313

The apostle shows that there are three parts to substitution, all concerning the state and condition of the Substitute. The first concerns the state and condition proper to the Substitute in and of himself, 'he knew no sin'. The second reveals what God wrought upon the Substitute in order that substitution might be effected for all the elect, God 'made him to be sin for us'. The last part sets forth the consequence of the substitutionary work for those on whose behalf substitution was made, 'that we might become the righteousness of God in him.'

The first part of this summary, II Cor. 5:21, declares the worth and suitability of the Substitute. Of necessity the work of substitution first requires the perfection of the Substitute. 'He knew no sin.' How could this be? Because the body prepared for the Son of God by the operation of the Holy Ghost, and by the overshadowing of the power of the Highest, was that 'holy thing' formed from the seed of the woman, without the least taint of the inbred corruption otherwise passed by natural generation to all mankind. He, Christ, conceived of the Holy Ghost, born of the virgin, was without sin, he knew no sin, it was not in the seed, not in the body, not in the soul, not in the humanity which the Son of God took into union with his divine nature in one holy Person, so as to become the Substitute of his people on the tree.

Equal in his spotless humanity, unblemished substance, and impeccable soul to take the place of any one of his people, in the mystery of his divinity, the infinity of his power, and the absoluteness of his ability, there appeared a resource more than sufficient to enable him to stand in, and at once, for all the countless myriads whose place he was to take in the one substitutionary sacrifice. From his conception to his trial, poised before the cross, there sounded upon him from above the testimony of heaven, 'He knew no sin'. Far from this implying a past life of proxy law-keeping resulting in a substitutionary legal righteousness having been wrought before the atonement, these words imply nothing other than the perfection and worth of the Substitute on the eve of the work of substitution.

The second part follows immediately, 'he hath made him to be sin for us', or, more literally, 'him he made sin for us'. What awesome mysteries appear in this revelation. Truly this is the reconciliation, the substitution, the exchange of places, the 'thorough exchange'. Thorough, in that he really was united to his people in their actual condition by the creative power of God, 'For both he that sanctifieth and they who are sanctified are all of one.' 'Of one' he was made with them, in the place of substitution, by the supernatural work of God, who 'made him to be sin for us'; that is, for every one of his elect in whose real condition he was 'made' to be.

This speaks of the profound work of God. It was God that took him who knew no sin, and God himself who made him to be sin. This mystery evidently took place on the cross, but, in the nature of the mystery, it was unseen by the eye of man, there was nothing about it that was outwardly visible, it was an interior work of God upon the passive soul and inward being of the Crucified. There was no exterior evidence of this inward and spiritual work that God was doing. The Substitute, accepted in the stead of every last one of those whom he was pledged to reconcile, having exchanged places with them, was so wrought upon that the depth and totality of the sin that they were, he was 'made'. From the depth and totality of his sinlessness, in the place of substitution, he was made the depth and totality of their sin for whom he was Substitute. From 'knowing no sin' to being 'made sin'. This is the meaning of the words. It is the meaning of the 'change' inherent in the 'exchange' of places. It is the force of the 'thorough exchange' involved in substitution and implied in reconciliation.

By the being 'made sin' through the mighty power of the Creator, he was changed from what he was in and of himself, to what they were, whose place he had accepted, in and of themselves. He was united to them, and they with him, in a mystery. Person for person by exchange, state for state by change, God wrought the work so that he was made what they were. This union of him who knew no sin with all his people in their sin—so that he was 'made sin' for them—in which he was passive and God was active, is that which this part of the verse describes in the work of reconciliation. This is the beginning. Here came the cry 'My God, my God, why hast thou forsaken me? That was the cause.

Nothing is said in the text about his bearing sin away; of his agony; of the depth of his sorrow and suffering; of the cost to him of such a dreadful state; of the effect upon his consciousness. Nothing is said of the judgment; the punishment now due to fall and be executed upon what he had been 'made', that it might be his, that he might take it away; nothing of the curse of the law; nothing of the wrath of God. The place, indeed the verse, does not speak of his broken body, his shed blood; not even of the crucifixion, nor the circumstances of his death. The holy apostle is revealing the reconciliation, that this involved the exchange of places, and the change in the Substitute from 'knew no sin' to 'made sin'. That is the exchange, the thorough exchange, which took place, and to it the Holy Ghost confines the verse. What is described is the change in the Substitute, wrought by God from above, whilst in the place of substitution.

The next, and last, phrase follows: 'that we might be made the righteousness of God in him.' This reads literally, 'that we might become righteousness of God in him.' The phrase does not actually describe this as having taken place; it is given as the reason for which the previous statement—'he was made sin'—took place: that this might happen. It did happen. And what is more, it happened in the place of substitution, at the cross. Not in the resurrection, though that was the divine seal on all that was done in the substitution. Much

316

less in the glory, from whence the work of reconciliation wrought on earth is administered. Everything was done at the cross, everything is in the death of Christ. Reconciliation is in the death of Christ. And so is righteousness.

The first was done to him, that the second might be wrought for us. So that from our being sin in ourselves, because he was made sin for us, we become righteousness of God in him. That is what we become in him, because of what he was made for us. All the changes are in the Substitute. He was without sin. He was made sin. He manifests God's righteousness. For us he was made sin. In him we become God's righteousness. Then our sin and God's righteousness met in him. Righteous judgment would not, could not rest, till sin had been put away wholly and for ever. Thus nothing remained but righteousness of God in him for us on whose account he had been made sin. And if this be so, nothing could more aptly state the case than that we have 'become the righteousness of God in him.' The moment that righteousness was satisfied in judgment, there remained no more sin to judge. But righteousness remained, and remains to everlasting for all those for whom the substitution was made. When the work was concluded, sin was gone, righteousness remained, the Substitute was dead, and we were seen to be 'the righteousness of God in him'.

All the changes were wrought in him for us. Real changes: he was made sin, we are become righteousness of God in him; neither of which we feel, but both of which were felt by him in a way inconceivable to us, when he took our persons and conditions into himself as his own. Then the last phrase describes—in the place of substitution still—the work completed, with all the worth of that substitution already to the good of those for whom it was wrought. But at the cost of his life, who became obedient unto death, even to the death of the cross.

However it is to be stressed that the verse expounds the effect of the substitutionary work wrought of God upon Christ, and that people seen in him. Having said that he was made sin, who knew no sin, the verse makes no mention of sacrifice, atonement, or the judgment of that sin. Rather, the next phrase, following immediately, declares the purpose of his being made sin: 'that we might become the righteousness of God in him.' Then, that righteousness met us absolutely in him who was made sin for us, and, having done so, could find no cause of offence, nothing to judge, thereafter. Thus that righteousness was at rest, and at rest with us in him. If so, we became the righteousness of God in him. Of this—though the verse does not mention it—his shed blood was witness. The verse, concerned solely to open the effect of the reconciliation upon him, speaks of what he was, what he was made in order to achieve substitution, and what we became in him as a consequence of this work of God.

This remarkable summary of the reconciliation, or substitutionary change of places, tells of God making Christ to be sin as though his doing that to him meant in and of itself our becoming righteousness of God in him. Of course the judgment in righteousness intervened. Yet it is not mentioned. The reason for this being that the entire emphasis is placed on the changes effected by his being in our place and our being in his place. That is the exchange. And that divinely wrought mystery is what the apostle reveals in this verse. Here it is not righteousness being imputed, or even being wrought out on our account: it is what happened to Christ—and of necessity to us in Christ—when the reconciliation—the exchange of places—took place. It is what he was in himself as a result of that work; and, because we were, and are, joined with him, what we were, and are, as found in him: 'become the righteousness of God in him.' That is, found in the place of death, with righteousness of God wholly at rest in the crucified Substitute.

At precisely this point reconciliation and justification meet, and from this place of divine mystery, and of love beyond compare, the doctrine of justification springs. Nevertheless II Cor. 5:21 itself expounds the reconciliation, showing the perfection, not to say exactitude, of the exchange of the Substitute for each one of his people, the whole of the election, whereby, through everlasting divine righteousness, they became the righteousness of God in him at the place of substitution.

In much the same way as some have misconstrued II Cor. 5:21, others have given a false gloss to I Cor. 1:30, 'But of him are ye in Christ Jesus, who of God is made unto us wisdom; both righteousness, and sanctification, and redemption.' Here the apostle speaks of the exclusion of all boasting and glorying. The word 'but' cuts off the occasion of supposing that any come to Christ as a result of their own intellectual convictions or in consequence of the activity of their own will. There were those who thought that they knew everything in religion, called 'the wise and the prudent', I Cor. 1:20. 'But' they were excluded. There were those who imagined that they had power to perform religious duties, I Cor. 1:26. 'But' they were not called. In contrast with these, 'Ye see your calling, brethren.' They did not call God, God called them.

Whilst they were in darkness and under the power of Satan, the Lord said of them to Paul, 'I have much people in this city'. He knew them; they did not know him. He chose them; they did not choose him. 'God hath chosen', I Cor. 1:27, and again, 'God hath chosen', I Cor. 1:27; once more 'hath God chosen', I Cor. 1:28. It was God's choice of them, not theirs of him. It was not of themselves that they were in Christ Jesus, but it was of him that they were in Christ Jesus. It was not of the will of man, but it was of the will of God that they had received the least revelation or experience concerning his Son. None had an interest in Christ save that God himself had drawn him, and revealed Christ to him: 'But of him are ye in Christ Jesus.'

As to that revelation of Christ to his people, it is sufficient in and of itself, it is complete. There is nothing for man to add. No knowledge, no perception, no work, no strength; nothing. Then where is the room either for boasting or for glorying? Yet, naturally, the Corinthians gloried in wisdom, and boasted of intellectual powers. But there was no place for such things in the gospel, as if they should aid the believer, or be of profit in the knowledge of Christ. Not only was it all of God that they had come to Christ, but as to the knowledge of Christ, that was all of God also. 'Of him are ye in Christ Jesus': that is one thing; 'who of God is made unto us wisdom': that is another thing. Here is a realm, a spiritual realm, in which both all the wisdom of man, and all man's attempts to be wise, are utterly excluded. All is of God.

As to the wisdom of God in Christ, it is altogether beyond and outside of that to which man's intellectual powers can attain, just as the object of that wisdom is beyond the ability of man to experience through his natural faculties. 'The natural man receiveth not the things of the Spirit of God', I Cor. 2:14. And again, 'The things of God knoweth no man but the Spirit of God.' Nevertheless, to those naturally poor, base, ignoble, nothing in the world, whom God had chosen, that no flesh should glory in his presence, these things were made known by revelation, and experimentally: 'Now we have received, not the spirit of the world, but the spirit which is of God', I Cor. 2:12.

This wisdom of God, which stands in the knowledge of Christ, could never become the curriculum of students, or the subject matter for academic study, or a body of learning to which scholars might apply themselves. How could it? Then it would be the wisdom of man. But it is the wisdom of God, and the subject is the spiritual knowledge of Christ, and the way in which this knowledge is made known is by revelation. This is God's way of teaching. 'Who of God'—mark that, of God—'is made unto us'—unto us, observe—'wisdom.' This wisdom is hidden from the wise and prudent, Mt. 11:25-27. But every one that hath heard, and hath learned of the Father, cometh unto the Son, for this is his manner of teaching, and the effect of it.

The sum of the knowledge of Christ, which is all of God, and must be taught of God, follows: 'both righteousness, and sanctification, and redemption.' This comprehends the knowledge of Christ in the gospel. Righteousness embraces all that was wrought in his death, sanctification encompasses all that he administers from the glory, and redemption speaks of all that he shall bring to fruition at his coming again. Thus Christ is assured, by God himself, to all his people. Everything is in him, he is the first and the last, and everything that is in him is spiritually conveyed to the elect by the Father through the Holy Ghost. 'Who of God is made unto us wisdom; both righteousness, sanctification, and redemption.'

The Spirit of truth takes the truth of Christ, in a vital, living and interior manner, and reveals it to the saints, thus glorifying Christ. As to righteousness, the revelation of righteousness of God in Christ is brought home to faith as the justification of the ungodly, wherein the convicted sinner rejoices to know the blessedness of the man unto whom God imputeth righteousness without works. It is to be noted that the Greek reads, 'who was'—note the tense, was—'made unto us wisdom from God'. A wisdom standing first and foremost in righteousness, wrought and accomplished when Christ died for his people on the cross.

I Cor. 6:11 is a scripture employed by the Anglican—Roman Catholic International Commission on Justification (ARCIC II), in their paper called 'Salvation and the Church', in order to provide an appearance of legitimacy for their technique of confusing justification with salvation—and I know not what else—until justification by faith quite disappears beneath the confounding together of things that differ. But neither this text nor any other will serve their purpose, which is to inform us that the Roman Catholics have professed justification by faith all along, only with a different—and more balanced—emphasis, as opposed to the unjustified bias of the Reformers. And so say the Anglicans.

The text reads, 'And such were some of you: but ye are washed, but ye are sanctified, but ye are justified in the name of the Lord Jesus, and by the Spirit of our God.' In this place there is no question of the apostle teaching the Corinthians about justification as such: that doctrine lies elsewhere. Here the doctrine is assumed. In this context the Apostle Paul shows the experience accompanying the imputing of righteousness to the ungodly: the change that this causes. I Cor. 6:11 describes the application of a previously accomplished work to the present experience of the saints.

The text shows that justification, effectually wrought at the cross, preached in the gospel, was applied with power to the Lord's people at Corinth 'in the name of the Lord Jesus, and by the Spirit of our God'. The chosen vessels of mercy, upon whom God would make known the riches of his glory, were afore prepared unto glory when Christ died for them. Everything was in the death of Christ. In terms of I Cor. 6:11 the death of Christ afore secured their washing, their sanctification, and their justification.

How can we tell this? First, as to washing being secured by the death of Christ, before ever it was applied by the Spirit of God, observe Rev. 1:5, 'Unto him that loved us, and washed us from our sins in his own blood.' Here his love, which is from everlasting—'I have loved thee with an everlasting love'—preceded his dying for them, which was on the cross, when the shedding of his blood cleansed—or washed—their sins away. It was this that the Spirit applied to them: 'but ye are washed.'

Next, as to sanctification being secured by the death of Christ, before ever it was applied by the Spirit of God, observe Heb. 13:12, 'Wherefore Jesus also, that he might sanctify the people'—here is their sanctification—'with his own blood, suffered without the gate.' Where sanctification doubtless is secured by the death of Christ. 'For by one offering he hath perfected for ever them that are sanctified.' The sanctification, the securing for them the Spirit of God, was wrought for the people of God in its entirety by the blood of Christ.

The same is true, lastly, as to justification. As we have seen over and over again, this was secured by the death of Christ. Rom. 5:9 'being now justified by his blood.' Justification was achieved when Christ's blood was shed. When Christ died, righteousness of God was already to the account of all those that had been, or ever should be, brought to faith.

These things, all of these things, washing, sanctification, justification, were already fully secured through the finished work of Christ at the cross for an elect and foreknown people. In the process of time, and the experience of that people,—'I have much people in this city', see Acts 18:1,9,10—the Spirit of God was sent to apply the work of Christ to those for whom it had been wrought. Why? Otherwise they would never receive it, because 'it is not of him that willeth, nor of him that runneth, but of God that showeth mercy.'

So filthy, so base, so wayward, so perverse, so corrupt were these people—'such were some of you', I Cor. 6:11—that, were the love of God in Christ displayed before their very eyes, of themselves they would turn away. But for such Christ died, and to such the Spirit is sent, and come they shall, for come they must, that 'no flesh should glory in his presence', I Cor. 1:29. From their birth in the flesh they will not come, but from their birth in the Spirit they shall come, for it is written, 'which were born, not of blood, nor of the will of the flesh, nor of the will of man, but of God', John 1:13.

And so the Greek reads, I Cor. 6:11, 'But ye *were* washed, but ye *were* sanctified, but ye *were* justified', referring in the past tense to their actual experience of what had been wrought for them before they were born.

When the mighty converting power of God turns the heart of the ungodly, there ensues a great yearning to be washed from filth, set apart from the world, and to be justified by faith. This longing shall never be in vain. Not many days shall pass before it is said, 'But ye are washed, but ye are sanctified, but ye are justified in the name of the Lord Jesus, and by the Spirit of our God.' This encourages the ministers of the gospel to say, 'Knowing, brethren beloved, your election of God.' But how do they know it? Because 'our gospel came not unto you in word only, but in power also, and in the Holy Ghost, and in much assurance', I Thess. 1:4,5. This assurance was because they knew that Christ had washed them from their sins by his own blood, when it was shed; that he had sanctified them with his own blood, when he had suffered without the camp; and that he had justified them by his blood, when he had brought in to their account righteousness of God at the cross.

All this was in the counsel and purpose of God. What was in the life and experience of the saints was, firstly, the washing of regeneration. By the revelation of Jesus Christ, and the quickening operation of the Holy Ghost, the interior new man was raised up in newness of life, and illuminated by the light of the glory. It was as if cleansing streams of water washed away the old filth and corruption, purging out the guilty stains. As the word came with power, so the living streams issued forth, and thus the cleansing work was done. This was called, The washing of water by the word: 'but ye are washed.'

Moreover, the saints were 'all full of the Holy Ghost'. They were strengthened with might by his Spirit in the inner man, their bodies the temple of the Holy Ghost, who took up his dwelling within their hearts. They loved this holiness, or sanctification, caused by his inward divine presence. This set them apart, within and without, from the world, the flesh, and the devil. They were not conformed to this world, nor to worldly things, they walked in the Spirit, were spiritually minded, and were led by the Spirit. The Spirit led them into all truth, glorifying Christ before their interior eyes, bringing them into an inward union and communion with the Father and the Son. 'But ye are sanctified.'

Likewise the church of God which was at Corinth, all of whom were the sanctified in Christ Jesus, called saints, by definition knew the blessedness of the man whose transgression was forgiven, whose sin was covered, to whom the Lord imputed not iniquity. By definition, because it was nothing other than the common experience of the work of God in justifying the ungodly that had constituted the church. All the saints had the same 'like precious faith', the 'faith of God's elect'. They were justified by faith, and had come together in consequence. They were the church at Corinth precisely because every individual in the city without exception who had eschewed his own righteousness, fled from the wrath to come, and had experienced the blessedness of righteousness being imputed without works, was in and of that company, gathered under the preaching of the apostle, called the church of God at Corinth.

They had been justified in the name of the Lord Jesus, and by the Spirit of our God. This was their spiritual experience: the church had not wrought it, it was not wrought by the church, God had wrought it, and all upon whom it was wrought were the church. Every one of the saints, the sum of whom was the church, had felt the Spirit witnessing with his spirit that he was a child of God, justified freely by grace. From within his inmost being welled up the cry, Abba, Father. All heaven was open to him, the old yoke clean gone, the obscuring veil taken away, the glory in the face of Jesus Christ as the body of heaven in his clearness.

The joy of the Lord was their strength; they rejoiced with joy unspeakable and full of glory, filled with all joy and peace in believing. By grace they had been saved through faith, and that not of themselves, it was the gift of God, not of works, lest any man should boast. But what man could boast? Where was boasting? It was excluded. By what law? of works? Nay: but by the law of faith. Therefore they concluded that a man was justified by faith without the deeds of the law, and found this a most wholesome doctrine, and very full of comfort. This was both the experience and the witness of the entire church of God which was at Corinth, every one of the sanctified, all the saints, to whom the apostle could say in spirit and in truth, 'But ye are justified'.

And yet some, perhaps most, of the saints at Corinth had been fornicators, idolators, adulterers, effeminate, abusers of themselves with mankind, thieves, covetous, drunkards, revilers, extortioners, without God in the world, and without inheritance in the world to come. 'But ye are washed.' That is, washed clean from every stain, all their guilt, besides every inward corruption that had brought forth such vile works. Not for them the background sanctity of a 'Christian' home, or of a sheltered 'church' upbringing. They were converted out of the world, they had been filthy, lawless, given over to greediness, fleshly lusts and worldly pleasures their selfish and ardent pursuit. But in a moment, in the twinkling of an eye, 'Ye were washed ... in the name of the Lord Jesus, and by the Spirit of our God.'

They were sanctified. Born of the Spirit in a moment, filled with the Spirit thenceforth, they were led by the Spirit away from their old companions in worldly pleasures and diversions, openly testifying of the wrath of God upon the world, and of salvation in the name of the Lord Jesus. Separate from every form of idolatry and worldly religion, they loathed the things which before they loved. Humbled, lowly, walking with self-distrust and self-abhorrence, shame and joy mingled as they received with meekness the ingrafted word, kept in the fear of God, and rejoicing in Christ Jesus, having no confidence in the flesh. The old things were passed away, behold, all things had become new. A new creation had come in an instant, the moment of regeneration, and they knew that they were sanctified. Though the pleasures of sin were still in the city, though the enticements of the world were ever in their environment, though the swellings of corruption were yet felt within them, nonetheless they were indwelt by the Holy Ghost, Christ filled their hearts, the Father's good pleasure was always before them, and they could see eye to eye with the word of God, 'but ye were sanctified ... in the name of the Lord Jesus, and by the Spirit of our God.'

They were justified. God himself had imputed righteousness to them without works, freely by his grace. Instantaneously they had received the blessing. As it was said of Peter with the Gentiles, likewise it was true of them, 'While Peter yet spake these words, the Holy Ghost fell on all them which heard the word.' The hearing of faith was their blessing, they were of those 'who by him do believe in God', having 'obtained like precious faith with us', that is, with the apostles. They had obtained faith, that is, it had come from God himself. This was their joy, God had done the work, and, if so, he would complete it. Nothing would stand that was of man, or of man's will. But, in Corinth, 'as many as were ordained to eternal life believed.' God had imputed righteousness, and they felt that God had imputed righteousness, just as they felt that God had quickened their faith into being. Faith was not of themselves, any more than righteousness was of themselves, all was of God, it was not of works, that is, not of the works of their will or choice, they could not boast, it was the work of God that they believed, and it was all their joy and song: God had done the work. This would stand, and this would both bring about and secure their recovery. 'But ye were justified ... in the name of the Lord Jesus, and by the Spirit of our God.'

All this, every part of it, washing, sanctifying, justifying, from first to last, from heaven to earth, from God to man, from eternity to eternity, was 'in the name of the Lord Jesus, and by the Spirit of our God'. Now, this brought justification by faith worth the name. It is justification by faith with a threefold divine witness. Justification by faith is of the essence, it is the heart of the gospel. It is the answer to the ancient cry, 'I know it is so of a truth, but how shall man be just with God?' It is of the essence, it is the heart of the ministry of Christ from the glory, the ministration of righteousness. It is of the essence, it is the heart of the answer to the sinner's cry, the prodigal's lament, the leper's entreaty, the blind man's plea, and the yearning of the penitent. The imputing of accomplished justifying righteousness to every heart-broken, mourning sinner is the occasion of the Spirit of the Lord GOD being upon Christ. Justification is the good tidings which the LORD hath anointed him to preach to the meek, it is that which binds up the broken-hearted, proclaims liberty to the captives, and the opening of the prison to them that are bound.

Justification is Christ's heavenly message, the divine proclamation of the acceptable year of the LORD, and the day of vengeance of our God. Justification by faith is comfort to all that mourn, the divine appointment to all that mourn in Zion, it is the consolation in Christ, the comfort of love, the fellowship of the Spirit, and the bowels of mercies of our God. Justification gives beauty for ashes, the oil of joy for mourning, the garment of praise for the spirit of heaviness: that they might be called trees of righteousness, the planting of the LORD, that he might be glorified. Justification is the tree of life, the blood of atonement, the Lamb slain from the foundation of the world, the righteousness of God, the blessing of Abraham, the blessedness of David, and the bliss of all that hunger and thirst after righteousness.

Justification takes in and sounds out the death of Jesus Christ at Golgotha. Justification answers the cry, Eloi, Eloi, lama sabachthani? Justification pronounces the word, Verily, I say unto thee, Today shalt thou be with me in paradise. Justification pleads the cause, Father, forgive them, for they know not what they do. Justification cries in triumph over sin, death, the fall, over every enemy, over the last enemy, over the judgment to come, justification cries, I say, with a loud voice, 'It is finished!' Justification preaches redemption through the blood of Christ, the forgiveness of sins, the pardon of the sinner, the ransom of the slave, the release of the bondman, the dissolution of the old yoke, the rending of the legal veil. Justification declares the reconciliation, proclaims substitution, shows the atonement, and affirms propitiation through faith in his blood.

Justification smiles upon the ungodly, stoops sweetly to the foul, answers mercifully to the sinful, declares God's righteousness for the remission of sins, God's justice in imputing righteousness by faith of Jesus Christ, disclosing the meeting-place of mercy and truth, the tryst of righteousness and peace. Justification is the foundation of Zion, the door of salvation, the banner of liberty, the key of the kingdom, the hope of Israel, the establishment of the world to come, the dwelling-place of righteousness, the assurance of the inheritance, and the pledge of everlasting glory. Justification is of the essence, the heart, of the gospel: it is the gospel, it is the evangel from which all else takes its rise, in which each doctrine is founded, upon which every truth rests, because it is that by which the death of Christ is opened, expounded, communicated and magnified in the name of the Lord Jesus, and by the Spirit of our God.

Justification was the substance of Paul's evangelism, it was the evangelism of the apostles, by which remission of sins was preached in Christ's name to all nations, beginning at

Jerusalem. When Paul evangelised, all who believed that evangel were justified by faith. They were of the church: they were the church. This was the church. There was no 'membership', there were no other bodies, societies, or exterior organisations in the Lord's name, no rival 'churches', the very idea was antichristian; there was one church. There was one body, and one Spirit, even as they were called in one hope of their calling; one Lord, one faith, one baptism; one God and Father of all, who was above all, and through all, and in them all. This was the church which was in God the Father, and in our Lord Jesus Christ. The preaching of the gospel—of justification by faith—by the apostolic ministry brought this into being, for by it the saints were gathered together in one.

The preaching of justification, and the belief of it, formed and united the saints in the house of God, the church of the living God, the pillar and ground of the truth. All who received the blessing were of the church, they were visibly united together in love, and all others outside of this body—including the vast religious edifice of formal priestly religion centred upon the outward temple—were not of the church, had not received the blessing, and were not of God's elect. This was the city set on an hill, the one pool of light in a sea of darkness, the one true love in a world of enmity, the only life in a realm of death.

All the saints, in the simplicity which was in Christ, and by the power which was in the Spirit, were united with one heart and one mind under the apostolic preaching of the gospel in the beginning. It was for this that the ministry of Christ was sent. Anything else, or anything gathered on any other foundation, of necessity would have defied the will of God, and would have stood in the apostacy, ministering to the future disintegration of the single testimony to the unity of Father, Son, and Holy Ghost, one God, blessed for evermore. Amen.

The apostles preached doctrinally, expounding the word of God. They brought home to the heart the condition of sinners under the law and under wrath, whilst opening the righteousness of God by faith of Jesus Christ, hour after hour, by day and by night, day after day, the gospel becoming a savour of life unto life, and death unto death to every hearer in all places. They were hated by the world, outcast of men, persecuted by the authorities, but loved by heaven, embraced of Christ, and favoured by God and the Father.

Far from the pragmatic acceptance of the divisions, of the apostacy, of denominationalism, these uncompromising, God-taught, heaven-sent, Christ-glorifying preachers of justification by faith, the evangelists of the word of God, gathered the believers into one body, one church, the one unity, as it was in the beginning, is now, and ever shall be. That is, it shall be, when justification takes its rightful place again, when men who fear God alone, and who are full of the Holy Ghost, who are not disobedient to the heavenly vision, leave all, forsake their nets, and follow him, to preach the glorious gospel of the blessed God, declaring the righteousness of God by faith of Jesus Christ through all the world abroad.

What message can compare with justification by faith? Nothing can compare with this glorious, spiritual, heavenly, divine, and saving doctrine. Here is a doctrine determined in the ancient settlements of eternity; ordained before all worlds in the bonds of the everlasting covenant; established in the eternal counsels of Father, Son, and Holy Ghost; sworn by the immutable oath of the Almighty; ratified by the blood of the Surety; sealed with the sevenfold seal of the Holy Ghost from heaven; and secured to the infinite reaches of everlasting glory. Justification by faith was determined in purpose before the world was, promised in anticipation at the dawn of time, established in the blood of Christ in the midst of the ages, and shall stand to everlasting when time is no more.

When the last judgment has had the last word, when the great earthquake has shattered the earth; when the sun becomes black as sackcloth of hair, and the moon becomes as blood; when the stars of heaven fall unto the earth as a fig tree casteth her untimely figs, shaken by a mighty wind; when the heavens depart as a scroll which is rolled together, and every mountain and island are moved out of their places; when the kings of the earth, the great men, and the rich men, and the chief captains, and the mighty men, and every bond-man, and every free man, hide themselves in the dens and in the rocks of the mountains, and say to the mountains, Fall on us, and hide us from the face of him that sitteth upon the throne, and from the wrath of the Lamb, for the great day of his wrath is come; and who shall be able to stand? then shall the justified stand. Then shall justification by faith, and the doctrine thereof, shine in her true lustre. For the ungodly shall not stand in the judgment, nor sinners in the congregation of the righteous. But justification shall stand; and the justified shall stand. For it is God that justifieth: Who is he that condemneth? Heaven and earth shall pass away, but these words shall not pass away.

Justification by faith shall abide the fire. When the wicked shall go away into everlasting punishment; when the devil, the false prophet, Babylon, and the two beasts, are cast into the lake of fire and brimstone that burneth for ever and ever; still justification shall abide. Justification shall abide the fire. When the heavens shall pass away with a great noise, and the elements shall melt with fervent heat; when the earth shall reel to and fro like a cottage, and all faces shall be as flames; when the earth shall be burned up and the works thereof; then justification shall abide the fire. Then shall this wonderful, this pre-eminent, this saving doctrine be marvellous in our eyes, and the LORD shall bring forth the headstone with shoutings, crying, Grace, grace unto it!

Justification shall attend the righteous into the very portals of the new heavens and the new earth wherein dwelleth righteousness. Ever sure, ever fresh, justification shall rest in fulfilment in the place where there is no night, where the Lord God Almighty and the Lamb are the light thereof. In the place where the Lamb which is in the midst of the throne shall lead the justified, now glorified, unto living fountains of waters. The place where God shall wipe away all tears from their eyes, where the ransomed of the LORD shall come to Zion with everlasting joy upon their heads, where they shall obtain joy and gladness, where all sorrow and sighing shall flee away. In that place shall justification by faith, having fulfilled her office, rest content, world without end, Amen.

INDEX

TO OTHER PUBLICATIONS

PSALMS, HYMNS AND SPIRITUAL SONGS

THE PSALMS

OF THE

OLD TESTAMENT

The Psalms of the Old Testament, the result of years of painstaking labour, is an original translation into verse from the Authorised Version, which seeks to present the Psalms in the purest scriptural form possible for singing. Here, for the first time, divine names are rendered as and when they occur in the scripture, the distinction between LORD and Lord has been preserved, and every essential point of doctrine and experience appears with unique perception and fidelity.

The Psalms of the Old Testament is the first part of a trilogy written by John Metcalfe, the second part of which is entitled *Spiritual Songs from the Gospels*, and the last, *The Hymns of the New Testament*. These titles provide unique and accurate metrical versions of passages from the psalms, the gospels and the new testament epistles respectively, and are intended to be used together in the worship of God.

Price £2.50 *(postage extra)*
(hard-case binding, dust-jacket)
ISBN 0 9506366 7 3

v

SPIRITUAL SONGS
FROM
THE GOSPELS

The *Spiritual Songs from the Gospels*, the result of years of painstaking labour, is an original translation into verse from the Authorised Version, which seeks to present essential parts of the gospels in the purest scriptural form possible for singing. The careful selection from Matthew, Mark, Luke and John, set forth in metrical verse of the highest integrity, enables the singer to sing 'the word of Christ' as if from the scripture itself, 'richly and in all wisdom'; and, above all, in a way that facilitates worship in song of unprecedented fidelity.

The *Spiritual Songs from the Gospels* is the central part of a trilogy written by John Metcalfe, the first part of which is entitled *The Psalms of the Old Testament*, and the last, *The Hymns of the New Testament*. These titles provide unique and accurate metrical versions of passages from the psalms, the gospels and the new testament epistles respectively, and are intended to be used together in the worship of God.

Price £2.50 *(postage extra)*
(hard-case binding, dust-jacket)
ISBN 0 9506366 8 1

THE HYMNS

OF THE

NEW TESTAMENT

The *Hymns of the New Testament*,. the result of years of painstaking labour, is an original translation into verse from the Authorised Version, which presents essential parts of the new testament epistles in the purest scriptural form possible for singing. The careful selection from the book of Acts to that of Revelation, set forth in metrical verse of the highest integrity, enables the singer to sing 'the word of Christ' as if from the scripture itself, 'richly and in all wisdom'; and, above all, in a way that facilitates worship in song of unprecedented fidelity.

The *Hymns of the New Testament* is the last part of a trilogy written by John Metcalfe, the first part of which is entitled *The Psalms of the Old Testament*, and the next, *Spiritual Songs from the Gospels*. These titles provide unique and accurate metrical versions of passages from the psalms, the gospels and the new testament epistles respectively, and are intended to be used together in the worship of God.

Price £2.50 *(postage extra)*
(hard-case binding, dust-jacket)
ISBN 0 9506366 9 X

'THE APOSTOLIC FOUNDATION OF THE CHRISTIAN CHURCH' SERIES

FOUNDATIONS UNCOVERED

THE APOSTOLIC FOUNDATION
OF THE
CHRISTIAN CHURCH

Volume I

Foundations Uncovered is a small book of some 37 pages. This is the introduction to the major series: 'The Apostolic Foundation of the Christian Church'.

Rich in truth, the Introduction deals comprehensively with the foundation of the apostolic faith under the descriptive titles: The Word, The Doctrine, The Truth, The Gospel, The Faith, The New Testament, and The Foundation.

The contents of the book reveal: The Fact of the Foundation; The Foundation Uncovered; What the Foundation is not; How the Foundation is Described; and, Being Built upon the Foundation.

'This book comes with the freshness of a new Reformation.'

Price 30p *(postage extra)*
(Laminated cover)
ISBN 0 9506366 5 7

THE BIRTH OF JESUS CHRIST

THE APOSTOLIC FOUNDATION
OF THE
CHRISTIAN CHURCH

Volume II

'The very spirit of adoration and worship rings through the pages of *The Birth of Jesus Christ*.

'The author expresses with great clarity the truths revealed to him in his study of holy scriptures at depth. We are presented here with a totally lofty view of the Incarnation.

'John Metcalfe is to be classed amongst the foremost expositors of our age; and his writings have about them that quality of timelessness that makes me sure they will one day take their place among the heritage of truly great Christian works.'

From a review by Rev. David Catterson.

'Uncompromisingly faithful to scripture ... has much to offer which is worth serious consideration ... deeply moving.'

The Expository Times.

Price 95p *(postage extra)*
(Laminated Cover)
ISBN 0 9502515 5 0

THE MESSIAH

THE APOSTOLIC FOUNDATION
OF THE
CHRISTIAN CHURCH

Volume III

The Messiah is a spiritually penetrating and entirely original exposition of Matthew chapter one to chapter seven from the trenchant pen of John Metcalfe.

Matthew Chapters One to Seven

GENEALOGY · BIRTH · STAR OF BETHLEHEM
HEROD · FLIGHT TO EGYPT · NAZARETH
JOHN THE BAPTIST · THE BAPTIST'S MINISTRY
JESUS' BAPTISM · ALL RIGHTEOUSNESS FULFILLED
HEAVEN OPENED · THE SPIRIT'S DESCENT
THE TEMPTATION OF JESUS IN THE WILDERNESS
JESUS' MANIFESTATION · THE CALLING · THE TRUE DISCIPLES
THE BEATITUDES · THE SERMON ON THE MOUNT

'Something of the fire of the ancient Hebrew prophet .... Metcalfe has spiritual and expository potentials of a high order.'
The Life of Faith.

Price £2.45 *(postage extra)*
(425 pages, Laminated Cover)
ISBN 0 9502515 8 5

THE SON OF GOD AND SEED OF DAVID

THE APOSTOLIC FOUNDATION
OF THE
CHRISTIAN CHURCH

Volume IV

The Son of God and Seed of David is the fourth volume in the major work entitled 'The Apostolic Foundation of the Christian Church.'

The book refers to the irreducible summary of the apostolic gospel in Romans 1:3-4, attention being drawn to truths which the modern 'gospel' never mentions, much less considers foundational.

'The author proceeds to open and allege that Jesus Christ is and ever was *The Son of God*. This greatest of subjects, this most profound of all mysteries, is handled with reverence and with outstanding perception.

'The second part considers *The Seed of David*. What is meant precisely by 'the seed'? And why 'of David'? With prophetic insight the author expounds these crucial verities.'

Price £1.10 *(postage extra)*
(250 pages, Laminated Cover)
ISBN 0 9506366 1 4

CHRIST CRUCIFIED

THE APOSTOLIC FOUNDATION
OF THE
CHRISTIAN CHURCH

Volume V

Christ Crucified the definitive work on the crucifixion, the blood, and the cross of Jesus Christ.

The crucifixion of Jesus Christ witnessed in the Gospels: the gospel according to Matthew; Mark; Luke; John.

The blood of Jesus Christ declared in the Epistles: the shed blood; the blood of purchase; redemption through his blood; the blood of sprinkling; the blood of the covenant.

The doctrine of the cross revealed in the apostolic foundation of the Christian church: the doctrine of the cross; the cross and the body of sin; the cross and the carnal mind; the cross and the law; the offence of the cross; the cross of our Lord Jesus Christ.

Price £6.95 *(postage extra)*
Hardback 300 pages
Laminated bookjacket
ISBN 1 870039 08 4

OTHER TITLES

DIVINE FOOTSTEPS

Divine Footsteps traces the pathway of the feet of the Lord the Son of man from the very beginning in the prophetic figures of the true in the Old Testament through the reality in the New; doing so in a way of experimental spirituality. At the last a glimpse of the coming glory is beheld as his feet are viewed as standing at the latter day upon the earth.

Price 40p *(postage extra)*
(Laminated Cover)
ISBN 0 9502515 1 8

THE RED HEIFER

The Red Heifer was the name given to a sacrifice used by the children of Israel in the Old Testament—as recorded in Numbers 19—in which a heifer was slain and burned. Cedar wood, hyssop and scarlet were cast into the burning, and the ashes were mingled with running water and put in a vessel. It was kept for the children of Israel for a water of separation: it was a purification for sin.

In this unusual book the sacrifice is brought up to date and its relevance to the church today is shown.

Price 75p *(postage extra)*
ISBN 0 9502515 4 2

THE WELLS OF SALVATION

The Wells of Salvation is written from a series of seven powerful addresses preached at Tylers Green. It is a forthright and experimental exposition of Isaiah 12:3, 'Therefore with joy shall ye draw water out of the wells of salvation.'

Price £1.50 *(postage extra)*
(Laminated Cover)
ISBN 0 9502515 6 9

NOAH AND THE FLOOD

Noah and the Flood expounds with vital urgency the man and the message that heralded the end of the old world. The description of the flood itself is vividly realistic. The whole work has an unmistakable ring of authority, and speaks as 'Thus saith the Lord'.

'Mr. Metcalfe makes a skilful use of persuasive eloquence as he challenges the reality of one's profession of faith ... he gives a rousing call to a searching self-examination and evaluation of one's spiritual experience.'

The Monthly Record of the Free Church of Scotland.

Price £1.20 *(postage extra)*
ISBN 0 9502515 7 7

OF GOD OR MAN?

LIGHT FROM GALATIANS

The Epistle to the Galatians contends for deliverance from the law and from carnal ministry.

The Apostle opens his matter in two ways:

Firstly, Paul vindicates himself and his ministry against those that came not from God above, but from Jerusalem below.

Secondly, he defends the Gospel and evangelical liberty against legal perversions and bondage to the flesh.

Price £1.45 (postage extra)
(Laminated Cover)
ISBN 0 9506366 3 0

A QUESTION FOR POPE JOHN PAUL II

As a consequence of his many years spent apart in prayer, lonely vigil, and painstaking study of the scripture, John Metcalfe asks a question and looks for an answer from Pope John Paul II.

Price £1.25. (postage extra)
(Laminated Cover)
ISBN 0 9506366 4 9

'TRACT FOR THE TIMES' SERIES

THE GOSPEL OF GOD

'TRACT FOR THE TIMES' SERIES

The Gospel of God. Beautifully designed, this tract positively describes the gospel under the following headings: The Gospel is of God; The Gospel is Entirely of God; The Gospel is Entire in Itself; The Gospel is Preached; The Gospel Imparts Christ; and, Nothing But the Gospel Imparts Christ.

Price 25p *(postage extra)*
(Laminated Cover)
No. 1 in the Series

THE STRAIT GATE

'TRACT FOR THE TIMES' SERIES

The Strait Gate. Exceptionally well made, this booklet consists of extracts from 'The Messiah', compiled in such a way as to challenge the shallowness of much of today's 'easy-believism', whilst positively pointing to the strait gate.

Price 25p *(postage extra)*
(Laminated Cover)
No. 2 in the Series

ETERNAL SONSHIP
AND TAYLOR BRETHREN

'TRACT FOR THE TIMES' SERIES

Eternal Sonship and Taylor Brethren. This booklet is highly recommended, particularly for those perplexed by James Taylor's teaching against the eternal sonship of Christ.

Price 25p *(postage extra)*
(Laminated Cover)
No. 3 in the Series

MARKS OF THE
NEW TESTAMENT CHURCH

'TRACT FOR THE TIMES' SERIES

Marks of the New Testament Church. This exposition from Acts 2:42 declares what were, and what were not, the abiding marks of the church. The apostles' doctrine, fellowship and ordinances are lucidly explained.

Price 25p *(postage extra)*
(Laminated Cover)
No. 4 in the Series

THE CHARISMATIC DELUSION

'TRACT FOR THE TIMES' SERIES

The Charismatic Delusion. A prophetic message revealing the fundamental error of this movement which has swept away so many in the tide of its popularity. Here the delusion is dispelled.

Price 25p *(postage extra)*
(Laminated Cover)
No. 5 in the Series

PREMILLENNIALISM EXPOSED

'TRACT FOR THE TIMES' SERIES

Premillennialism Exposed. Well received evangelically, particularly through the influence of J.N. Darby, the Schofield bible, and the Plymouth Brethren, Premillennialism has assumed the cloak of orthodoxy. In this tract the cloak is removed, and the unorthodoxy of this system is exposed. A remarkable revelation.

Price 25p *(postage extra)*
(Laminated Cover)
No. 6 in the Series

JUSTIFICATION AND PEACE

'TRACT FOR THE TIMES' SERIES

Justification and Peace. This tract is taken from a message preached in December 1984 at Penang Hill, Malaysia. In this well-known address, peace with God is seen to be based upon nothing save justification by faith. No one should miss this tract.

Price 25p *(postage extra)*
(Laminated Cover)
No. 7 in the Series

FAITH OR PRESUMPTION?

'TRACT FOR THE TIMES' SERIES

Faith or presumption? The eighth tract in this vital series exposes the difference between faith and presumption, showing that faith is not of the law, neither is is apart from the work of God, nor is it of man. The work of God in man that precedes saving faith is opened generally and particularly, and the tract goes on to reveal positively the nature of saving faith. Belief and 'easy-believism' are contrasted, making clear the difference between the two, as the system of presumption—called easy-believism—is clearly shown, and the way of true belief pointed out with lucid clarity.

Price 25p *(postage extra)*
(Laminated Cover)
No. 8 in the Series

EVANGELICAL TRACTS

xxx

EVANGELICAL TRACTS

1. *The Two Prayers of Elijah.* This tract, first printed in 1972, was reprinted in 1982. It shows the spiritual significance of the drought, the cloudburst, and the two prayers of Elijah. Green card cover, price 10p.

2. *Wounded for our Transgressions.* An evangelical message taken from Isaiah 53. Declaring the salvation of God, this is a tract intended to help those seeking the Saviour and his work. Gold card cover, price 10p.

3. *The Blood of Sprinkling.* Taken from Hebrews 12:24 this booklet expounds the things to which the people of God are not come, besides those to which they are come. Obvious from the context, this is striking in the exposition. The saving grace of God is clearly preached in this evangelical tract. Red card cover, price 10p.

4. *The Grace of God that brings Salvation.* An evangelical message preached in South East Asia in 1985, this tract brings home to the heart the work of God in ⸺e salvation of the sinner. Blue card cover, price 10p.

These tracts may be ordered directly from the Trust, or through Bookshops. If money is sent with order, please add letter post allowance.

MINISTRY BY JOHN METCALFE

TAPE MINISTRY BY JOHN METCALFE
FROM ENGLAND AND THE FAR EAST
IS AVAILABLE.

For Tapelist please contact the John Metcalfe Publishing Trust, Church Road, Tylers Green, Penn, Buckinghamshire, HP10 8LN.

Owing to the increased demand for the tape ministry, we are unable to supply more than two tapes per order, except in the case of meetings for the hearing of tapes, where a special arrangement can be made.

THE MINISTRY OF THE NEW TESTAMENT

The purpose of this 32 page A4 gloss paper magazine is to provide spiritual and experimental ministry with sound doctrine which rightly and prophetically divides the Word of Truth.

Readers of our books will already know the high standards of our publications. They can be confident that these pages will maintain that quality, by giving access to enduring ministry from the past, much of which is derived from sources that are virtually unobtainable today, and publishing a living ministry from the present. Selected articles from the following writers have already been included:

ELI ASHDOWN · JOHN BUNYAN · JOHN CALVIN · JOHN CENNICK
J.N. DARBY · JOHN FOXE · WILLIAM GADSBY
WILLIAM HUNTINGTON · WILLIAM KELLY · HANSERD KNOLLYS
JAMES LEWIS · MARTIN LUTHER · JOHN METCALFE
ROBERT MURRAY McCHEYNE · ALEXANDER—SANDY—PEDEN
J.C. PHILPOT · J.B. STONEY · JOHN VINALL · GEORGE WHITEFIELD

Price £1.75 *(postage included)*
Issued Spring, Summer, Autumn, Winter.

NEWLY PUBLISHED

The Elect undeceived

TRACT FOR THE TIMES 9

The Elect undeceived, the ninth Tract for the Times, earnestly contends for 'the faith once delivered to the saints' in a way that is spiritually edifying, positive, and subject to the Lord Jesus Christ according to the scriptures.

The Tract is a response to the pamphlet 'Salvation and the Church' published jointly by the Catholic Truth Society and Church House Publishing, in which the Anglican and Roman Catholic Commissioners agree together about JUSTIFICATION. The pamphlet shows how they have agreed.

The Elect undeceived responds by revealing that not only have the R.C.-C. of E. Commissioners struck at the heart of Article XI of the Church of England, 'JUSTIFICATION BY FAITH ONLY', but, in so seeking to overthrow the massive bulwarks of the Reformation, they have also threatened the very foundations upon which our fathers built for our future. 'If the foundations be destroyed, what shall the righteous do?'

The Tract is subsidised to a fraction of its real cost because of the love and concern of godly men and women. Please do help us to distribute THIS VITAL RESPONSE.

Tract for the Times No. 9. Special laminated gloss finish stiff cover, price 25p.

Price 25p (*postage extra*)
(Laminated Cover)
No. 9 in the Series

Order Form

Please send to the address below:-

		Price	Quantity
A Question for Pope John Paul II		£1.25	......
Of God or Man?		£1.45	......
Noah and the Flood		£1.20	......
Divine Footsteps		£0.40	......
The Red Heifer		£0.75	......
The Wells of Salvation		£1.50	......

Psalms, Hymns & Spiritual Songs (Hardback edition)

		Price	Quantity
The Psalms of the Old Testament		£2.50	......
Spiritual Songs from the Gospels		£2.50	......
The Hymns of the New Testament		£2.50	

'Apostolic Foundation of the Christian Church' series

		Price	Quantity
Foundations Uncovered	Vol.I	£0.30	......
The Birth of Jesus Christ	Vol.II	£0.95	......
The Messiah	Vol.III	£2.45	......
The Son of God and Seed of David	Vol.IV	£1.10	......
Christ Crucified (Hardback edition)	Vol.V	£6.95	......
Justification by Faith (Hardback edition)	Vol.VI	£7.50	......

Tracts

		Price	Quantity
The Two Prayers of Elijah		£0.10	......
Wounded for our Transgressions		£0.10	......
The Blood of Sprinkling		£0.10	......
The Grace of God that Brings Salvation		£0.10	......

'Tract for the Times' series

		Price	Quantity
The Gospel of God	No.1	£0.25	......
The Strait Gate	No.2	£0.25	......
Eternal Sonship and Taylor Brethren	No.3	£0.25	......
Marks of the New Testament Church	No.4	£0.25	......
The Charismatic Delusion	No.5	£0.25	......
Premillennialism Exposed	No.6	£0.25	......
Justification and Peace	No.7	£0.25	......
Faith or presumption?	No.8	£0.25	......
The Elect undeceived	No.9	£0.25	......

Name and Address (in block capitals)

. . . .

. . . .

. . . .

If money is sent with order please allow for postage. Please address to:- The John Metcalfe Publishing Trust, Church Road, Tylers Green, Penn, Bucks, HP10 8LN.

Magazine Order Form

Name and Address (in block capitals)

. . . .

. . . .

. . . .

Please send me .... current copy/ies of The Ministry of the New Testament.

Please send me .... year/s subscription.

I enclose a cheque/postal order for £ ....

(Price: including postage, U.K. £1.75; Overseas £1.90)
(One year's subscription: Including postage, U.K. £7.00; Overseas £7.60)

Cheques should be made payable to The John Metcalfe Publishing Trust, and for overseas subscribers should be in pounds sterling drawn on a London Bank.

10 or more copies to one address will qualify for a 10% discount

Back numbers from Spring 1986 available.

Please send to The John Metcalfe Publishing Trust, Church Road, Tylers Green, Penn, Bucks, HP10 8LN

All Publications of the Trust are subsidised by the Publishers.